MANAGING CONVICTED OFFENDERS IN AN ORDERLY SOCIETY

Elmer H. Johnson

Southern Illinois University Press
Carbondale and Edwardsville

Library of Congress Cataloging-in-Publication Data

Johnson, Elmer Hubert.
  Japanese corrections : managing convicted offenders in an
orderly society / Elmer H. Johnson.
    p. cm.
  Includes bibliographical references and index.
    1. Corrections—Japan. 2. Correctional institutions—Japan.
3. Prisons—Japan. 4. Community-based corrections—Japan.
I. Title.
HV9813.J64 1996
364.6′0952—dc20   95-20808
ISBN 0-8093-1736-2   CIP

The paper used in this publication meets the minimum requirements of American National Standard for Information Sciences—
Permanence of Paper for Printed Library Materials, ANSI Z39.48-
1984. ♾

To the Japanese Fulbright Alumni and
Yoshiharu Shino of Osaka, whose
generous contributions to increase the
number of Fulbright Awards to Americans
for research and study in Japan
made this book possible

Contents

PLATES

TABLES

xi

PREFACE

$\mathcal{A}$ growing number of books and articles in English have described and analyzed Japanese society and its "miracle economy." Now and then the "safe streets" have been mentioned, but little of substance and reliability has been said about the approaches of the Correction Bureau and the Rehabilitation Bureau.

The unique features of Japanese corrections aroused my curiosity in 1970 while attending the United Nations Congress on the Prevention of Crime and Treatment of Offenders in Kyoto. As Visiting Expert on community corrections in 1985 at the United Nations Asia and Far East Institute for Prevention of Crime and Treatment of Offenders (UNAFEI) in Tokyo, I had an exceptional opportunity for an extensive observation of correctional institutions and community-based programs in Japan.

These initial contacts had impressed me with the importance of understanding the operations of the Correction and Rehabilitation Bureaus. My feeling was that, on a scale not yet accomplished, the what, why, and how of those operations should be recorded and made available to the public and criminologists.

With my retirement from the faculty of Southern Illinois University at Carbondale scheduled for the fall of 1987, I wanted to satisfy my curiosity by studying in detail the workings of Japanese corrections. Ideally, such analysis would be undertaken by a person with sound knowledge of the history, sociocultural setting, and political system of Japan, competent in the language, and familiar with international corrections. A Japanese criminologist experienced in comparative research would be preferred. Since no more-qualified person had assumed an analysis of Japanese corrections, I seized an unusual opportunity for a meaningful investigation, in spite of my limited acquaintance with Japan, its history, and its language.

In January of 1987 I proposed to Minoru Shikita, then director general of the Correction Bureau, that a book be prepared on Japanese prisons. His enthusiastic response and a grant from the Takeuchi Foundation of Hitachi, Ltd., in 1988 made possible three months of preliminary research in Japan. The coverage of the project was expanded to include community-based corrections when suggested by Keiji Kurita, director general of the Rehabilitation Bureau.

An extensive literature on Japanese history, institutions, and beliefs was available for my study and provided background for the analyses that follow. My unfamiliarity with the Japanese language has been partly remedied by English-speaking officials of both bureaus. Some forty staff members of the Correction Bureau were students at the Center for the Study of Crime, Corrections, and Delinquency, Southern Illinois University at Carbondale. They knew my approach to corrections and served as effective guides and translators.

A Fulbright award supported nine months of research in 1990–1991. After completion of the draft chapters, I returned to Japan in 1992 for two months at my expense to obtain additional information and to check on the accuracy of my discussion. Findings and analysis are entirely my responsibility and do not necessarily represent the points of view of the Ministry of Justice, the Correction Bureau, and the Rehabilitation Bureau.

During those years of research, the career system of

Japanese corrections brought other persons to the positions of directors general of the Correction and Rehabilitation Bureaus, components of the Ministry of Justice. The directors general continued their indispensable executive support that made the project feasible and meaningful. Kazuyoshi Imaoka, Kazuo Kawakami, Kiyohiro Tobita, and Noboru Matsuda headed the Correction Bureau in turn and Keiji Kurita, Kunpei Satoh, Tsuneo Furuhata, and Hiroyasu Sugihara the Rehabilitation Bureau.

Fulbright awards immediately after World War II brought to American universities many Japanese who now occupy important positions in business, industry, and higher education in Japan. These Japanese "Fulbrighters" decided to supplement the Fulbright program financially to bring more American scholars to Japan. The purpose was two-fold: to express gratitude for their earlier experiences in the United States and to promote congenial relationships between the two countries. When the effort to collect these funds was announced, Yoshiharu Shino of Osaka contributed a very generous sum, the interest from which supported my Fulbright award. In appreciation, I dedicate this book to him and to the Japanese Fulbrighters. My wife, Carol, and I remember with pleasure the cordiality and assistance of the Japan-United States Educational Commission (JUSEC) before and during our stay in Japan.

Of the staff members of the Correction Bureau and the Rehabilitation Bureau, many contributed generously of their time and knowledge to strengthen my understanding of the corrections, culture, and people of Japan. Listing all of them would exceed the space available here, but several were exceptional in that regard. Ko Akatsuka, Takehisa Kihara, Masaru Matsumoto, Keisei Miyamoto, and Toshiaki Okumura gave essential service as executives. Koichi Watanabe was my translator, guide, and friend during three of my stays in Japan. Among others in these roles, I must mention Akira Murata, Satoru Ohashi, Masaharu Ozawa,

Kenichi Sawada, Kenji Teramura, Hiroshi Tsutomi, Mitsuyo Yoshitake, and Junko Fujioka. John Wilson at Southern Illinois University Press edited the manuscript with care and competence. Darrell L. Jenkins and his Social Studies staff, Morris Library of Southern Illinois University at Carbondale, provided access to the basic literature. During our 48th, 49th, and 50th years of marriage, Carol Holmes Johnson has been indispensable to the project as a companion, constructive critic, and operator of the word processor.

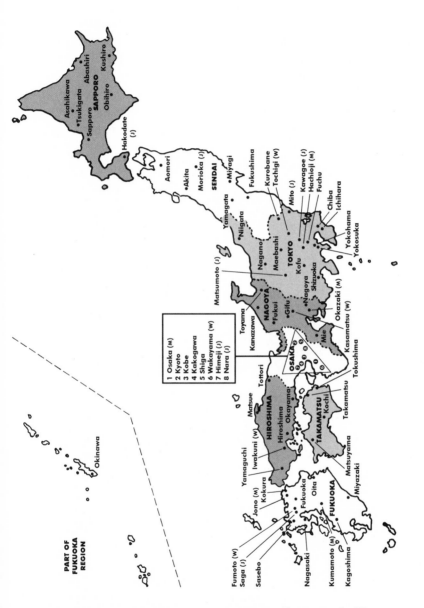

Map 1. *Adult correctional institutions in Japan. Shown are the 59 primary prisons, including 5 medical (M) and 5 women's (W) prisons, plus 8 juvenile (J) prisons.*

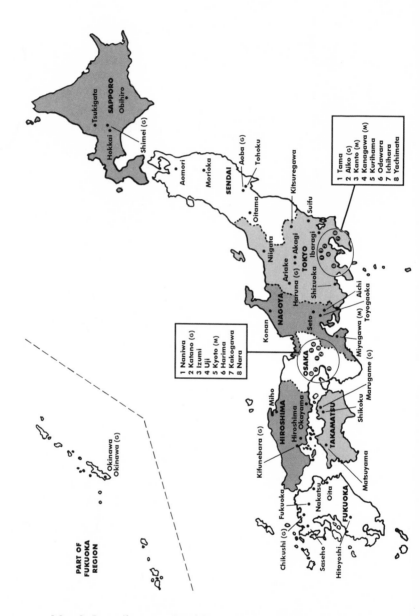

Map 2. Juvenile correctional institutions in Japan. Shown are the 53 Juvenile Training Schools, including 4 medical (M) and 9 girl's (G) schools.

JAPANESE
CORRECTIONS

INTRODUCTION

Among industrialized societies, Japan sends remarkably few of its convicted criminals to prison. Its imprisonment rate per 100,000 persons was only 32.3 in 1990, compared with approximately 292 in the United States (see table 1.1). The number of Japanese prisoners present on the last day of 1990 (39,892) was less than that in the federal correctional institutions alone of the United States (50,403); the prisons of the American states added another 689,596. Between 1960 and 1991 the number of Japanese prisoners dropped by 34.7 percent and the number in American prisons increased by 247.5 percent (Research and Statistics Section 1991a, 24; Flanagan, Pastore, and Maguire 1993, 608, 610).

The contrast also is found for juvenile training schools. The American public and private institutions (training schools, ranches, and camps) held 44,618 juveniles in 1989, at a rate of 175 persons per 100,000 aged ten years through the statutory-defined age of majority. Japanese training schools receive youngsters aged fourteen to twenty years, making for a discrepancy in the range of ages, but the crude comparison still is to Japan's advantage. On the last day of 1989, the Japanese training schools held 3,104 juveniles. For all Japanese age fourteen to twenty, the rate per 100,000 was 26.0. Taking the American age continuum (ten to twenty years), the rate per 100,000 was 16.4. (Flanagan and Maguire 1992, 597; Research and Statistics Section 1988, 89).

Table 1.1

Pattern of Imprisonment in Japan and U.S., 1926–90

| | Japanese Prisoners | | U.S. Prisoners | | |
| | | | | | Ratio of Rates |
Year	No.	Rate	No.	Rate	(Japan/U.S.)
1926	39,513	65.1	97,991	83	.78
1930	41,188	63.9	129,453	104	.61
1935	51,094	73.7	144,180	113	.65
1940	38,599	53.7	173,706	131	.41
1945	36,824	51.1	133,649	98	.52
1950	80,589	96.9	166,123	109	.89
1955	67,813	76.0	185,780	112	.68
1960	61,100	65.4	212,953	117	.56
1965	52,657	53.6	210,895	108	.50
1970	39,724	38.3	196,429	96	.40
1975	37,744	33.7	240,593	111	.30
1980	41,835	35.7	315,974	138	.26
1985	46,105	38.3	480,568	200	.19
1990	39,892	32.3	739,980	292	.11

Sources: Research and Statistics Section 1991a; Maguire, Pastore, and Flanagan 1993.

Note: The number of prisoners in both countries is counted from 31 December of the given year. The rate is calculated as the number in prison per 100,000 of the general population.

COMPARING JAPANESE AND AMERICAN RATES OF INCARCERATION

Japan has trailed the United States since 1926 (when comparable data were first available) in the total number of convicted offenders in prison, and that difference has consistently and sharply enlarged since World War II. The total population of Japan is about half the population of the United States; the effects of different-sized general populations are ruled out in table 1.1 by the calculation of imprisonment rates per 100,000 population.[1] Without any change in criminogenic factors and operations of the criminal justice system, an increase in the general population would generate a proportionally greater number of criminals and prisoners.

The Japanese rate dropped considerably in the 1940s when military mobilization removed many males from the community and aroused patriotic sentiments. During the socioeconomic chaos immediately after the war, the imprisonment rate peaked briefly but dropped precipitously thereafter. The American rate rose rapidly until the nation entered World War II and then declined sharply. Until 1965, the postwar trend was modestly upward; the early 1970s witnessed a decline before a sharp rise began to the present day.

Japan has consistently placed less reliance on imprisonment as a means of dealing with criminals than has the United States. The smaller the ratio between the two rates shown in the last column in table 1.1, the relatively less have the Japanese depended on imprisonment in a given year. Until the end of World War II, the ratios reflected the erratic trend of greater American reliance. In 1950 the peaking of the Japanese prison population brought the Japanese imprisonment rate closest to the American rate. From then on, the two rates progressively diverged, the Japanese rate declining from about two-thirds of the American rate in 1955 to just one-ninth in 1990.

According to Blumstein (1988), determinate sentencing policy in the United States has pushed prisons increasingly into being instruments of toughness and the demands of interest groups press judges to send more people to prisons and for longer terms. Most prosecutors and judges are elected and must compete for votes by promising to increase satisfaction of the demand. The prison population has grown at a rapid rate, prison sentences are longer, and the prisoners younger on average.

The rapid escalation of prison population in the United

States has aggravated the always formidable difficulties of prison administration. Overcrowding affects the physical and psychological well-being of inmates and appears to lead to more violence through destabilization of inmate social networks (Porporino 1986). Data derived from nineteen prisons operated by the federal government of the United States show that assaults increased with overcrowding (Gaes and McGuire 1985). Stastany and Trynauer (1982) speak of the pluralization of prison subcultures as the "walls" became more permeable to developments in society at large. Fox (1982) calls attention to shifts in prisoner values towards greater acceptance of interracial victimization, predatory violence, and use of collective action for the resolution of problems. "Institutional programming is becoming more restricted in response to violence and the need to control it, to the point where we may be producing a malignant cyst of violence in places like readjustment centers" (Toch 1976, 44)

Reluctant use of imprisonment has enabled Japan to avoid the crisis of overburdened prisons and its effects. Prison environments are havens of tranquility, and inmates are remarkably submissive to their keepers. Forced confinement inevitably will favor the development of distinctive inmate values, but Japanese inmates are far less inclined to mount subcultural opposition to the prison staff and its official goals. Those conditions, of course, are encouraged by the avoidance of crowded cells, but both the uncrowded prisons and the relative tranquility of their environments are also due to the Japanese culture and its expression by inmates and by employees.

CULTURAL HERITAGE
AND PERCEPTION OF CRIME

To understand Japan's low imprisonment rate and to trace its profound effect on the programs of criminal corrections, we must examine the intermingling of ideas and institutions imported from the West with indigenous traditions. The Tokugawa regime (1603 to 1867) unified a collection of warring feudal domains into a centralized state that was near collapse when Commodore Matthew C. Perry forcibly ended the isolation from the outside world. In 1868 a group of feudal lords took over the imperial court in Kyoto in the "Meiji Restoration" that terminated the Tokugawa shogunate and proclaimed the emperor's direct responsibility for government.

The Meiji Restoration initiated a series of reforms for modernizing the Japanese social and legal institutions, including those of criminal justice. Lessons learned from studies of Western institutions were adapted to Japanese traditions and style of government. The intermingling of imported and indigenous ideas marks contemporary policies and practices of the Correction and Rehabilitation Bureaus; the differences and similarities with Western corrections are most attractive for the research of comparative criminology.

The feudal principles of a hierarchical social order linger in the Japanese social psychology today: knowing one's place in the societal scheme, fulfilling the Confucian obligations that the ruler be benevolent and the ruled be obedient, and holding the respect of others by maintaining social harmony, even at the expense of self-interest. Within that normative system, the law-breaker is expected to be repentant and to undertake self-correction.

In spite of the effects of urban life, the Japanese have retained what Luhmann (1979) calls "system trust." The urban scene tends to lose its taken-for-granted familiarity, because daily experience can only envisage or recall it in a fragmentary way. He sees trust as a leap beyond what one's own reasoning and experience would justify. In personal trust, confidence is placed in other persons with whom one has friendship, love, and other relatively intimate relationships. Lacking direct experience with the chain of events that lead to the delivery of products or services, urbanites also must have system trust, in the sense of having confidence in whatever organization is supposed to deliver such benefits.

A strong system trust favors avoidance and deterrence of crime as an expression of frustration and alienation; it encourages the defendant and convicted offender to expect the criminal justice system to reward repentance and a will to be rehabilitated. Personal trust underlies the faith (whether that of the public or of officials) that offenders are capable of self-correction without further intervention of the courts and correctional agencies.

From the Japanese perspective, penal incarceration and its consequences are viewed differently than they are in the United States. As evidence of the difference, Hamilton and Sanders (1992) offer conclusions of their survey in Detroit, Yokohama, and Kanazawa: First, the Japanese are more likely to identify the severity of incarceration with separation from other persons sharing their usual social network. Second, they have less regard for the law as an instrument for resolving disputes. The residents favored rehabilitation, specific deterrence, and denunciation as justifying rationales, while Detroiters preferred retribution, incapacitation, and general deterrence.

Low Imprisonment Rate: Cause and Effect

The public prosecutors and sentencing judges follow those values in extending leniency to those offenders expressing repentance and showing willingness and capacity for self-correction. Legal standards and procedures, within certain limitations, permit public prosecutors to divert defendants from trial and judges to suspend the prison sentences they have just ordered. Thus, the imprisonment rate of Japan is remarkably low; it is even lower than would be expected from the low incidence of crime.

The courts believe that probationary supervision is an unnecessary burden on those convicted offenders capable of self-correction. When they suspend a prison sentence, they have the choice of returning the individual to the community without restriction or requiring probationary supervision. The attitude of the judges, the choice left to them, and the criteria permitted by the law result in some serious offenders being "punished" by being put on probation.

The prisons and juvenile training schools receive an even smaller residue of the offenders received by the public prosecutors. The selective decisions of the public prosecutors send the least promising individuals to the correctional institutions: those who were in penal incarceration previously, the old veterans of imprisonment, the members of criminal syndicates, and those otherwise possessing "advanced criminal tendencies."

Nevertheless, the prisons for adults are remarkably tranquil and orderly. The infrequency of violence may be attributed to the environment of constraint characteristic of security prisons generally, the extensive industrial production in Japanese prisons, the strict enforcement of official rules, and the behavior of both the keepers and the kept in accord with the social psychology of the Japanese. Two-thirds of the adult prisoners are in the workshops for a forty-hour work week; that notable characteristic of Japanese penology is given full attention in chapter 5.

The juvenile training schools are also the responsibility of the Correction Bureau. The decline of their population has been slowed by the greater official concern about juvenile drug abuse and traffic offenses. The juvenile justice system places great emphasis on protecting the young from victimization and meeting their needs through therapeutic and educational approaches.

The Rehabilitation Bureau is responsible for probation, parole, and aftercare; the responsibilities make the bureau a representative of community corrections. Participation in community affairs has a particular meaning to the Japanese as an expression of their cultural heritage and their more recent experiences with urban existence.

An outstanding feature of the bureau's operation is the overwhelming reliance on unsalaried volunteers for almost all supervision of probationers and parolees. Also the halfway houses, mostly for discharged prisoners, are operated by private organizations. The heavy dependence on private citizens is a prime example of two major qualities of Japanese government: Japan prefers to turn over to the private sector some of the functions usually carried out by the government, and the bureaucracy of the Japanese government has been held at an unusually small size.

The two qualities illustrate the basic principle of comparative criminology that the policies and practices of correctional agencies mirror the culture and structure of the society they serve. The Correction and Rehabilitation Bureaus are not exceptions, as is also demonstrated by their following of the managerial system of the large-scale organization in Japan's private sector. The bureaus enjoy well-trained and competent personnel through the recruiting scheme of the national government and through in-service training of the recruits. The managerial system receives special attention in chapter 4, partly because, as indicated by the title of this book, the management of convicted offenders is its key theme.

MANAGING CONVICTED OFFENDERS IN AN ORDERLY SOCIETY

"Management" can be interpreted as "making or keeping the convicted criminals submissive" or as a defense of "artful manipulation of convicted criminals." For my purposes, management is better defined as handling or directing operations with a degree of skill and a well-chosen approach, or as success in accomplishing legitimate organizational goals. I am complying with the advice of Foucault (1980, 38): "With the prisons there would be no sense of limiting oneself to discourses *about* prisons; just as important are the discourses which arise within the prison, the decisions and regulations which are among its constituent elements, its means of functioning, along with its strategies."

In the preparation of this book, more than eighteen months in Japan were dedicated to gathering information about the operations of the Correction Bureau and the Rehabilitation Bureau, twin agencies within the Ministry of Justice. The information was acquired from field visits and interviews, collected documents, and other materials prepared by Japanese and foreign experts.[2] The data were gathered and processed to bear on three general questions: What are the characteristics of major programmatic elements? How do various personnel carry out programmatic responsibilities? Why are the various duties and activities carried out in a particular way? Of course, the three questions are abstract and must be fleshed out as the following chapters take up in turn the major programs. In short, in my research I have endeavored to learn *how* and *why* these instruments of society carry out their responsibilities the way they do.

The "orderly society," the other element of the book's title, emphasizes that the correctional agencies are creatures of Japanese society and culture. The Japanese are a remarkably orderly people, in keeping with their structural framework and social psychology. Their orderliness underlies the correctional system serving them. What is "normal," "typical," or "natural" in the society colors the agency environment and the conduct of the staff and its "clients."

Japanese Corrections focuses on the *management* of the offenders who are the subjects of the programs of the Correction and Rehabilitation Bureaus. The discourses, decisions, and strategies reported for Japan in this book sometimes resemble those in other countries, yet there also are fundamental differences. The similarities of correctional agency operations with those of other societies stem, first, from fundamentals in the managing of unwilling clients and, second, from the calculated importation of Western ideas and institutions some 120 years ago. During the Allied Occupation after World War II, other Western ideas were added, but the imported elements were adapted to Japanese traditions. Corrections followed suit.

A REMARKABLE OPPORTUNITY FOR COMPARATIVE CRIMINOLOGY

My curiosity about Japanese corrections has been an extension of my long-term study of correctional work in the United States and other countries. While teaching courses in criminology at North Carolina State University at Raleigh, I became convinced that textbooks of that time ignored the practicalities of criminal justice administration. As a kind of postdoctorate education, I attended classification sessions at nearby Central Prison and Dix Hill Mental Hospital. In 1950, Clarence Patrick, a professor then serving as chair of the North Carolina Board of Paroles, authorized my service for a summer as a parole supervisor in three rural counties. In 1958, William F. Bailey, then director of the North Carolina Prison, invited me to become assistant director. "What a wonderful postdoctorate course in practical penology for the criminologist!" I told myself.

I had joined a prison administration dedicated to modernizing what had been a "chain-gang" system. Staff members, who had survived the almost complete personnel turnover of the "spoils system" after each election, described conditions of county-operated prison camps in the 1920s and 1930s: insufficient food budgets that had to be stretched at the end of the month; broken windows in the cell blocks that let in winter snow in the mountain camps; prisoners handcuffed to the bars when they were whipped; baking soda spooned through the bars to prisoners with upset stomachs. As a novice in prison administration, I was shocked by the poverty of resources and programmatic alternatives. The prison administration of North Carolina, as well as that of other American states, has made impressive progress since the early 1960s.

North Carolina prisons were the first in the United States to introduce work release for felons and suggested to me the usefulness of work release as a tool for reform (E. Johnson 1967; 1969). Other publications of mine have dealt with other aspects: prison "rats" (E. Johnson 1961); introduction of social work (E. Johnson 1963); staff in-service training (E. Johnson 1966a); correlates of rule violations of inmates (E. Johnson 1966b); prisoner self-injuries (E. Johnson 1973), and the potential of administrative statistics for criminological research (E. Johnson 1965; 1968).

By being exposed to the practicalities of institutional and community-based corrections in America, I have been able to recognize similar patterns in Japan and, more important, the unique features of the history and current practices of Japanese agencies. The extraordinarily detailed statistics published annually by the Ministry of Justice have been a resource for the preparation of this volume. Independent scholars should evaluate the operations of criminal justice agencies, urges Miyazawa (1990). He believes that participation would strengthen the methodological and theoretical quality of criminological research by the Japanese. Japanese criminologists, I hope, will join the effort in greater numbers.

2

Parsimony in Resort to Imprisonment

"From the initial police interrogation to the final judicial hearing on sentence," Haley (1989, 495) summarizes, "the vast majority of those accused of criminal offenses confess, display repentance, negotiate for their victims' pardon and submit to the mercy of the authorities. In return they are treated with extraordinary leniency."

That set of procedures results in a remarkably reluctant use of imprisonment in Japan. Diversionary procedures of the public prosecutors and judges are most visible in reducing the number of suspects and accused persons who end up in prison or a juvenile training school. Since the Meiji Restoration some 120 years ago, the Japanese government has preferred to leave to the private sector functions usually held to be the responsibility of government. The preference persists today to limit the allocation of resources to correctional agencies and thus adds to motivations for reducing the number of convicted offenders entering prison.

The procedures of the public prosecutors and judges are embedded in the legal codes, in judiciary philosophy, and, more fundamentally, in the Japanese culture that encourages the public to at least tolerate official leniency. The diversionary practices of the procuracy and judiciary rely on the authority of Japanese values to put pressure on the defendants in order to enlist their sense of obligation to the group and to bring about their abandonment of criminal ways. When the defendant fails to be repentant, penal incarceration is likely to be chosen in an exercise of official power.

This chapter dips into the history of feudal Japan and the Meiji Restoration and, from that background, summarizes major facets of contemporary Japanese social psychology. While making clear the relevance of values to the reluctant resort to penal incarceration, the review of some relevant literature provides a background for other topics in chapters that follow.

Feudal Japan: Platform for Today

The period 1336 to 1608 was turbulent with inter-clan warfare that preoccupied the feudal lords (the *daimyo*). "The whole of Japan was torn by factions and plagued by incessant civil war until late in the sixteenth century, when a process of national unification by force of arms was begun" (Sansom 1963b, v). Each lord and his retainers were dedicated to protect the clan members, to assure survival of the clan and its domain, and to penalize those who served the interests of a rival clan.

Crown Prince Taishi Shotoku (572–622) is credited with promoting the growth of Buddhism, encouraging learning, and laying down the basis for political reform (Sansom 1963a). The first article of his Code of State Ethics expressed high regard for harmony: "Harmony is to be valued and an avoidance of wanton opposition is to be honored. All persons are influenced by class-feelings, and there are few who are intelligent. Hence there are some who disobey their lords and fathers or who maintain feuds with the neighboring villages. But when those above are harmonious and those below are friendly, and there is concord in the discussion of business, right views of things spontaneously gain acceptance. Then what is there that cannot be accomplished?" (Singer 1973, 62).

Confucian philosophy was the ethical foundation of feudal society. "It was the ruler's duty to reward or discipline with the attitude of a father watching over his children. The individual ... was important only as he completed the unity of his society" (Scalapino 1953, 6–7). The rulers were expected to be benevolent and the people obedient. A rigid class hierarchy placed the *samurai*, as warriors and administrators, at the top of the social pyramid, and their obligation was to teach the others higher morality and selflessness. The farmers came in a poor second on the social scale; but, as producers of rice, they had a crucial role in the economy. The artisans were the third class, and the merchants at the bottom because they were believed to put profit ahead of duty.

"Most Japanese scholars find that the traditional rural community provided the prototype of conformity which characterizes Japanese society," claims Ishida (1983, 35). The rural communities were relatively isolated from one another by mountains and, by living together for centuries, the families developed affinity. The values and nature of contemporary Japanese have been attributed to social rhythms and labor demands peculiar to rice cultivation at that time. Rice growing required the entire village to work so closely together that cooperation became second nature. The tasks were not specialized; everyone performed all the chores. The work was repetitive from year to year; perseverance was more required than innovation. Successful techniques could not be kept secret; Japanese learned to imitate innovations without considering Western ethical standards. The repetitive tasks could be conducted through village consensus without strong individual leadership (Hayashi 1988).

The Tokugawa Era (1603 to 1867) transmitted feudal characteristics that still linger in contemporary Japan; the ultimate collapse of the Tokugawa state ushered in the Meiji Restoration that followed (Scalapino 1953). Ieyasu Tokugawa used clever military leadership, skillful political treatment of defeated adversaries, and the binding of daimyo to him by awarding fiefs. Initially he made concessions to foreign missionaries and merchants in the hope of developing Japan's foreign and domestic trade, establishing shipbuilding, and acquiring foreign knowledge. However, the policy of the *bakufu* (the Tokugawa state) was reversed by prohibition of the Christian faith; decrees in 1633, 1635, and 1639 forbade foreign contacts (Sansom 1963c).

The Tokugawa feudal empire was based upon hierarchical control of all phases of life: occupation, behavior, and the possession of weapons. The values of the agricultural population were clan orientation; submissiveness to superiors; reliance on fellow villagers for help, tempered by suspiciousness; alertness to others in order to obtain favorable treatment and to avoid negative reports to superiors; and a strong work ethic (Tatai 1983).

As a step toward centralized government, the bakufu employed several means of controlling the daimyo. They were divided into either *fudai* (vassal daimyo) or *tozama* (allied daimyo who mostly had submitted only after Tokugawa military victories). The tozama were kept in distant regions and were required to send hostages to Edo (now Tokyo). They were weakened economically by being required to provide materials and manpower for construction of the great castle in Edo and fortifications in key areas. The shogun recruited the highest counselors from the fudai and the samurai for administrative and political offices, and the bakufu sent auditing officials to the domains to check on their wealth, administration, military strength, and size of population (Duus 1969).

Restoration: Catching Up with the West

Commodore Matthew C. Perry entered Edo Bay in February 1854 with his Black Fleet of eight American warships.

The following March a convention was signed, opening two ports for obtaining naval stores, authorizing consuls, and making vague provisions for trade. Similar agreements obtained by the British, Russians, and Dutch accelerated the opening of the nation to foreign influence. The term "Meiji Restoration" refers to a coup d'état carried out in Kyoto on 3 January 1868, when a group of feudal lords took control of the imperial court, terminated the bakufu, and proclaimed the emperor's direct responsibility for government. They began a series of reforms that established the institutional structure of a new Japan (Beasley 1972).

The feudal system had been in decline for several centuries and something like the Meiji Restoration may have come ultimately (Craig 1961). Previous isolation had led to similarities of language, customs, and values that, coupled with the threat of Western powers, served as the foundations for the new nation-state, but the Japanese reaction, stemming from internal factors, differed from that of other Asian nations. The limited Dutch trading concession gave enough information so that Japan knew more about the West than the West knew about Japan (Levy 1970).

By 1866 economic power had shifted to the great merchants of Edo and Osaka and to the merchant-landlord-industrialists of the towns and villages. The feudal lords and their retainers suffered serious losses of income. Wandering samurai had lost affiliations with feudal lords. Peasants were burdened with rising taxes and debt. Food prices soared in Kyoto and Edo. By the end of 1865, Edo became dangerous at night. "Prison records of Edo indicate that after a modest decline in the rate of commoner and minor *samurai* jailings in the city during 1864 there was a sharp increase in such jailings the following year" (Totman 1980, 217).

A series of secret and unconnected plots by the samurai began in the 1850s and gradually became a national revolutionary movement in the 1860s with the support of many nobles in the emperor's court in Kyoto. The display of Western military might made clear that resistance to modernization was suicidal. Forced on the Tokugawa government, the treaties specified that foreign nationals in Japan would be subject to the laws of their countries, not the laws of Japan. Aware of the fate of China, the new government realized that the principle of extraterritoriality would result in the loss of Japan's independence and ultimately would lead to dominance by Western imperialism (Beckman 1957).

The Meiji reformers undertook modernization of institutions to strengthen Japan's capacity to resist Western imperialism. Change was carefully controlled. Foreign experts were invited for advice and other services. Delegations went to Europe and the United States for quick studies of Western social institutions, including legal codes and criminal justice systems (Noda 1976; Beasley 1990).

Once military opposition was overcome, the violence implied by the usual interpretation of "revolution" did not occur. The graft and corruption of the bakufu simplified its overthrow, and the restoration of the emperor had great symbolic appeal. The peasants were accustomed to sacrifices demanded by their rulers. The bakufu policy was confiscation of the land of dissident daimyo and favored the Meiji switch of capital to industrialization. The merchant class had gained economic power in the later stage of the bakufu rule and were prepared to take new roles in the modernization. The Tokugawa elite was prepared to step down, and the reigning shogun voluntarily surrendered his power to the emperor (Levy 1970). Tokugawa Japan had already attained a high level of urbanization and population growth. By requiring the feudal lords to be in the capital city for part of the year, the shogunate encouraged the construction of roads and inns. Creation of castle towns and a money economy increased urban demand for goods and service. Improved irrigation methods and rice yield was accompanied by cottage industries. Literacy was surprisingly high (Fuse 1975).

Agrarian changes in the preceding century and a half made possible the modernization of Japanese society. In the Tokugawa period, district officials administered the villages and collected taxes without military support and were dependent on the loyalty of peasants and the corporate integrity of the villagers. The spread of tenancy, rural-to-town migration, and official trade monopolies created a political crisis, instability in villages, and political divisions among the samurai. The Meiji reformers used the language of feudal and family ethics to enlist loyalty to the emperor. The approach appealed to the peasants; their village social system lent stability to the society at large. The Tokugawa state had imposed a heavy tax burden on agriculture; the Meiji reformers depended on the continuity of that revenue for financing modernization (T. Smith 1959).

"By continued emphasis on the Japanese way," Levy (1970, 264) comments, "they [the reformers] were able to get individuals to adapt quickly the new ways in spheres in which they were essential and retain the old, at least long enough for a more gradual transition in other spheres of life." The rural villages became subunits within prefectures that became the administrative divisions of the central government. The Meiji government strictly limited associations between villages and attempted to extend the villages' strong sense of conformity to the national level (Ishida 1983).

The Meiji leadership was vested in the young samurai from southwestern Japan who were dedicated to transmitting many of the traditional values of their class. Most of them participated in the overthrow of the Tokugawa "with the intention of defending—not destroying—the feudal system as they knew it" (Scalapino 1953, 36). Because of the decline of agriculture, many of them already had added domestic trade and primitive manufacturing to their agrarian interests.

Contemporary Japan: Mosaic of Past and Present

The Tokugawa Era was transitional between the feudal age and the modernization initiated by the Meiji reformers. After reviewing contemporary trends in Japan, Passim (1968, 248) concludes that "we seem to see a mosaic of the past and present, fragmentation of the total society into old and new sectors, old patterns persisting in their entirety or in parts, new patterns displacing the old or re-organizing total areas of experience." The intermingling of Japanese traditions with the ideas and practices imported from the West complicate any assessment of contemporary Japan. Cross-cultural research always tests the foreign observer's ability to avoid the traps of ethnocentrism and the view that modernization is only westernization.

Broadly speaking, the Japanese are among those peoples emphasizing the subordination of self to the interests of the group, whereas Americans are among those peoples giving priority to the interests of individuals. Drawing such a contrast, however, tends to exaggerate the distinctions between highly urbanized contemporary societies and encourages acceptance of caricatures of Japan and America.

A voluminous and diverse literature presents the disagreements among experts on the uniqueness of Japanese values and behavioral patterns. The *nihonjinron* literature claims the superiority of Japanese social consensus over Western individualism (Mouer and Sugimoto 1986). Nihonjinron is nothing more than empty ethnocentrism, Dale (1986, 205) concludes: "Uniqueness becomes a code word applied to exotic phenomena whose attractiveness lay precisely in the way they give lively contemporary witness to a world and life style transcended by the march of time and progress in the West." American scholars also sometimes exaggerate the dichotomy of "American individualism" versus "Japanese groupiness": "Attraction to the opposite, to the different, to the exotic, has characterized the intellectual stance of Americans, and perhaps other Western scholars as well. To individualistic Americans ... the group phenomenon defines the problematics for Americans" (Befu 1992, 31).

Descriptions of a totally harmonious society also draw objections. Areas of conflict are ignored when the *ideal* of social harmony is treated as a complete reality. "The lines of overall social cleavage—class conflict, urban-rural conflict, sex-role conflict—seem less salient, intense, or widespread in Japan than in many Western societies," argue Steinhoff, Krauss, and Rohlen (1984, 377–78). However, they also insist that recognition of "ubiquitous conflict" is a realistic foundation for understanding contemporary Japan.

De Vos (1973, 3) declares, "What makes a Japanese 'Japanese,' that is to say, what comprises Japanese cultural psychology, has persisted in spite of changes in legal institutions, in technology, and in spite of an absorption of a great deal of scientific and aesthetic tradition from the industrial West." He sees this persistence as an example of "psychological lag." The dynamics of political, economic, and social changes inevitably modify human behavior, but interpersonal relationships respond more slowly. Block transfer of foreign ideas is countered, first, by the slowness of a people to change their familiar ways and, second, by the necessity to accommodate new ideas to the existing complex of institutions and values.

In Western societies, relationships tend to be along the horizontal dimension: with work colleagues, persons of similar age, and other peers. In Japan, social ties are along the vertical rather than the horizontal dimension through attachments of *oyabun* (persons of superior rank: parent, patron, boss, and so on) with the *kobun* (persons of subordinate rank: child, client, employee, and so on). The vertical dimension favors group cohesion in spite of rank differences among members (Nakane 1984).[1]

In his study of a bank, Rohlen (1974) discovered the concepts of social harmony and oyabun-kobun linkages served to inextricably interrelate in "one-great-family" the interests of the employees and those of the bank. The bank's motto, "harmony and strength," conveys the themes: cooperation, warmth, trust, hard and efficient work, and fellowship. Every employee's duty is to promote the well-being of the "family." Different roles and degrees of authority are to be respected, and each should be loyal to his or her rank. Like fathers, leaders are responsible for the welfare of followers.

The feudal principles of a hierarchical social order persist in the great importance placed on duty and on the location of the individual within the status-oriented relationships among group members. From their cultural heritage, Japanese recognize social obligations to one another in friendliness or benevolence, rather than relying on civil rights (Kawashima 1967, 263–66). In the West a person "can *demand* that other people, particularly his own government, respect, or refrain from infringement upon, the interests which are vital for his existence as a human being." Instead of demands derived from the rights of individuals as individuals, Japanese give priority to the collective interest.

"We hate crime but not criminals" is a saying in Japanese with a double meaning. First, offenders should be punished according to their moral and legal responsibility. The merger of both kinds of responsibility contrasts with the Western concentration on legal responsibility. Second, criminals are "our fellow countrymen" and deserve to be accepted back into society "when they purify themselves from the tainted past" (Nagashima 1990, 4–6). The moral condition of becoming repentant and rehabilitated must be satisfied if the criminal is to be accepted into the community's fellowship.

Unlike the Western concentration on legal responsibility, the Japanese perspective emphasizes the moral failures of the offenders. In that vein, Wagatsuma and Rosett (1986,

477) note the Japanese premise that the deviant has an innate capacity for eventual self-correction: "Japanese not only believe that human character is mutable but view an excessively bad person as 'non-human.' When such persons reform, they are seen as 'returning to being a real human being' " when they purify themselves.

Noda (1976) emphasizes that the word *giri* is basic to Japanese social psychology and, although it evokes too many meanings for a clear-cut definition, does convey several important ideas. Duty locates the individual in relationships with others according to the status of the respective parties; the feudal principles of a hierarchical order persist today. The person benefiting from the observance of duty cannot demand the other individual's observance but must wait for voluntary observance. Giri obligations are perpetual; they cannot be extinguished even when a duty has been performed. Although selfish gain may be involved, the relationships carry feelings of affection. The obligations are sanctioned simply by a sense of honor.

Those ideas are important for the Japanese interpretation of deviance, according to Wagatsuma and Rosett (1986). First, the individual wishes to maintain or restore a positive relationship with another person who has been harmed by the individual. (The public prosecutor and sentencing judge emphasize the offender's restitution and expressions of regret to the victim as a condition for leniency.) Second, the apology places the forgiven person in a limitless obligation to the forgiver. (The offender's desire to counter the effects of the offense is perpetual; pressure toward "rehabilitation" persists.) Third, the apology typically receives a favorable response from others because the Japanese have faith in deviants' capacity for self-correction and their commitment to future harmonious relationships with other persons. (This implication of apology is consistent with the principle of giri that external demands should be withheld because the response of the offender must be voluntary.)[2]

Traditions and
the Emergence
of Modern Law

The contemporary operations of Japanese corrections may be attributed to a strong drive initiated in 1868 to learn from Western experiences, but the lessons were adapted to the Japanese traditions and style of government. Noting the prisons of the world present general similarities, Sykes (1958, xiii) postulates: "Perhaps this is due to a diffusion of ideas, customs, and laws; perhaps it is a matter of social structures arising independently from attempts to solve much the same problems. Most probably it is some combination of both."

Correctional work in the West, as an aspect of criminal law and the political institutional structure, emerged and evolved over time. Through many centuries, Europe moved through tribalism, feudalism, and nationalism in the development of political institutions. Gradually, the concept of individual responsibility for crimes was substituted for the tribal conception that the clan is responsible for its members' transgressions. The state's authority replaced that of the clan as the unit of justice (Jeffery 1969).

The evolution of political institutions in Japan followed similar general stages, but was compressed into a shorter time-frame and was based on a different brand of political authority, argues Koschmann (1978, 5–7). In the West "humanity advanced through an endless process of confrontation, conquest, and subjugation, and rebellion." Westerners came to regard the operations of the state with relative objectivity and learned that political authority depends upon their respect and consent. They became capable of saying "no" to government. "Outside influence was piecemeal: foreign authorities, gods, and techniques were generally subordinated to structures already in place rather than installed by force." Without serious challenge, a succession of rulers held political authority that was taken for granted by the people "as an inalienable part of the natural order." Not exposed to alternative conceptions of political authority, the Japanese were not prone to say "no" to the rulers whose power was woven into the fabric of tradition and morality.

As an island society, Japan did not suffer foreign political control until the end of World War II, and the few outsiders before then who came were compelled to adapt themselves to the indigenous culture rather than presenting alternative customs and norms. "Japan has been an exceptionally homogeneous nation for a long time because of the cultural unification of different influences in a relatively isolated chain of small islands" claims Ishida (1971, 9).

A full-fledged body of written law was not framed until Japan entered the modern age—after 1868. In a form based on Chinese ideas and resting essentially on custom and morality, a partial code in about A.D. 800 had an administrative and civil part (the *ryo*) and a part (the *ritsu*) that included provisions for arrest and imprisonment. The Joei Shikimoku in 1232 was the most important of the written laws and was the chief source of feudal law into the nineteenth century. Rather than being a full-fledged code, it was a set of guidelines for the shogun's court and the provincial constables and magistrates watching over the conduct of the common people. In the years of interclan warfare, 1336–1608, several feudal lords issued "house laws" intended to protect members of the clan and its domain and to penalize severely those who lent advantages to a rival clan. For the Tokugawa state, the Rules for the Military House (Buke Sho-hatto), revised later in some particulars, was similar to the previous house laws in safeguarding the regime and imparting a Confucian flavor by enjoining frugality and a moral life (Sansom 1963a; 1963b; 1963c).

Modern law in Japan has been largely imported from the West: "There may be a marked difference between the modern and the old law at the level of state law, but at the level of living law (that from tradition and custom) there was no break in continuity. The latter evolved spontaneously and unconsciously plays an important role in the social life of the Japanese people today" (Noda 1976, 39). Outside the sphere of written law and criminal justice bureaucracies, Japanese traditions and customs express moral values that order behaviors in families, communities, and other social groups. When they are influential, traditions and customs mobilize the conscience of persons so they accept group interests as their own from habit or a sense of duty. The Western concern about legal rights is lower in priority.

Limiting the Functions of Government

While introducing modern social institutions and their infrastructure with extraordinary rapidity, the Meiji Regime could amass only a fraction of the material and social-psychological resources that this movement required. The leaders recognized their need to cloak the profound changes in the language of feudal ethics and to extend the emotional appeal of family relationships to the contacts between citizens and the Japanese state as symbolized by the emperor. In addition, the slender material resources of the state were to be stretched by limiting the functions of government.

The leniency in the decisions of the public prosecutors and sentencing judges, as discussed below, is the most visible manifestation of a criminal justice system that diverts a substantial portion of offenders from the prisons. The lenient policy is derived from a culture that presses both offenders and nonoffenders to be committed to the restoration of harmony.

The efficacy of that policy rests on the adherence of the contemporary Japanese to the moral principles suggested by the brief description above of giri and the Japanese interpretation of apology. The Meiji reformers recognized the importance of preserving the authority of traditions and customs and wanted to continue their capacity to maintain social discipline in spite of the fundamental changes in the social, economic, and political spheres of society. Tightly organized all-embracing groups continued to hold the loyalty and devoted service of their members (Bellah 1971).

The Meiji government also faced the grave and very practical problem of stretching limited resources to create an entire infrastructure. An example directly relevant to the criminal justice system would be the managing of 27,000 prisoners who had been on the losing side in the Satsuma Rebellion in 1877; it was the largest of a number of samurai revolts. Checking the rebellion took six months and required the entire army, newly established in a modern style, and along with the pensioning of samurai, added substantially to the heavy costs of modernization. Rice warehouses and stables were hastily converted into inadequate places of confinement; rioting, arson, and escapes were frequent. The heavy expense of building prisons was begun (Hiramatsu 1973; Beasley 1990).

Suspended prosecution emerged informally as an immediate and practical solution, without being incorporated in the legal code. Public prosecutors seized opportunities to avoid prosecution of minor offenses, if reasonable grounds existed, even when evidence was sufficient for conviction. Well after its practical introduction, suspended prosecution was formally recognized and authorized in 1905 by the Law for Suspension of Execution of Sentences (Nishikawa 1990).

Today, Japan is unusual among industrial nations in its relatively small size and curtailment of the growth of the national bureaucracy. The National Personnel Authorization Law (effective in May 1969) fixed the maximum number of officials. The cabinet required each ministry to eliminate one of its bureaus and to reduce personnel by 5 percent over a three-year period (Pempel 1982).

The government left to the private sector many of the functions usually assumed by the government, although a number of improvements in social security programs were introduced in the early 1970s. The government preferred a "welfare society" to a "welfare state" and expected that the family, community, and private employers would assume the responsibilities for social welfare and health care (Watanuki 1986). In that spirit, the introduction of modern probation and parole avoided the costs of a professionalized supervision by relying on unsalaried voluntary probation officers.

During the early years of the Meiji Restoration, private enterprises had very little participation in industrial development because of reluctance to risk investments in unfamiliar sectors of the economy, because of the technical and organizational difficulties of starting machine production, and because of the shortage of capital. The government was especially active in developing communications, railways, mines, and shipyards. In 1880 the government began to sell many of the state-owned enterprises at bargain prices because they were losing money and capital was needed to promote exports (T. Smith 1955).

For the field of Japanese corrections, the industrial prison is another example of the dependence on the private sector. Two-thirds of the adult inmates spend a forty-hour week making products sold on the open market. Their labor meets some of the costs of operating prisons. Contracts with private companies make possible the active workshops in Japanese prisons. Chapter 5 considers the merits of the industrial prison, an institution that is controversial in some circles.

Principle of Discretionary Prosecutions

The principle of discretionary prosecutions is an example of the combination of Western law and adaptation to Japanese circumstances; it is a basic element in the minimal use of imprisonment. Japan has embraced the principle since the establishment of its public procurator system (B. George 1988). The courts accept and adjudicate cases instituted by the public prosecutors, as opposed to the principle of mandatory prosecution under which the prosecutor must pass on for trial every case involving a suspicion of guilt and the court decides whether or not the evidence warrants formal action.

The Japanese tend to accept wide discretion in the interpretation of legal codes during processing of specific cases, thereby tolerating the principle of discretionary prosecutions. There seems to be a "disposition to lay a greater emphasis upon intuitive sensible concrete events, rather than upon universals" (Hajime Nakamura 1964, 351). Christopher (1983, 168) describes the matter this way: "The letter of the law in Japan can change drastically with little or no notice and no legislative action whatever. Judges can and do take advantage of the imprecision of their language to radically reinterpret the meaning of legal statutes."

Customary ways of the Japanese regulating conduct resisted the introduction of Western principles of law that emphasize specificity in the definition of crimes and idealize uniformity in the administration of the penalties: "The substance of Japanese legal thought—not what was written in the law books, but what the people thought and felt about the law—resisted rapid transformation" (Ozaki 1978, 123).

The present Code of Criminal Procedure offers general criteria but leaves concrete rationale to the prosecutors' discretion. Article 248 reads: "If after considering the character, age and situation of the offender, the gravity of the offense, the circumstances under which the offense was committed, and the conditions subsequent to the offense, prosecution is deemed unnecessary, prosecution need not be instituted."

Suspensions of prosecution were a major disposition into the 1980s, when referrals for formal trial became preeminent, and continue to hold a large share of cases (see table 2.1). Shikita and Tsuchiya (1990) attribute the decline (initiated in 1961) in the use of suspended prosecution to increased prosecution of assault, bodily injury, and stimu-

Table 2.1
Disposition of Cases Involving Violations
of Penal Code and Special Laws, 1931–88

| | | Percentage Distribution | | | |
| | | Formal | Summary | Prosecution | Other Non- |
Year	Decisions	Trial	Proceedings	Suspended	Prosecutions
1931	334,277	9.2	15.8	52.1	22.9
1941	310,901	9.7	27.2	52.6	10.5
1951	1,057,303	13.5	18.9	56.8	10.8
1961	544,086	22.3	29.5	39.0	9.2
1971	434,139	20.2	34.2	37.4	8.2
1981	343,880	34.4	31.7	27.0	6.9
1988	241,819	38.5	24.4	28.8	8.3

Source: Shikita and Tsuchiya (1990).

Note: Professional negligence and road traffic offenses are not included.

lant-drug offenses. Suspension of prosecution is the major kind of nonprosecution, but discretion is not the sole basis. In 1991 suspensions were 78.8 percent of all instances of nonprosecution. The remainder were justified by insufficient evidence, 14.4 percent; lack of valid complaint, 2.5 percent; mental incapacity, .6 percent; and other reasons, 3.8 percent (Research and Training Institute 1992, 96).

The principle of discretionary prosecution is found in some other countries.[3] It enlarges the role of the public prosecutor in decision making for the sake of reducing the number of trials. The practice raises questions about the equality of justice and the deterrent effect of law enforcement. However, according to Satsumae (1977, 6–9) even serious criminals are favorably impressed by "such generous dispositions" by the procuracy and judiciary and are moved to reform themselves. He claims that "the practice is better able to reflect the individual circumstances in the case" and the worthy offender is protected from stigmatizing publicity.

I was told of the following case of suspended prosecution that illustrates the emphasis on the qualities of the offender and the crime situation: Housewives in a rural neighborhood asked the forty-two-year-old wife of a small shop owner to purchase clothing for them and their children when she went to the city. Obtaining a profit, she began to fill orders regularly on weekly shopping trips. One day at the urban textile store she realized that she had insufficient money to meet all the orders. She paid for some items on the third floor, believing she could leave unnoticed without paying the entire bill. However, a store detective stopped her outside the store and summoned the police. She admitted the theft and the police released her after taking her statement. Having no criminal record, she agreed to abandon the order business to avoid more temptation. The stolen items were returned to the store. The public prosecutor dropped the case without going to trial with the consent of the store manager and with her husband's assurance that he would supervise her.

Haruo Abe (1963) declares that official leniency has increased over the years in reduced imposition of the death penalty, preference for selecting the minimum sentences prescribed by statute, and granting probation. He advances several tentative explanations: Judges and prosecutors surpass the public in understanding the causes of crime and in humanitarian impulses, they are less emotionally shocked by offenses, they doubt that imprisonment has positive effects, and consciously or unconsciously, the judges sometimes want to demonstrate judicial broad-mindedness.

Public prosecutors and judges are careerists. By passing a national examination, a candidate becomes eligible to take an even more difficult examination and gain entry to a two-year course conducted by the Legal Training and Research Institute of the Supreme Court. Four months are devoted to civil and criminal procedures, sixteen months to field training, and four months to capstone instruction. Pending a final examination after completion of training, the apprentice is qualified to be an assistant judge, prosecutor, or lawyer. Full judges have had at least ten years experience in such roles (Hakaru Abe 1963; Hattori 1963).

"In some countries judges do not consider whether or not the suspect has compensated the victim because, they say, the rich can buy their freedom but the poor can not," a former public prosecutor told me in an interview.

> But we do not have any special mediation or reparation scheme. The most important advice of the defense counsel in Japan is to negotiate with the victim and his people for forgiveness and offer money as compensation. When the victim or his family write a statement that lenient treatment is acceptable, I, as the defendant's adviser, would take the piece of paper to the public prosecutor. If convinced by his own investigation that the victim is satisfied with the payment, the public prosecutor will take the statement in consideration. If the offender's past conduct has not been good or the amount of damage is too great to warrant suspension of prosecution, the case is highly likely to go to trial. The court will consider all those factors when passing sentence.

Suspension of Prison Sentences

The judge is authorized to suspend a sentence to prison under "extenuating circumstances." Article 25 of the Penal Code limits the leniency to persons who were sentenced to prison for no more than three years or, if previously imprisoned, had not been imprisoned again within five years after satisfaction of the previous prison sentence. In practice, "extenuating circumstances" are such as the following: The defendant has no, or a minimal, criminal record or is young enough to change attitudes and lifestyle; the victim excuses the offender, the victim and the defendant have agreed to terms for restitution, and the offender exhibits readiness for rehabilitation; the offense was accidental, not deliberate (Kouhashi 1985).

Blameworthiness is measured in practice by deliberateness in planning, and coldheartedness in execution, of the criminal plan, inflicting excessive pain on the victim, repetition of offenses, and other evidence of moral depravity (Suzuki 1979). Favorable social and psychological factors are considered in evaluating the offender's capacity for positive behavior. Previous imprisonment is a negative factor contributing to the concentration of recidivists in Japanese prisons. The effect, however, is mitigated by lifting that criterion if at least five years had passed since the earlier penal confinement ended.

The provision in the Japanese Penal Code for suspended sentences was modeled on the French-Belgian system (Ancel 1971). Alarmed by the increase of crime and recidivism, nineteenth-century France questioned the usefulness of imprisonment. Conditional suspension of prison sentences emerged in Belgian law in 1888 and French law in 1891 when the Meiji reformers were examining European legal systems. In Belgium and France, the prison sentences were pronounced to intimidate the convicted offenders, but the casual offender was believed to have the capacity to rehabilitate voluntarily, when so intimidated, without probationary supervision.

Over the decades, the suspensions of prison sentences have attained greater proportions in Japan (see table 2.2). As evidence of the approach's efficiency, revocations of the suspensions have fluctuated around only 10 to 20 percent. The suspensions usually do not require probationary supervision, because the judges tend to believe that official monitoring is excessive punishment of individuals who are capable of self-rehabilitation. Outcomes for 1991 indicate that the judges' expectations are usually justified by experience. For 28,021 persons granted suspensions of prison sentences without supervision in 1991, 2,337 were revoked (8.3 percent) for new offenses. For 4,647 granted suspensions with probationary supervision, 1,186 were revoked (25.5 percent) for new offenses. Another 189 individual revocations were due to previous offenses, violation of

Table 2.2

Suspended Prison Sentences, Probation, and
Revocation, 1931–91

Year	Prison Sentences	Suspended Sentences			
		No.	Suspension Rate (%)	Suspended w/ Probation (%)	Suspension Revoked (%)
1931	35,219	4,817	13.7	NA	10.5
1951	118,229	54,272	45.9	NA	18.6
1961	83,249	43,142	51.8	18.7	13.6
1971	69,467	40,361	58.1	16.0	8.2
1981	76,219	44,269	58.1	18.6	14.3
1991	54,557	32,668	59.9	14.2	10.8

Sources: Shikita and Tsuchiya (1990); Research and Training Institute (1993).

probation conditions, and other reasons (Research and Training Institute 1993, 73).

The rates of suspension vary among offenses because of differences in length of sentences as allowed by statutes. Crimes believed to pose greater threats to public security, of course, draw more sentences exceeding the three-year limit for suspensions. In publishing data on the suspension of prison sentences in 1990, the Supreme Court notes the judges' readiness to return to the free community, and not necessarily under probationary supervision, even those individuals convicted of violent crimes. These individuals had not been imprisoned in the previous five years; if granted a suspension of a previous prison sentence, they had not committed a crime during that period of suspension; and they had received a prison sentence of no more than three years for a recent crime. On those grounds, a number of violent cases were considered for suspension of the prison sentence: 82 cases of robbery, 186 of homicide, and 3,405 of bodily injury. Because the particular crimes were the least flagrant and the offenders presented favorable characteristics, a portion of those cases were granted suspensions: 54 percent of the robbery cases, 66 percent of the homicide, and 55 percent of the bodily injury. Those homicide cases were found to qualify as "mercy killings," and the robbery and bodily injury cases were found to be less aggravated.

SUMMING UP: A LOW RATE OF IMPRISONMENT

After assembling the various facets of criminal justice processing, we return to the fundamental point: Japan sends a remarkably small proportion of offenders to prison. Table 2.3 presents data in support of that statement by outlining the range of dispositions available to the courts and how the choices among the dispositions have changed over the decades.

The total number of defendants increased fourfold between 1951 and 1961 but declined irregularly thereafter, while always exceeding the 1951 level. Meanwhile, the actual number of imprisonments dropped with almost complete consistency. The number of death sentences and life sentences have been too few to have any effect on the imprisonment rate. In 1951, referrals to prisons took up 11 percent of the dispositions; thereafter, they have represented less than 3 percent. Table 2.2 documents the fact that suspensions have taken up a progressively increasing share of the prison sentences and that only a minor share of the suspensions have required the supervision that is the indispensable element of genuine probation.

Fines especially dominate the dispositions of summary courts and those reported in table 2.3. Penal detention is a mild version of imprisonment, being less than thirty days served in a detention facility. Article 18, Penal Code, authorizes penal detention in a detention house for persons unable to pay a fine in full. Imposed only in few instances, use of penal detention has declined over the years.

Type of Crime and Length of Sentence

The diversionary decisions, of course, affect the number of prisoners. Our data permit examination of two relevant variables: the crimes that sent convicted defendants to prison and the length of the prison sentences imposed upon them. Of course, in addition to the decisions of the procuracy and judiciary, the two variables are affected by changing conduct of criminals, the enactment of new criminal laws, modifications of old laws, revised law enforcement circumstances, and new sentencing policies.

The crimes of prisoners admitted to prison are grouped in table 2.4 according to commonly employed categories. Property crimes are most prevalent; larceny is numerically dominant, followed in turn by fraud, embezzlement, forgery, "intrusion upon a habitat," arson, and possession of stolen property. Property crimes dropped consistently, from half of all crimes in 1970 to 38 percent in 1992.

Violence against persons is predominately "bodily injury"; robbery and homicide are only a third of the number of bodily injury offenses. Assault has minor importance, and kidnapping is very infrequent. In crimes of "societal violence," the community has been victimized by illicit economic gain (typically, the transgressions of criminal syndicates known as the *yakuza* in Japan), by inflicting death or injury through negligence (mostly in traffic offenses), or by engaging in aggravated crimes with firearms and swords. Both general brands of violence declined over the years.

Traffic offenses punished by imprisonment stood third among the crime categories in 1970 and their share also dropped over the years. Rape, indecent assault, and pornography consistently drew a smaller share of admissions. Gambling and lottery as well as prostitution were of least importance.

Table 2.3

*Dispositions of Adjudicated Defendants by Court
of First Instance, 1951–89*

Dispositions	1951	1961	1971	1981	1989
Imprisonment	64,112	40,205	29,148	31,986	31,122
Capital Punishment	(44)	(29)	(4)	(2)	(2)
Life Sentence	(111)	(69)	(38)	(34)	(46)
Prison Term	(63,957)	(40,107)	(29,106)	(31,950)	(31,074)
Fine	452,758	2,462,134	1,807,006	2,121,880	1,208,575
Penal Detention	270	120	75	42	79
Suspended Imprisonment	54,272	43,142	40,361	44,269	35,528
Simple Suspension	NA	(35,075)	(33,910)	(36,052)	(30,409)
With Probation	NA	(8,067)	(6,451)	(8,217)	(5,119)
Acquittal	2,539	425	451	212	134
Other[a]	29,128	3,072	1,623	625	367
Total	603,079	2,549,098	1,878,664	2,199,014	1,275,805
			Percentage Distribution		
Imprisonment	10.63	1.58	1.55	1.46	2.44
Fine	75.07	96.59	96.19	96.49	94.73
Penal Detention	0.05	0.00	0.00	0.00	0.01
Suspended Imprisonment	9.00	1.69	2.15	2.01	2.78
Simple Suspension	NA	(1.36)	(1.80)	(1.64)	(2.38)
With Probation	NA	(0.32)	(0.34)	(0.37)	(0.40)
Acquittal	0.42	0.02	0.02	0.01	0.01
Other[a]	4.83	0.12	0.09	0.03	0.03
Total	100.00	100.00	100.00	100.00	100.00

Sources: Data modified from Shikita and Tsuchiya (1990); 1989 data supplied by Research and Training Institute, Ministry of Justice.

[a]"Other" includes guilty but no penalty, time of legal responsibility was exceeded, and summary sentence was sent but not received by defendant.

Table 2.4
Male Prison Admissions by Crime, 1970–92

Crime	1970	1975	1980	1985	1990	1992
	Percentage of Admissions for All Crimes[a]					
Property	49.5	46.6	39.4	38.6	37.9	38.1
Violence Against Persons	15.6	15.2	12.7	12.3	12.3	11.5
Societal Violence	9.8	9.8	8.4	7.8	8.2	7.6
Traffic	16.4	15.6	14.1	11.9	12.4	10.9
Sex	5.7	4.5	2.5	2.0	2.6	2.6
Gambling	2.2	1.5	0.8	0.6	0.6	0.5
Drugs	0.5	6.6	21.9	26.4	25.5	28.4
Prostitution	0.3	0.2	0.2	0.4	0.5	0.4
Total	100.00	100.00	100.00	100.00	100.00	100.00
Total No.	24,966	25,157	26,933	29,523	20,888	19,115
	Percentage of Admissions Excluding Drug Crimes[a]					
Property	49.8	49.9	50.5	52.5	51.0	53.2
Violence Against Persons	15.7	16.3	16.2	16.7	16.5	16.1
Societal Violence	9.8	10.5	10.8	10.6	11.0	10.6
Traffic	16.5	16.7	18.0	16.2	16.6	15.2
Sex	5.7	4.8	3.2	2.7	3.4	3.6
Gambling	2.2	1.6	1.0	0.8	0.8	0.7
Prostitution	0.3	0.2	0.3	0.5	0.7	0.6
Total	100.00	100.00	100.00	100.00	100.00	100.00
Total No.	24,837	23,498	21,047	21,710	15,564	13,677

Sources: Research and Statistics Section, *Annual Report of Statistics on Correction* for given years.

[a]Data exclude public order, other penal law, and other special law offenses.

Drug offenses deserve special attention because, alone among the crime categories, they had a drastic increase from their less than 1 percent share in 1970. Laws against opium have existed since 1879, against narcotics since 1948, and against stimulant drugs (amphetamines) since 1951. During World War II, drug abuse was limited to a few opium and cocaine addicts. During the postwar chaos, abuse of stimulant drugs became prevalent. One hypothesis is that stimulant drugs produced for the military in wartime had leaked out to the public. Arrests for drug offenses were dominated by violations of the Stimulant Drugs Control Law. Since 1985 the number of arrests each year have declined (National Police Agency 1992).

To demonstrate the major effect of stimulant-drug offenses on the number of prisoners, table 2.4 includes the percentage distribution of crime categories by year with the drug offenses removed. The total number of male prison admissions, minus drug offenses, declined rather consistently, from 24,837 in 1970 to 13,677 in 1992. The second general pattern in types of crime became more obvious: the increase in the percentage shares of prison admissions for property, violence, and traffic offenses.

A declining average length of sentence will reduce the number of prison inmates present in the long run. A person sentenced to three months of penal confinement probably would add to the prison population for only that year. The person sentenced to five years and released on expiration of sentence would be present for five consecutive years. When admissions of persons with long sentences became more and more frequent over the years, that factor alone would raise the imprisonment rate, but Japan's imprisonment rate *dropped* in spite of the growth of the mean length of sentence from 17.52 months in 1970 to 20.93 in 1990.

Only an Artifice of the Low Crime Rate?

"Of course, fewer Japanese go to prison," a Dutch lawyer told me. "They are less likely than most people to commit crimes." He implied that the imprisonment rate, essentially and merely, mirrors the crime rate. He overlooked the fact that, even for persons sentenced to prison, a substantial share are immediately returned to the community. The

Table 2.5

Crime Rates Compared with Imprisonment Rates, 1926–90

| Year | Rate per 100,000 Population | | Ratio |
	Crime[a]	Imprisonment[b]	
1926	1,171	65	18.01
1930	1,612	61	26.43
1935	2,183	72	30.32
1940	1,414	54	26.18
1945	984	68	14.47
1950	1,756	102	17.22
1955	1,608	74	21.73
1960	1,476	68	21.71
1965	1,367	54	25.31
1970	1,234	39	31.64
1975	1,103	34	32.44
1980	1,160	36	32.22
1985	1,328	38	34.95
1990	1,324	33	40.12
1992	1,400	30	46.67

Sources: Shikita and Tsuchiya (1990); Research and Training Institute (1993).

[a]Includes penal code violations other than traffic.

[b]Based on average daily prisoners present.

crime rates and imprisonment rates have diverged increasingly over the years since 1945 (see table 2.5).

The divergence would be even greater if the heavy reduction of traffic cases before imprisonment were included. Administrative processing of traffic violations has had some effect; the Traffic Infraction Fine System was introduced in 1968. A "violator ticket" is given for a minor violation. The fine may be paid within ten days at a post office or certain banks; failures to pay go to the public prosecutor. Traffic offenses aside, the police can terminate the "petty offenses" when the damage is negligible and has already been recovered, the victim does not desire punishment, the offense can be considered accidental, and repetition of the offense is unlikely (Tsubouchi 1973).

Japanese police enjoy high clearance rates; that is, the number of major, nontraffic offenses for which suspects are identified, divided by the total offenses reported to the police. Claimed as evidence of police efficiency, the high clearance rate also is due to stringent control of firearms and illicit drugs (Kasai 1973; Suzuki 1979). Japan's small area and lack of land border with another country also promote apprehension.

Japanese favor both effective law enforcement and lenient application of punitive sanctions: "The policy of limiting institutional treatment to the bare minimum could be adopted in Japan, partly because of high rate of clearance of crime by apprehending the criminals, thus allowing leniency, and partly because ... the public still sees the offenders as fellow countrymen who are believed to have shown sincere repentance for their wrongful acts" (Shikita 1985, 671).

The police benefit from considerable participation of citizens in crime prevention associations, the Traffic Safety Association, and juvenile guidance. *Koban* (miniature police substations) in urban neighborhoods and *chuzaisho* in the countryside collect information about local happenings and administer the official registration of persons living in the neighborhood. Those responsibilities enable the police to become aware of questionable activities (Van Wolferen 1989).

The remarkable clearance rate also has been explained as a consequence of less concern about civil rights. The Japanese police are "unencumbered by the concern with U.S. due process constraints on 'lawful' search and seizure, arrest, interrogations, and other 'taken-for-granted' entry-level rights of the suspect" (Fishman and Dinitz 1989, 122). Forced confessions have been found, but from the perspective of Japanese values, "being picked up by the police, is, in any event, shameful, and there is comfort in converting an overwhelming sense of shame into an admission of guilt" (Van Wolferen 1989, 189).

Plant Capacity When Inmates Are Few

Substantial growth in the number of prisoners raises questions about the adequacy of plant capacity. American experts have debated, without reaching a reliable conclusion, whether or not additional capacity has encouraged judges to sentence more offenders to prison (Blumstein 1988).

In spite of the long-term decline in Japan in the number of prisoners, the rated capacity of penal institutions (including detention facilities) has remained about the same. The number of inmates (including accused and untried defendants in detention centers) per 100,000 Japanese has dropped sharply and somewhat regularly. The failure to cut capacity is demonstrated more precisely by the general decline in the average usage per 100 available sleeping spaces, from 154.1 inmates in 1950 to 70.4 inmates in 1992.

The failure to cut capacity is especially noteworthy because obsolete plants and public opposition to existing prisons in their neighborhoods gave reason to abandon some sites. Urban growth has ended the previous geographical isolation of many prisons. Major prisons had been constructed on the design of American and European prisons of the 1930s and 1940s. The cellblocks and workshops were poorly lighted and sanitary facilities were introduced later in a provisional way. A major reconstruction program was undertaken in the late 1980s to modernize the large prisons by substituting well-lighted and spacious buildings. Instead of exploiting the opportunity to reduce operating costs by cutting capacity, the Correction Bureau has chosen to improve the quality of prison housing.

3

THE TWO BUREAUS:
THEIR PLACE, FUNCTIONS,
AND HISTORY

*U*nlike the American dispersal of correctional agencies at the federal, state, and local levels, Japan concentrates all operations in the Correction and Rehabilitation Bureaus in the national government. Since the origin of modern prison administration with the Kangokusoku (prison rules) in 1872, the trend has been toward unification. From 1872 to 1885 the Ministry of Home Affairs included a prison bureau. From 1885 to 1903 the Police and Public Peace Bureau took over. When all the prisons came under the central government in 1903, the Ministry of Justice again assumed jurisdiction, renamed the prison bureau the "Prison Administration Bureau," and set up a rehabilitation bureau as well. In 1943 the two bureaus were merged to become the Penal Administration Bureau. Another change in 1946 set up the Prison Administration Bureau and the Rehabilitation Section in the Ministry of Justice Secretariat. The current format emerged in 1952 as the Correction Bureau and the Rehabilitation Bureau (Correction Bureau 1967).

Centralized administration encourages fiscal efficiency, uniformity of policy and practice, systemized recruitment of personnel, and effective in-service training. The consolidation of correctional activities within two nationwide systems risks concentrating authority in the Tokyo headquarters, thereby favoring pathological bureaucracy. The risk has been minimized by the dispersion of the administration of the Rehabilitation Bureau to the probation offices and eight regional parole boards. For the Correction Bureau, the headquarters of eight correction regions stand between the central administration in Tokyo and the prisons, detention facilities, and juvenile training schools. Chances for recognition of local circumstances are enhanced: classification of arriving inmates is kept within the region; inmates are located closer to their families for visits; and the costs of transporting prisoners from place to place are minimized.

Three Distinct Correctional Ideologies

An ideology is a composite of beliefs that enable members of a particular group to work together toward the group's goals. The agency ideology captures what the agency as a group, or a segment of the more extensive group, *believes* it is supposed to accomplish and how that purpose is to be achieved. Whether or not the belief is widely held is of less importance to our analysis than, first, that the belief shapes what is done and, second, that the belief stems from characteristically *Japanese* perceptions.

The moral component in Japanese culture plays a crucial part in justifying the agency ideologies; it heightens the offender's remorse and strengthens the social rejection of offenders who are not repentant. Japanese social psychology goes beyond what Andenaes (1975) calls the price tariff of the criminal law: the punishment authorized by law that is supposed to stir fear and abandonment of any intention to commit a crime. "Criminal law is not only a price tariff, but rather also is an expression of society's disapproval which may work in subtle ways to influence behavior" (341).

Ideology of the Prisons

The prisons for adults turn to industrial labor and strict discipline as management strategies that in conjunction sustain an orderly environment. Like prison systems elsewhere, the Correction Bureau claims it produces benefits for prisoners when they return to the community: "Prison industry is organized to serve constructive purposes in the treatment of prisoners. Its objective is not only to provide inmates with vocational knowledge and skills, but to strengthen their will to work, sense of self help and spirit of cooperation through working together (Correction Bureau 1990b, 35–36).[1]

When Japanese offenders are repentant and try to cancel the effects of their crimes on the victims, the Japanese favor leniency for the offenders because they appear to show the capacity for self-correction Japanese expect of most rule breakers. Denied official leniency when they are not repentant, the adult prisoners appear to the general public to be socially unworthy and, therefore, proper candidates for stern control as prisoners. The ideology of adult prisons includes the justification of industrial labor. "Most prisoners have led a life of idleness, they did not work in society," I was told in an interview, "It is important that they learn to work. Control from outside the inmates develop their self-discipline in a kind of education."

Here "correctional training" refers specifically to enforced compliance to a circumscribed behavioral script that is expected to become ingrained habit. Even-handed administration of the prison's punishment-reward system is supposed to have blanket effects on all of the prisoners, regardless of differences among personalities in motivation, perceptions, and personal background. Profound study of individual differences is believed unnecessary. The routine tasks of prison labor are expected to cultivate discipline of persons unused to productive work. Rather simple diagnosis and classification of prisoners are deemed sufficient and are favored because time-consuming study of individuals is avoided. Correctional training can be carried out rapidly, it is argued, by custodial personnel knowledgeable in disciplinary measures but lacking competence in sophisticated therapeutic modalities.

Ideology of Juvenile Justice

The Juvenile Law, Article 1, expresses the official philosophy of the family court, juvenile classification homes, and juvenile training schools: "The object of this Law is, with a view to the wholesome rearing of juveniles, to carry out protective measures relating to the character correction and environmental adjustment of delinquent juveniles and also to take special measures with respect to the criminal cases of juveniles and adults who are harmful to the welfare of juveniles" (UNAFEI n.d., 165)

Japan has a long history of treating juveniles differently than adult offenders. Young lawbreakers usually are not considered serious threats to the community. Their youth encourages faith that any deviant tendencies can be corrected before they are ingrained in habits and a particular social perspective. The young are believed to be especially susceptible to change. "Juveniles are malleable," the superintendent of a training school for boys told me. "The staff must try to rid them of the effects of bad experiences. Adults have many choices and know the value of choices; they must take the responsibility for their misdeeds. Juveniles do not know there are choices; we want to teach them the choices and the good way of living." Another superintendent said: "The real goal of corrections is to try to change the individual within and not to attempt to control him or her from outside. If the problem that brought the juvenile here is discovered, the staff has to help him or her to solve it." A third superintendent said: "We try to take care of the needs of each inmate in an individualistic way. The inmates are not the same, but there are limitations of time."

Applying the casework method, the family court is expected to concentrate, not exclusively on the delinquent acts, but on the unmet needs of individual youngsters brought before it, their unfavorable living circumstances, and their failures to control antisocial impulses. In keeping with the Japanese faith in deviants' capacity for eventual self-correction, the official philosophy is to mobilize community resources to assist the juveniles and, thereby, to avoid sending them to training schools.

Established in 1949 during the reorganization of the juvenile justice system, the juvenile classification homes are the responsibility of the Correction Bureau. Their fundamental mission is to diagnose juveniles referred by the family courts. Psychologists conduct diagnostic interviews, administer psychometric tests, and prepare reports.

Ideology of the Rehabilitation Bureau

In a videotape orienting the public to the work of the Rehabilitation Bureau, a spokesman says in part: "The rehabilitation system is based on the concept of trusting people who unfortunately have committed crimes or have been delinquent so they can reform by developing a greater awareness of themselves and their circumstances. . . . Imprisonment isolates criminals from society, and they often return to crime when they are released. Consequently, the crime rate never decreases. Therefore, the prevention system is very important in assisting offenders when they return to society, supporting their social rehabilitation and making them productive members of society."

The Rehabilitation Bureau voices the same claims made for community corrections in the West but, unlike in the West, relies heavily upon private persons and groups to achieve its purposes. Volunteer probation officers (VPOs) conduct almost all supervision of probationers and parolees. Rehabilitation aid associations operate halfway houses, serving parolees chiefly, that receive government subsidies but rely more on private funding.

Japanese volunteers and the Rehabilitation Bureau are effective partners, claims a former director general of the Rehabilitation Bureau (Satoh 1989). Taking advantage of traditions of cooperation between citizens and the government, the bureau guides, offers treatment methods, and develops plans for the participation of private organizations and volunteers. Private organizations and volunteers hold the confidence of local employers, business enterprises, and local residents for reintegration of the probationers and parolees into the local economy and fellowship. Private parties are more familiar with the neighborhood and its institutions.

ORGANIZATIONS WITHIN ORGANIZATIONS

The central offices of the Correction Bureau and the Rehabilitation Bureau each occupy one floor in one of the two twenty-story skyscrapers in Hibiya, overlooking the Emperor's Palace. The two skyscrapers and a smaller older building hold the offices of the Ministry of Justice. The proportion of space allocated to the two bureaus and the organization of the ministry attest to the dominance of the procuracy in the affairs of the Ministry of Justice. The organizational dominance is consistent with the vital contributions of the public prosecutors and the courts to the low imprisonment rate of Japan and the effects of their contributions on correctional affairs (see chapter 2).

As an executive department in the national government, the Ministry of Justice drafts laws and ordinances related to the judicial system and carries out its administrative business through seven bureaus. The constitution, enforced in 1947, invests all business pertaining to courts under the jurisdiction of the judiciary, independent of the executive branch.

The Civil Affairs Bureau specializes in the bases for the rights of people, such as nationality, family registration, and registration of immovables and commercial enterprises. It also drafts laws and ordinances pertaining to civil matters. The Criminal Affairs Bureau has general supervision and control over the work of the prosecutors and drafts legislation on those matters. The public prosecutors investigate criminal cases, institute prosecution when deemed appropriate, and conduct prosecution at trials. The Litigation Bureau is concerned with civil and administrative suits that involve the interests of government. The Civil Liberties Bureau is responsible for protection of the basic rights of people, including investigation and disposition of infringements upon their rights. The Immigration Bureau specializes in the administration of measures dedicated to control of alien and Japanese nationals entering and leaving the country, and the registration of alien residents.

The ministry also carries out investigations required by the Subversive Activities Prevention Law and, when action against particular organizations is found appropriate, refers the case to an agency outside the ministry, the Public Security Investigation Agency.

The United Nations Asia and Far East Institute for the Prevention of Crime and Treatment of Offenders (UNAFEI), located in Fuchu, a suburb of Tokyo, has been in operation since 1962 under the joint auspices of the United Nations and the Ministry of Justice. The government of Japan assumed all financial obligations in 1970. The institute brings senior officials and experienced workers of countries in the Asian region for three or four training courses and seminars each year. In addition to the regular faculty, visiting experts invited from abroad teach the courses.

ORGANIZATION OF
THE REHABILITATION BUREAU

The organizational sinews of the Rehabilitation Bureau consist of fifty probation offices, thirty branch probation offices, and eight regional parole boards. The probation offices are responsible for supervising those adults who are granted release into the community under probationary supervision, juveniles placed on probation by the family courts, and inmates released on parole from prisons and training schools. The probation officers are responsible for supervision of parolees as well as probationers.

The eight regional parole boards (RPBs) are located in Tokyo, Osaka, Nagoya, Hiroshima, Sendai, Sapporo, Takamatsu, and Fukuoka where high courts and high public prosecutors are located. The Penal Code, Articles 28 and 30, authorizes the boards to grant or revoke paroles from prisons and to grant provisional releases from detention houses. The RPBs also decide when inmates serving indeterminate sentences will be released and grant paroles and irrevocable releases from juvenile training schools.

The central office in Tokyo has a staff of 22 and the field offices have 1,316 staff members, including 855 probation officers in probation offices and 95 attached to regional parole boards, as of 1 January 1991. VPOs carry out preparole investigations and supervise probationers and parolees.

During 1990 the personnel of the Rehabilitation Bureau processed 179,997 cases. Table 3.1 shows that the bureau's total 1990 budget was $103,597,838, or about $575 per case processed. The supervision of probationers and parolees absorbed a considerable share of the total budget. Supervision costs are estimated to include a portion of office expenses, $8,599,838; central office salaries, $46,877; probation officer salaries, $49,660,600; and expenditures for volunteer probation officers, $21,359,423; for a total of $79,666,738. Responsibilities other than supervision are subsumed into

Table 3.1

Budget of Rehabilitation Bureau, FY 1990–91

Budget Items	Expenditure in U.S. Dollars	Percentage of Budget
Office Expenses	8,599,838	8.30
Salaries	60,756,662	58.65
Central Office	(46,877)	(0.05)
Parole Boards	(11,049,185)	(10.66)
Probation Offices	(49,660,600)	(47.94)
VPOs	21,359,423	20.62
Expenses Repaid	(21,019,800)	(20.29)
Training	(297,961)	(0.29)
Other Expenses	(41,662)	(0.04)
Hostels	12,592,223	12.15
Reimbursement	(12,284,954)	(11.86)
Subsidies	(272,015)	(0.26)
Training	(35,254)	(0.03)
Training, Supervision of Volunteer Association	133,592	0.13
Material Aid	88,677	0.09
Crime Prevention Actions	67,423	0.06
Total	103,597,838	100.00

Source: Data provided by Central Office (Tokyo), Rehabilitation Bureau.

Note: The Japanese fiscal year ends 31 March. All dollar amounts are computed on the basis of 130 yen per $1 (U.S.).

that total; the costs of supervision are exaggerated, but for the total cases processed in 1990, the estimate for supervision is only $443 per case. In 1990 hostels received 8,393 individuals, and the probation offices gave material aid to 6,451 in the form of food, clothing, medical treatment, or travel expenses (Research and Statistics Section 1991c, 152–53). Expenditures were $1,500 per person referred to hostels and less than $14 per inmate receiving material aid.

Advocates of community-based corrections frequently note lower costs as a major advantage over imprisonment. In very broad terms, the total costs of the Correction Bureau ($48,864 per adult prisoner, juvenile training school inmate, or juvenile classification home resident) is much greater than the total costs of the Rehabilitation Bureau ($1,410 per probationer, parolee, or aftercare client). In a rough way, the item "managing inmates" suggests the Correction Bureau's costs of direct contacts per client: $3,537 for adult prisons and detention houses, $4,991 for juvenile training schools, and $352 for juvenile classification homes for juveniles received from the family courts.

The heavy use of VPOs has considerable effect on the Rehabilitation Bureau's costs. Moreover, the period of parole or probation supervision is shorter than confinement in a correctional institution. Correctional institutions are expected to deal especially with the more threatening offenders, and daily costs are greatly inflated by around-the-clock custody and maintenance of inmates.

ORGANIZATION OF
THE CORRECTION BUREAU

The headquarters of the correction regions also are located in Tokyo, Osaka, Nagoya, Fukuoka, Hiroshima, Sendai, Sapporo, and Takamatsu. Each supervises the correctional facilities in several prefectures, coordinates the transfer of inmates and operations of prison industries, inspects institutions periodically, and operates a branch center for training personnel.

Adult prisons are differentiated by function and type of inmates; each correction region has a classification center. Pretrial detention is handled in 7 large detention houses and 102 branches.[2] Five prisons and one branch prison receive women only. Four institutions for adults are designated as hospitals. One prison specializes in foreign prisoners, 2 others receive foreigners along with Japanese inmates, and 8 juvenile prisons receive young adults under twenty-six years of age.

The juvenile training schools are classified into four types (primary, middle, special, and medical) distinguishing juvenile inmates according to age, physical or mental difficulties, and criminalistic tendencies. Certain schools are designated for formal education, vocational training, and medical care.[3] The Correction Bureau also manages 53 juvenile classification homes providing diagnostic services for family courts and 1 women's guidance home for sentenced street prostitutes.[4]

The Correction Bureau is allocated 50 positions in the central office in Tokyo and 175 in the headquarters of the eight correction regions. The personnel of the prisons and detention houses number 17,018, the juvenile training schools 2,474, the juvenile classification homes 1,211, and the women's guidance home 6. The grand total is 20,934 executives and staff members.

At the end of 1990, the prisons and detention houses held 46,890 persons and the juvenile training schools 3,529 juveniles (Research and Statistics Section 1991a, 18; 1991b, 94). The prisons and detention houses averaged 2.75 inmates to personnel; the juvenile training schools had a ratio of 1.43 inmates to personnel. The juvenile classification homes, of course, had an especially heavy flow of juveniles referred for diagnoses and a few for detention. The homes received 18,831 cases and averaged a daily population of 1,078 in 1990. The homes received an average of 15.5 cases

Table 3.2
Budget of Correction Bureau, FY 1990–91

Budget Items	Expenditure in U.S. Dollars	Percentage of Budget
Central Office[a]	131,123	0.00[b]
Regional Headquarters	1,267,216,523	50.36
Adult Institutions	1,028,391,361	40.87
Administration	(727,304,238)	(28.90)
Managing Inmates	(165,863,638)	(6.59)
Prison Industries	(21,287,485)	(0.85)
Building Maintenance	(113,936,000)	(4.53)
Juvenile Training Schools	150,830,077	6.00
Administration	(117,510,885)	(4.67)
Managing Inmates	(17,613,215)	(0.70)
Building Maintenance	(15,705,977)	(0.63)
Juvenile Classification Homes	69,153,554	2.75
Administration	(59,345,000)	(2.36)
Managing Juveniles	(6,634,346)	(0.26)
Building Maintenance	(3,174,208)	(0.13)
Women's Guidance Homes	621,792	0.02
Administration	(551,569)	(0.02)
Managing Residents	(70,223)	(0.00)[b]
Total	2,516,344,430	100.00

Source: Data provided by Central Office (Tokyo), Correction Bureau.

Note: All dollar amounts are computed on the basis of 130 yen per $1 (U.S.).

[a]This item is an underestimate because some expenditures are woven into the budget of the Ministry of Justice.

[b]Less than 0.01 percent.

per staff member; in terms of average daily population, the ratio was .89 juveniles per staff member, a particularly high level of staffing (Research and Statistics Section 1991b, 2–3).

The Correction Bureau averaged an expenditure of $48,864 per individual in 1990 (see table 3.2). More specifically, if the costs of the headquarters in Tokyo and the correction regions are ignored and the population of the institutions at the end of 1990 is used for the calculation, the average expenditure was $21,947 for each of the 46,898 inmates of adult prisons and detention houses, $42,740 for each of the 3,529 inmates of juvenile training schools, and $3,718 for each of the 18,599 clients held in juvenile classification homes after referral by the family court.

Consolidated Organization of Detention

The detention facilities of the Correction Bureau hold three general kinds of persons. "Suspects" are being held while the police and public prosecutors complete their investigation. The "accused" have been ordered to stand trial and are awaiting appearance before the court. The "convicted" have been found guilty at their trials and begin their imprisonment at the detention facility. The detention houses also hold prisoners sentenced to death and carry out the executions. The facilities are gatekeepers to the prisons. Inmates are assigned to that type of prison appropriate to their general characteristics. Staff of the detention houses study the qualities of new inmates and assess their background, biography, and criminal history. Information from the police and courts is acquired to determine security risk and for forwarding to the assigned prison.

The convicted inmates are distributed among the prisons according to a classification scheme that takes into account their sex, nationality, kind of penalty, age, length of sentence, degree of "criminal tendency," and physical or mental disabilities (Correction Bureau 1990b, 30–31). The category codes are: females (W); foreigners (F); persons sentenced to imprisonment without forced labor (I); juveniles sentenced to adult prisons (J); persons serving sentences more than eight years in length (L); adults less than twenty-six years of age (Y); persons without advanced criminal tendencies (A); persons with "advanced criminal tendencies" (B); individuals who are mentally retarded or need treatment as such (Mx); psychopaths or persons with a considerable psychopathic tendency (My); psychotics, serious neurotics, and drug or alcohol addicts (Mz); those who are physically handicapped, pregnant, or need care for a considerable time (Px); the physically handicapped needing special treatment and the blind, deaf, or mute (Py); and persons older than sixty years of age who need special treatment (Pz).

Classification Centers for Young Adults

The classification centers receive newly admitted male prisoners of the given region who are less than twenty-six years of age, sentenced for at least a year, and in prison for the first time. The centers are a distinct exception to the usual security orientation of Japanese prisons for adults. Seven prisons called "juvenile prisons" are designated for vocational training in automobile maintenance, information processing, electrical work, hair dressing, and so on.

In 1972 the centers, with psychologists as directors, were established in each of the eight correction regions. The Tokyo region's center is the only one in a juvenile prison, Kawagoe Juvenile Prison. Another in Osaka is a detention house. The others are in class-B prisons. The center at Kawagoe stands out as a model for further development of diagnostic services and elaboration of the operations of the other classification centers. It is the only classification center receiving from other prisons in its region those inmates with behavioral problems, although the referrals are few. The Kawagoe center has followed up the subsequent progress of inmates who had been at the center.

A long room at Kawagoe is for group administration of psychometric tests, and another for orientation sessions. Among the smaller rooms are one for psychodrama, two for group treatment, one with devices for measuring vehicle driving aptitude, one for vocational aptitude testing, and several for psychological interviewing. The group-treatment rooms have one-way windows for observation. In the room for sandbox diagnosis, the inmate selects plastic objects and creates in a sandbox a scene such as a farm, a home and its environs, or a forest. The psychologist questions the inmate about the meaning of the scene.

The Kawagoe center has three sections. The classification section administers psychometric instruments, case investigations, and various techniques for diagnosis, and conducts reclassification and reeducation of noncenter inmates. The parole evaluation section gathers information on Kawagoe inmates being considered for parole. The parole and community section arranges for investigation of community factors for Kawagoe inmates to be released on parole at expiration of sentence.

The guidelines for classification centers call for procedures lasting fifty-five days. For the first two weeks, a medical examination is conducted, group and individual psychometric instruments administered, and inmates interviewed. Inquiry letters are sent to the police, courts, juvenile classification homes, and families. If appropriate, hospitals are contacted and the inmate given a medical examination at the prison. In the four-week middle stage, the inmates are employed in the center's workshop assembling simple objects while their behavior is observed. They are trained in military marching and the duties of a prisoner. Their physical agility and vehicle driving aptitude are tested. Individual and group psychological testing is conducted. As a diagnostic method frequently used in Japanese corrections, the young men write essays about themselves, their families, or their perceptions of the future.

Family Courts and Juvenile Classification Homes

Since 1949 the family court has been the entry point for the juvenile justice system. The family court is important to our analysis because, first, it refers some juveniles to the juvenile classification homes and, second, it is the gate-keeper determining the flow of juveniles to the training schools.

Juvenile Law, Article 17, authorizes the family court to send a youngster to the juvenile classification home for diagnosis for up to two weeks, with an additional two weeks in event of "particular necessity." Article 9 describes the investigations conducted by the classification homes: "Every effort shall be made to make efficient use of medical, psychological, pedagogical, sociological and other technical knowledge, especially the result of the physical and mental examination conducted in the juvenile classification home, in regard to the conduct, career, temperament and environment of the juvenile, his guardians or other persons concerned" (UNAFEI n.d., 67).

Upon receiving a juvenile case, the family court has the option of sending the boy or girl to the juvenile classification home for detention within twenty-four hours in either of two circumstances. First, Articles 11 and 26 of the Juvenile Law permit the family court to issue a summons to the juvenile or his or her guardians when necessary for investigation. If the summons is disobeyed "without good reason," the family court may issue a warrant of detention. Second, Articles 12 and 26 permit a family court warrant against the juvenile when "necessary for the welfare of a juvenile who is in urgent need of protection." The latter covers situations when the offense is grave, serious personality problems seem to be present, or keeping the juvenile in a family residence is not feasible. Detention is limited to seven days.

Juvenile Training Schools

The juvenile training school is something of a community, a superintendent told me, serving as an educational facility, a place of work, a home, and a community center. There are many events: field days, athletic meetings, birthday parties, Christmas celebrations when families come, the holiday when every Japanese reaches adulthood, and many other Japanese holidays. Training schools compete in annual chorus competitions. Club activities include painting, calligraphy, haiku (seventeen-syllable poems), volleyball, handball, flower arranging, the tea ceremony, and so on.

The juvenile training schools are differentiated according to a four-type scheme. The "primary" and "middle" classes receive persons who are not "seriously defective mentally or physically." The primary class singles out juveniles fourteen or more years of age but generally less than sixteen. The middle receives those sixteen through nineteen. The "special" (or advanced) class deals with juveniles, age sixteen to twenty-three, without serious mental or physical defects, but with "advanced criminal tendencies." Medical schools treat juvenile inmates, regardless of age, with serious mental or physical disabilities or ailments.

The Juvenile Training School Law, Article 11, specifies that inmates be released when they become twenty years of age but makes certain exceptions. When the inmate is "considered defective physically or mentally or his criminal tendency has not been corrected," the school superintendent may apply to the court for an order that the juvenile be held beyond age twenty but not beyond twenty-three (UNAFEI n.d., 237–38). The court may order continued custody in a medical training school until age twenty-six if the inmate is mentally defective to a remarkable degree.

THE MANAGERS:
THOSE WHO WORK
IN CORRECTIONS

Factories manufacture inanimate products such as automobiles, clothing, and processed foods. Employees are
the only people managed so that their work is consistent
with the factory's purposes. In contrast, people are the
"products" of schools, hospitals, and military boot camps.
In addition to the employees who must be managed,
schools have students to be taught, hospitals have patients
to be treated, and boot camps have recruits to be prepared
for military service. Correctional agencies are among the
"people-processing institutions" that must lend direction
to activities of staff members, as well as to their "clientele."

This chapter focuses on the scheme whereby the Rehabilitation and Correction Bureaus recruit, prepare, and motivate staff members for managing probationers, parolees,
and inmates. They are *individuals* but the two bureaus
transform them into staffs of remarkable loyalty, dedication, and quality by following principles of personnel administration characteristic of Japanese government and
large-scale private companies.

JAPANESE MANAGERIAL SYSTEM

In Japan large-scale organizations have a personnel
policy variously identified as lifetime employment, the

Japanese managerial system, or welfare corporatism. It is reserved primarily for key male employees in large-scale industrial organizations and for government employees.[1] The managerial system provides a conceptual framework for an analysis of personnel administration by the Correction and Rehabilitation Bureaus. The features are lifetime employment as a "corporate citizen," recruitment directly from schools, in-service training to teach specific skills and management philosophy, career paths for further development of competence, a seniority-based reward system through rotation along the vertical job hierarchy, and a set of tangible welfare benefits (Yoshino 1968; Okochi, Karsh, and Levine 1973; Abegglen 1973; Dore 1987; Lincoln and Kalleberg 1990).[2]

Ishida (1971, 46) explains the lifetime employment scheme: "When a student graduates and joins a company or enters the civil service, his life is already mapped out, since lifetime employment is the norm and there is little horizontal mobility. Of course, there is still competition for promotion, but it is confined within a framework of promotion by seniority."

Around the turn of the century, employers encountered the heavy demand for skilled labor and the tendency of artisans to move from job to job in quest of higher wages (Yoshino 1968; Crawcour 1978). Because of "appallingly primitive working conditions," the Factory Act was passed in 1911, but the business community objected and proposed that, instead of unionization of labor, familial benevolence and reciprocity would be the model for employer-employee relationships (Yoshino 1968, 75). "The paternalistic management ideology based on the familial tradition was a deliberate and rational response on the part of Japanese business leaders to the specific and social strains they faced" (84). Industrialization had broadened the disparity between the idealized family and the contemporary family in reality, but the familial tradition was emphasized as a substitute for the outmoded authoritarianism of earlier industrial relations.

To curb turnover and absenteeism, the managers set out to elicit workers' loyalty in the familial mode by offering guarantees against dismissal, scheduling salary advancements, and emphasizing dependability in assessing recruits. Young unskilled workers were recruited directly from secondary schools. To meet the needs of a more sophisticated industrial technology and to promote loyalty of workers, the young unskilled workers were trained by in-plant instruction in specific skills. Temptation of skilled workers to go elsewhere was curbed by group insurance, retirement benefits, and other nonwage advantages.

In-service training is especially crucial for private and public institutions in Japan because the educational system does not significantly prepare students for occupational careers. "The technical training in business that Japanese universities offer is, as a rule, minimal, and there is today no more than a handful of graduate schools of business," Rohlen (1974, 193) says. "In fact, it has been public policy to leave technical training to the nation's companies."

Recently, doubts have been raised about the lifetime employment policy. The "bubble" of extraordinary economic growth has been burst and the firms have reasons to wonder whether the policy serves their interests in a time of limited, if any, growth. Saso and Kirby (1982, 158) observed the following more than a decade ago: "At present the older generation of Japanese managers, approaching retirement and looking for successors, frequently aver that they cannot find successors who are not only qualified to replace them but also are motivated to do so."

In meeting past recessions, Colignon and Usui (1994) report, Japanese companies typically avoided layoffs and abandonment of factories. Other strategies were preferred: reduction of overtime work, ending for at least a year the hiring of new employees, reassigning workers, dismissing part-time and temporary workers, extending vacations, cutting salaries of managerial personnel, closing factories temporarily, and voluntary retirement and dismissal of workers. The government subsidized the retention of workers as a way of easing the impact of welfare measures on the public purse. In spite of considerable employment adjustment during the recession of the 1990s, companies cling to lifetime employment by resorting to the above measures. Observers disagree on long-term prospects; some believe the scheme is obsolete, but others contend that long-term employment is feasible and essential for Japan.

Even before the current recession, employees' enthusiasm for lifetime employment was far from universal. A survey of white-collar respondents (chiefly middle-aged and older workers in large companies) found 90 percent agreeing that "work is an important part of my life, but it is not everything." Only 6.5 percent believed "the company I work for means everything in my life"—the workaholics (Sakuma 1988, 12). Cheng (1991) drew on a national sample of male adult work histories to determine whether or not workers remain with their first employers. Overall, 33 percent were still with the first employer, but government agencies were among the employing organizations with the highest retention rates.

Lifetime employment has served the correction agencies well; it would continue to do so even if the scheme were to wither in the private sector. As elements of the scheme, selection among recruits, in-service training oriented to the contemporary conceptions of correctional work, and career awards have created a dedicated and loyal work force. Insulated from the effects of an economic downturn, the bureaus and their employees are more likely to accept the scheme.

CAREER: GENERALIST VERSUS SPECIALIST

According to the concept of career, the employee sees work as giving benefits beyond immediate income. Career commitment implies a succession of jobs filled by an individual who is motivated to increase the degree and expanse of competence because of expectations of higher compensation and status through promotion, tenure, retirement benefits, and various nonfinancial rewards. The term "career enlargement" refers to the efforts of employees to increase their eligibility for greater rewards by additional formal education, in-service training within the employing enterprise, or on-the-job experience (Cole 1979).

The Japanese private and public institutions follow the generalist, not the specialist, approach in most personnel decisions. Most employees and organizations ignore the idea of an exclusive occupation. In the generalist approach, personnel departments, rather than supervisors, decide when some employees are moved among departments; a manager will rotate through different functional departments. Employees are hired, not for specific occupations, but to become lifetime members of the corporate "family" (Hirono 1969).

The generalist model promotes the commitment to the long-term interests and practices of the agency. Training inculcates the agency's values and imparts the knowledge and skills the agency deems crucial. Training develops careers within the agency following a series of jobs requiring different knowledge and skills.

The specialist model assumes increased complexity of industrial production, delivery of services, and scientific knowledge. Industrial experts specialize in machine design, testing of materials, maintaining the flow of raw materials, or other aspects of factory operations. Such specialists must acquire a particular sphere of knowledge and skills crucial to the organization's ultimate purposes. The physician is the prototype of the high-level specialist. Through intensive and long-term study of a particular pathology of the human organism, the medical specialist is better prepared to cope with that pathology than any other physician.

Some of the sophisticated knowledge and skills that

have been developed in society at large are also relevant to progressive correctional administration. Examples can be noted in fields as diverse as business management, administrative procedures, industrial production, and behavioral science. In-service training in the generalist model tends to become self-centered in shutting out intellectual and technical advances external to the agency. In-service training by the employing agency is not equipped to impart the higher order of competence of the small cadre of specialists of various kinds. The specialist model favors preservice education and cultivates linkages with developments external to the agency. The model is less likely to favor loyalty to the agency; it serves the career interests of the individual in a series of employing enterprises and hones knowledge and skills within a narrowly defined occupation.

Employees make sacrifices for career enlargement; the identification with the corporate family may be so self-fulfilling for some employees that self-denial is not perceived. The candidates selected for future executive positions are likely to be transferred to other cities when promoted within a nationwide organization. Parents are reluctant to change the permanent residence when additional transfers come during the career sequence, especially when the children are in a highly desirable school and the home is owned. Many Japanese work so hard for their employers that they sacrifice their family interests (Hirono 1969). Many fathers become *tanshin funin* (field office bachelors) who work and live a considerable distance from their families. Some companies even have bachelor dormitories, according to Rohlen (1974): "There is nothing uncommon in this for a large Japanese company, particularly one that must transfer men from place to place" (212).

From the perspective of Japanese personnel administration, the transfers are sound policy for management but, I was told, are also in the interest of the persons being transferred. Job rotation gives the future top executives a wide range of experiences. The individual is saved from the boredom of being in the same position for a long period of time; being transferred often sharpens one's interest in meeting responsibilities.

Psychologists and the Specialist Model

The psychologists are a primary example of specialists in correctional work and the need for sophisticated knowledge and techniques. For both counseling and clinical branches of psychology, competence requires long-term study under qualified faculty. Intervention in the lives of others demands solid grounding in the principles of counseling psychology. Clinical psychology specializes in the interpretation of the results of psychometric instruments. Japanese institutions of higher education are only beginning to prepare students for careers in clinical psychology, and involvement in counseling psychology has proceeded at an even slower pace. The correctional field is contributing to the tentative trend; several clinical psychologists, after years of service in the Correction Bureau, have joined university faculties.

Clinical psychology offers diagnostic expertise of particular value to juvenile classification homes and the classification centers for young adult inmates. Counseling psychology, of course, is applicable to probation and parole; the program of Kawagoe Juvenile Prison could be a forerunner for rehabilitation-oriented treatment in adult prisons.

Psychologists are recruited to the prison service in two ways: a special test administered by the National Personnel Authority (NPA) and recruitment by correctional institutions of persons holding a master's degree in psychology.[3] As the third possibility, ordinary prison officers may administer group tests and gain on-the-job experience under a senior staff psychologist.

Depending on the budget, 5 to 8 psychologists have been recruited for each of the years 1987 to 1992 through NPA examinations, plus 42 directly recruited on basis of master's degrees.[4] There are 420 allocated positions for psychologists in the Correction Bureau: 25 in the central or regional headquarters, 104 in the prisons, 26 in the juvenile training schools, 264 in the juvenile classification homes, and 1 in the women's guidance home. The total number of qualified psychologists, however, falls short of the need. Promotion to managerial positions is encouraged by the in-service training program and the limited opportunity for career advancement as practicing psychologists. The gain from recruitment just about matches the loss of retiring psychologists.

University graduates in psychology are not necessarily skilled in the interpretation of psychometric instruments. Some majored in other fields of psychology; it is even more likely that while on campus they had not received any on-hand experience in diagnostic instruments. In-service training after entering the correctional service is enlisted to remedy the deficiency.

After one year of service, twenty psychologists attend the basic specialized course at the branch training center at Nakano, Tokyo. For a month they attend lectures on psychological topics. Then three weeks are spent in on-the-job training at correctional institutions. Five years after recruitment, forty psychologists are selected for a specialized course of 80 hours offered in alternate years by the Training Institute for Correctional Personnel (TICP). In the tenth year of service, TICP offers a more advanced training course in alternate years for forty psychologists.

The curriculum of the basic course is for 152 hours: introduction to criminal policy and correctional administration, 8 hours; psychological theory and method, 76 hours; psychology-related field, 12 hours; study of actual cases and practice in classification work under the supervision of an expert from a juvenile classification home, 40 hours; and administrative routines, 14 hours. In "psychological theory and method," university professors teach personality interpretation, 4 hours; interview theory, 4 hours; and interview practice, 8 hours. The superintendent of a juvenile classification home deals with classification and psychological tests, 4 hours. The chief of a prison classification section reviews the theory of the Rorschach test, 8 hours; supervises practice of the test, 8 hours; and supervises practice of the Thematic Apperception Test, 8 hours. The chief of the classification section of a detention center deals with the theory, 6 hours; and practice of the picture drawing test, 4 hours. Fourteen hours are devoted to behavioral observation, role playing, intelligence testing, and administration of group tests.

Personnel Administration of the Bureaus

The Rehabilitation and Correction Bureaus follow the lifetime employment system. The staff is recruited from universities and high schools, instructed in the agency ideology and body of knowledge, and motivated by career rewards in corrections. Career enlargement of executives and middle managers is through in-service training in the generalist fashion. Management positions, short of that of the director general, are in career tracks of regular employees of the Correction Bureau or Rehabilitation Bureau. Promotions and career rewards are seniority based. A university education receives the best career prospects.

The occupant of the Minister of Justice position is a politician representing the current government. The positions of director general in the Correction and Rehabilitation Bureaus are elements in the career system of public prosecutors and judges in the Ministry of Justice. That career system extends beyond the two bureaus in the ministry to include the position of assistant director and director of the United Nations Asia and Far East Institute for the Prevention of Crime and the Treatment of Offenders (UNAFEI) and the several status-levels for public prosecutors.

The personnel scheme of the bureaus consists of a series of offices or job positions, each of which has its particular duties and demands for competence. Each position is subject to formal or implied rules of conduct and offers authority and prestige for motivating the occupant. Individuals differ in behaviors as they move into positions of greater authority along the career ladder, but the Japanese culture influences conduct. For example, the executive is less pressed to maintain physical distance for gaining the respectable diffidence of subordinates. Dore (1987) notes that symbols of aloofness and physical separation that bolster authority are more common in Britain than in Japan. In the open plan of typical Japanese offices, directors work in one huge room with a number of subordinates. "The locations, size, and emptiness of desks permit rankings to be identified. But there is little sense that the integrity of the hierarchy will be endangered if superiors are observed to be picking their noses or nodding off to sleep in the middle of a memorandum" (90).[5]

Generalist Model for the Bureaus

New personnel are recruited for general potential and trained for responsibilities after being hired. Job rotation for executives and rising middle-level managers occurs every two or three years, usually in April. Promotions are in the generalist mode; a variety of work situations are experienced in a career. Promotions are along the vertical dimension of the job hierarchy and are seniority based. For example, in the Rehabilitation Bureau, the positions of directors of probation offices differ in prestige with Tokyo at the top, Osaka in second position, Nagoya in third position, and so on. If the Tokyo position is open, the vacancy probably will go to the occupant of the Osaka position, and so on down the line of positions.

The employees of the two bureaus prepare their credentials and preferences for future assignments. Along with assessments of immediate superiors, the documents move through the administrative hierarchy to reach eventually the General Affairs Division of the respective bureau's headquarters in Tokyo. ("General affairs" is the title of the section in all levels of administration that specializes in personnel and fiscal matters.) There the year's personnel changes are decided. The individual is told informally in advance of the move; repeated refusals to accept the job change may mean risking one's career advancement.[6]

Information on personnel turnover in the Correction Bureau indicates that the Japanese managerial system has gained the career commitment of correctional workers. Approximately half of the withdrawals from service in fiscal 1989 were for retirement and 4 percent for illness or death. Retirements in 1989 should be especially high because, assuming that persons usually join the correctional service at about twenty years of age, these were persons who were recruited in about 1949 when the number of inmates was particularly great. In that year, modern corrections was being established in Japan, and the postwar conditions gave advantages for employment in criminal justice agencies. Resignations comprised 44 percent of the withdrawals and were especially prevalent among physicians and psychologists who have specialist rather than generalist orientations. Managers avoided resignation completely. Resignations of prison officers and training school instructors were numerous because usually they had fewer years of service and probably had not been promoted.

Nationwide Recruiting Scheme

Recruitment benefits from the nationwide system administered by the National Personnel Authority (NPA) for all the national government. In addition to five annual NPA examinations for the correctional bureaus, other routes offer entry into the Correction Bureau. Psychologists and others with a master's degree, vocational training instructors, and academic teachers may be recruited without taking NPA examinations. Wardens and superintendents are authorized to administer their own tests[7] and recruit individuals recommended to them as being qualified in techniques such as martial arts or industrial production.[8]

The NPA I examination is prepared for graduates of senior colleges and universities who have majored in psychology, sociology, education, law, economics, architecture, public administration, physics, chemistry, and so on. Those applicants who pass the examination are interviewed by agencies with vacancies in which the particular applicant is interested. Because these individuals are regarded as promising prospects for ultimately becoming senior executives, they enter the service in higher pay grades and are admitted earlier to advanced training.

The NPA II examination is for graduates of junior colleges or persons who have not specialized in a particular academic field as undergraduates in senior colleges. Those qualified by the NPA II examination begin in-service training with the basic course and have inferior eligibility for advanced instruction. The NPA III examination is primarily for high school graduates, but some college graduates also take it. Expectation for upward mobility through the agency and accessibility to advanced instruction are even less. An NPA examination designed specifically for officers in adult institutions has a long history.[9] The fifth NPA examination was introduced in recent years for juvenile training personnel who are in direct contact with inmates.

Several methods are used in recruiting Correction Bureau personnel. Management vacancies are filled entirely through internal promotion, as is true to a lesser degree for administrative jobs. Direct recruitment by wardens or superintendents is followed primarily for physicians and maintenance workers; to a lesser extent than physicians, psychologists also are recruited directly. Otherwise, prison officers and training school instructors dominated entry through NPA examinations, but for both groups, some are brought into the service through the direct method.

The Rehabilitation Bureau interviews those who pass the NPA I examination and wish to become probation officers. Accepted candidates are assigned to a probation office or regional parole board. After six months as trainees, they become probation officers and, after a year, are eligible for in-service training. University graduates prefer to be in metropolitan offices; other offices have difficulty attracting and holding them. Tokyo has about 30 percent of the staff from the NPA I group; other metropolitan offices have about 15 percent. Staff members entering the Rehabilitation Bureau via the NPA II examination spend four to six years in administrative tasks. Thereafter, they are eligible to become probation officers and to begin entry-level training. For persons passing the NPA III examination, at least eight years of administrative tasks are required before promotion to probation officer.

Career Tracks and Rewards

The agencies develop personnel along career tracks that are seniority based, and the reward scheme attracts recruits and holds qualified personnel. In-service training moves persons along vertical career tracks according to certain types of eligibility. The first criterion is the level of the NPA examination taken and passed; graduates of universities and senior colleges who take NPA I are favored by a higher pay grade at entry and earlier access to training courses. Regular pay increases, promotions, and access to advanced training are all dependent on seniority.

Salary schedules for adult prison personnel and for juvenile correctional personnel are specified by the Public Security Service Wage Tables I and II, respectively, of the Ad-

Table 4.1

Pay Grades of Correction Bureau Personnel, FY 1989–90

Position	Pay Grade	Monthly Pay in U.S. Dollars	
		Minimum	Maximum
Regional Headquarters			
Directors, Division	(10–11)	2,431	3,874
Director, Section	(7–9)	1,869	3,325
Correction Expert	(5–7)	1,606	3,081
Subsection Chief	(4–6)	1,351	3,023
Adult Prisons			
Warden	(9–11)	2,225	3,874
Director, Division	(8–10)	2,011	3,475
Warden, Branch Prison	(5–9)	1,606	3,325
Director, Section	(6–8)	1,738	3,225
Correction Expert	(3–8)	1,049	3,225
Asst. Director, Section	(5–7)	1,606	3,081
Director, Branch Prison Sect.	(5–7)	1,606	3,081
Asst. Captain	(3–5)	1,049	2,875
Subsection Chief	(3–5)	1,049	2,875
Senior Prison Officer	(2–3)	929	2,697
Prison Officer	(1–2)	858	2,505
Juvenile Training Schools[a]			
Superintendent	(9–11)	2,225	3,874
Deputy Superintendent	(8–10)	2,011	3,475
Principal Specialist	(7–8)	1,869	3,225
Section Chief	(6–8)	1,738	3,225
Chief Specialist	(6–8)	1,738	3,225
Specialist	(3–6)	1,215	3,025
Subsection Chief	(3–5)	1,215	2,627
Officers	(2–3)	1,028	2,146

Source: Data provided by Central Office (Tokyo), Correction Bureau.

Note: All dollar amounts are computed on the basis of 130 yen per $1 (U.S.).

[a]For Juvenile Classification Homes, the pay grades were the same for these positions, except deputy superintendent (8–9), $2,011 to $3,325.

ministrative Service. Both tables award 10 percent more to frontline staff than for other governmental personnel engaged in similar work. The policy recognizes the intrinsic difficulty of dealing directly with adjudicated offenders. The pay scales are fixed according to the rank of one's position and years of service. There are eleven pay grades, with the amount of pay increasing progressively according to the degree of responsibility, authority, and prestige. The pay grades and minimum and maximum pay for the various positions are listed in table 4.1.

Within each pay grade, the employee moves up one step every year; seniority is rewarded. A supervisor can reward merit by recommending 15 percent of the staff for an additional step a year. Annual bonuses add about five months' wages. The general personnel principles also apply to the Rehabilitation Bureau, but the salary scales for major categories of personnel are different; they are summarized in table 4.2.

All public employees receive several allowances including those for family, commuting to work, living quarters, overtime, service in a cold climate, and the higher living costs in urban areas. There are twenty paid holidays a year, but Japanese employees generally take only a portion of the holiday days. Correction employees are even more reluctant, taking thirteen days vacation on average. A maximum of ten days can be accumulated for the following year. In 1991 the National Personnel Authority reduced the forty-four-hour work week to forty-two hours on average; in 1992 the forty-hour week was introduced.

Like all public employees, correctional personnel retire on the earliest 31 March after age sixty. Retirement allowances vary by length of service, rank, and reason for retirement. For example, if a prison officer had entered the service upon high school graduation, retirement at age sixty would produce a total allowance of approximately $140,000 (U.S.).

Table 4.2

Pay Grades of Rehabilitation Bureau Personnel, FY 1989–90

Position	Pay Grade	Monthly Pay in U.S. Dollars Minimum	Maximum
Regional Parole Boards			
Board Members	(9–11)	2,404	4,409
Director, Secretariat	(9–10)	2,404	3,885
Director, Section	(7–8)	1,993	3,419
Parole Officer	(3–7)	1,348	3,234
Subsection Chief	(3–6)	1,348	3,156
Officers	(1–3)	983	1,348
Probation Offices			
Director	(9–11)	2,404	4,409
Director, Section	(6–8)	1,853	3,419
Probation Officer	(3–7)	1,348	3,234
Subsection Chief	(3–6)	1,348	3,156
Officer	(1–3)	983	1,348

Source: Data provided by Central Office (Tokyo), Rehabilitation Bureau.

Note: All dollar amounts are computed on the basis of 130 yen per $1 (U.S.).

In-Service Training: Merging Policy and Practice

The Rehabilitation Bureau follows the multiple-agency model of in-service training.[10] The Research and Training Institute serves several components of the ministry: probation officers, civil affairs officers, and immigration service officers. The institute draws a sufficient number of trainees to justify the facilities, faculty, and other resources. Each full-time instructor specializes in one of three personnel classes; two handle the courses for probation and parole personnel. Their duties are supplemented by experienced probation officers, regional parole board personnel, and other adjunct instructors. Trainees from all over Japan attend the institute's courses in Tokyo. They stay in a dormitory and the institute pays their expenses.[11]

The entry-level course is divided into fifty-day and thirty-day segments of residential instruction. In the six-month interim, the trainees are at probation offices for on-the-job experience. The residential instruction deals with laws, legal procedures, and Rehabilitation Bureau procedures, with counseling, casework, and underlying concepts, and with fieldwork. Almost all probation officers take the course. A few have been transferred from prisons or juvenile training schools, and the bureau's budget limits the number of trainees.

The secondary courses are carried out by regional parole boards; these refresher courses involve few students. For the courses, the parole boards are divided into east and west areas. A board in each region organizes a short course (usually fifteen days in length) that focuses on practical aspects of probation and parole. Other boards in the area may send their people. At the institute in Tokyo, the special courses of twenty days are for experienced probation officers. Generally, the courses deal with casework and special categories of offenders, and also a particular theme such as treatment methods, rehabilitation aid hostels, and so on. Participants in senior courses of thirty-two days are probation officers with fifteen or twenty years experience. The subject matter is procedures, legal matters, interviewing, casework, and other practical aspects. Graduates are candidates for positions as section supervisors. The appointees take another course of thirteen days in the philosophy and techniques of management.

In-service training of the Correction Bureau is in the independent-academy model.[12] The Training Institute for Correction Personnel (TICP) in Fuchu, a suburb of Tokyo, is the hub of the nationwide scheme. It prepares course materials, offers advanced and some specialist courses, and orients new instructors of the branch training centers. TICP occupies its own modern plant. The Museum of Corrections is in an adjacent building. TICP is staffed by a director with the rank of superintendent of a regional correction headquarters, a deputy director selected from among wardens and superintendents, twelve full-time instructors, and an administrative staff.

At each of the eight regional headquarters, a branch training center occupies a separate building with offices, classrooms, and a trainee dormitory. The superintendent of the regional headquarters also is director of the branch training center and has direct responsibility. The deputy director of the branch has immediate supervision of the faculty of three to six full-time instructors. All entry-level instruction of new officers is at the branches, with assistance of the TICP faculty, for 120 prisons, detention houses, juvenile training schools, and juvenile classification homes. The 1990 primary course at the Tokyo training branch illustrates the contents. The emphasis was on laws and regulations (39.4 percent of the instructional hours) and custodial matters such as weapons, restraints, and martial arts (27.5 percent). The total of 284 instructional hours were widely distributed: behavioral and social therapy, correctional policy, personnel affairs, special programs in corrections, physical education, administration, report writing, and ethics. In addition to the 284 instructional hours, 96 were devoted to visits to correctional institutions, outdoor activities, marching, ceremonials, roll call, discussion groups, conferences, and club activities.

TICP offers special advanced courses and regular advanced courses. Special advanced courses are offered for either middle-management personnel or executives who must be recommended by a warden or superintendent. These courses concentrate on the particular responsibilities of a category of personnel such as a medical problem, change in administrative procedures, or a new policy. To be eligible for a regular advanced course, the individuals who had passed NPA II or NPA III examinations must also pass a qualifying test administered by TICP. The regular advanced courses are intended to prepare selected persons for executive positions. Completion of these courses must be matched by further years of experience before promotion is obtained. For those who had passed the NPA I examination, the regular advanced course at TICP is for six months, orients them to the correctional service, and gives them the basic knowledge essential for executives.

Persons recruited directly without NPA examinations or by NPA III examination move through primary and junior courses at branch training centers. The branch training centers also offer courses for personnel below the middle-management level. The subject matter varies from year to year and concentrates on the responsibilities of a particular category of personnel. No qualifying test is necessary for admission to courses.

Tradition of Correctional Training

Training of prison personnel has existed in Japan for a century. In Europe the first documented school for prison officers was in Ghent, Belgium (1834) but was soon discontinued. A fully developed school for recruits existed at Luneburg Prison from 1859 to 1868, when it was abandoned. Other programs were begun at Louvain Prison, France (1867) and at Regine Coeli Convent (1873) in Italy (Sellin 1935). During the Meiji Restoration, Kurt von Sebach of Germany was invited to come as an adviser on prison administration. He played a prominent role in the establishment of a training center for prison officials of all Japan on 22 January 1890, at Central Prison in Tokyo. Kanagawa-ken Prison had initiated training in 1884, but the center in Tokyo offered the first nationwide program.

Personnel training in Japan was interrupted by developments in the society; a private association made possible the resumption of training. Two courses were conducted at the center in Tokyo, but it was closed in 1891 because of von

Sebach's death and insufficient funding. In 1899 training was resumed with the opening of the Institute for Police and Prison Officers at a former army training center near the Emperor's Palace in central Tokyo. The curriculum for correctional personnel was expanded to include penal procedures, penology, prison construction, budgetary accounting, and correction of juveniles. By 1904, 415 persons had completed a series of six-month courses, but training was ended on 31 March 1904 because of the war with Czarist Russia (Correction Bureau 1990a).

Training was resumed in 1909 because a considerable number of prison officers had been fired for unreported reasons and because new regulations had to be explained. Then the Japanese Prison Association—a private organization now known as the Japanese Correctional Association (JCA)—assumed responsibility.[13] Special courses were introduced for middle managers, rising captains, nurses, medical technicians, industrial managers, and prison officers needing advanced instruction.[14] By 1943 the association had introduced a format followed today: a central institute specializing in advanced training and locating courses for prison officers in seven major prisons (Correction Bureau 1990a).

In 1947 the Cabinet authorized the Ministry of Justice to assume responsibility for training. Courses were expanded to include staffs of juvenile training schools and juvenile classification homes. The current scheme of primary, middle, and advanced courses was introduced. In March 1966 the central institute was moved from a location near the Emperor's Palace to Fuchu and came to occupy its current plant in 1969 when it was named the Training Institute for Correctional Personnel (Correction Bureau 1990a).

THE INDUSTRIAL
PRISON

The industrial prison arose in the United States along with the industrialization of the society in the early nineteenth century, but by the end of the century that model of the American prison was already disappearing. The industrial prison also appeared in Japan in connection with the industrialization of the society, but the model continues to thrive there because of linkages with the private industrial sector.[1]

THE FACTORY SYSTEM AND THE PRISON

Before the industrial revolution in Europe, workers sometimes were brought together in central shops, but the factory system emerged with the introduction of machine techniques between 1750 and 1825 in England. The factory system arranges a series of specialized machines in a sequence for manufacturing a product. A predetermined scheme routinizes each worker to the demands of the assigned task within the division of labor set by the machines. Failures to perform the task are obvious when the product is inspected. The relationships between the worker and the supervisor—as opposed to contacts between individual workers—are magnified in importance. In abstract terms, individuals "come together in a strict hierarchical framework, with no lateral relation, communication being possible only in the vertical direction" (Foucault 1977, 238). The employer gains a new opportunity for close supervision of workers.

By introducing the disciplinary potential of machine-production, the industrial prison both gave wardens an unprecedented way to manage prisoners and magnified the demands that long-term imprisonment exerts on their executive and managerial skills. In 1834 a prison director in France told an official inquiry: "I do not know how to concede that work exercises an *essentially reforming* effect on them [the inmates]. But I do consider work in any large prison to be the surest guarantee of order, peace, and quiet" (quoted in O'Brien 1982, 183–84).

Before long-term confinement in prisons, detention houses had only held offenders briefly until execution, exile, corporal punishment, or fines were imposed. With imprisonment being added to the arsenal of measures, wardens had to exhibit greater executive and managerial skills in providing basic necessities of life for inmates and controlling their conduct (Rothman 1971). Machine-based production added other demands: coordinating the phases of production, supervising the task performance of inmate-workers, motivating them to maintain product outcome, and sustaining positive ties with the consumers, whether outside contractors, retail firms, or the public.

The merger of the factory and prison has received mixed reviews. Wardens and their staffs tend to welcome the workshops as another phase of the routinized regimentation lulling most prisoners into habitual conformity. Lopez-Rey (1958) views the industrial prison in a positive way, arguing that regular work grants inmates self-respect, self-responsibility, and self-reformation without the prison investing in treatment. Factory production has been condemned for replacing the pleasures of craftsmanship with the drudgery of standardized tasks. Foucault (1977, 242–43) sees the industrial prison as a tool for forced compliance, "a scheme of individual submission and of adjustment to a production apparatus." Noting that production dictates the nature and timing of the prisoner's allocated task, Melossi and Pavarini (1981) argue that pursuit of economic gain blunts the effect of punitive supervision because willing and competent participation in production requires the prospect of positive rewards for the prisoner.

Along with the "guarantee of order, peace, and quiet," the industrial prison increased the importance of inducing the inmates to perform assigned tasks. Measures to motivate inmate laborers have ranged from the threat of severe punishment to inducements such as early release, privileges in recreation or housing, allocation to favored work assignments, or modest financial rewards. Most inmates welcome labor for relieving the cancer of idleness and speeding psychologically the passage of time to discharge.

Opposing Outcomes in the U.S. and Japan:
The Political Aspect

According to Yanagimoto (1970, 216), "Japan has experienced neither systematic opposition to prison industries from outsiders, representing business and labor unions, nor legislative action to limit the inmate's employment in order to protect the free market. Therefore, the atmosphere of all the industrial prisons is close to that of a factory." Japanese, as well as Americans, protest the construction of prisons in their neighborhoods, but opposition to prison-made goods has been exceptionally high, especially in times of prosperity and labor shortages.[2]

The industrial prison emerged in the early nineteenth century with the Auburn system in New York state. After flourishing in other states, it suffered a progressive decline. Japan adopted the model in the late nineteenth century and it flourishes today. Why the opposing outcomes? The answers reflect differences in cultures and in the judgmental baggage of the industrial prison.

The industrial prison was developed experimentally at Auburn Prison in the years 1821–24. Prisoners were assembled in workshops during the day but in separate cells at night. Inmates marched in lockstep between the cells and workshops. Perpetual silence was enforced by flogging to prevent criminogenic contamination, escape plots, and rebellion. Inmates were expected to labor diligently and not look up from their work and were not "to laugh, dance, whistle, sing, run, jump, or do anything that will have the *least tendency* to disturb or alarm the prison" (Powers 1826, 3).

In nineteenth-century America, prison industries were likely to play a part in the development of a new state's economy. The industrial prison flourished initially, largely because it was believed to meet at least a major portion of the prison's costs. Prison output, especially contracting, soon became the target of political interest groups protesting the competition of prison-made goods. As the decades passed, the percentage of inmates at factory work declined consistently: 90 percent in 1885, 71 percent in 1895, 53 percent in 1932, and 10 percent in 1979 (Funke, Wayson, and Miller 1982, 20–21).

Competition among political interest groups—sometimes called "pressure groups" or "lobbies"—has been prominent in policy making because of the particular nature of American politics (Keefe et al. 1990). Federalism divides power between the national government and the several states; national, state, and local governments offer many targets for exerting influence. Politicians of differing ideologies are in each of the political parties. Party discipline is weakened by candidates competing for the support of interest groups.

Initially, organized labor was most active in lobbying the state legislatures; their primary argument was that prisoners competed unfairly with free workers (Lewis 1967).

By the 1860s and 1880s labor gained political influence in a number of northeastern states. Certain manufacturers who opposed contracting with prisons assembled in Chicago in 1886 and organized the National Anti-Contract Association. The final blow came during the Great Depression with passage of the Hawes-Cooper Act (1929) and the series of Ashurst-Summers Acts (1935–40). Federal legislation authorized state legislatures to prohibit in their jurisdiction the sale of goods manufactured in the prisons of other states. (The Constitution otherwise reserves control of interstate commerce to the federal government.) The states seized the opportunity enthusiastically and responded to lobbyists' demands by also restricting sale of goods made in their own prisons (Flynn 1951).

The absence of crime as a major public issue in Japan has insulated the industrial prison there from intensive political pressure. Since there is only the national prison system, one prefecture cannot forbid the sale of goods of another prefecture. Lobbying is part of Japan's politics, but access to governmental policy making has been obtained chiefly by big business and agriculture. Correctional issues do not arouse sufficient nationwide concern to produce major interest-group lobbying. The political structure is under strain at this writing; political reform is possible, but the industrial prison is unlikely to become a major issue. Political maneuvering within the national bureaucracy is more in prospect; the development of CAPIC, reported later in this chapter, is an example.

Opposing Outcomes in the U.S. and Japan: Judgments of Contracting

The industrial prison in the nineteenth century had to attract entrepreneurs willing to contract for prison labor, but the contractors also had to be assured that the production would meet their requirements. Prison officials knew that a profitable institution improved prospects for their job tenure. Nevertheless, they husbanded their authority and initially admitted to the prison the contractors only if all work instructions to the inmates would go through the keepers. Experience demonstrated that the keepers did not know enough about the work processes to serve competently as surrogate foremen. A physician at Auburn Prison described how the contract scheme was so dominant in the prison's economy that it was uncertain whether the state or the contractors were the real governing power: "Each alternation of party ascendancy suddenly changes every official from the warden to the gate tender; while the contractors may be, and often are, connected with the institution for many years in succession" (Fosgate 1866, 29). In only a tenth of the prisons in 1880 were industries managed by the prison administration (Wines 1880, 108).

Patronage has been the heritage of the "spoils system" since the presidency of Andrew Jackson (1829–37), in the belief that capable storekeepers could do any government job. A prison official pronounced "politics to be the greatest handicap to progress in penal reform" (Stutsman 1926, 52). "A comparatively short time ago few wardens were appointed because of efficiency," he declared. Patronage shortened the tenure of many wardens.

The hesitant introduction of personnel training also handicapped the quality of the prison service (Schade 1986; Stutsman 1931). As recently as 1966, over half of the American correctional agencies lacked training of even minimal quality (President's Commission 1967, 100–101). Most training programs of correctional agencies and college curricula in corrections appeared in the 1960s and 1970s when federal funding became available.

The Japanese have avoided the conditions that sparked the American opposition to contracting. Subcontracting, vital to Japan's industrial system, has given the industrial prison an accepted place in the production system of private companies.[3] The industrial prison draws support from government in general because it funnels revenue directly to the national treasury and contributes significantly to the internal orderliness of Japanese prisons. Recruitment and in-service training of staff for Japanese prisons avoid any effects like the consequences of the gross "political spoils" system in earlier American prisons.

PRISON LABOR VERSUS CHARACTER REFORMATION

American prison reformers and some wardens placed priority on the reformation of the inmates's character; they especially challenged the industrial prison. The early debate pitted Auburn Prison's congregate labor system against Eastern Penitentiary at Cherry Hill, outside Philadelphia, where solitary confinement without labor was the initial policy. The Pennsylvania Quakers shut off human communication except with prison officials, moral instructors, official visitors, and the guards who brought meals. Criminal contagion by other inmates would be prevented and only the positive influences, including that of the Bible, would have effect. Handicraft labor within the cell was permitted later because it, too, prevented communication among prisoners, worked less havoc on the mind and body, taught an honest trade, and allowed the inmate to contribute to the costs of the prison (Lewis [1922] 1967).

In the 1850s, religious evangelism was considered the major means of rehabilitation. Wardens wanted to make prison labor pay, but the American faith in public education began to enter prison practice. Commutations of sentences and some assistance for released prisoners appeared. At the 1970 meeting in Cincinnati where the National Prison Association (now the American Correctional Association) was founded, reform wardens favoring industries clashed with reform wardens who saw reformation as the purpose of prisons (McKelvey 1977).

Labor agitation in the state of New York succeeded in

1881 in having the legislature prohibit contracts; by 1900, New York prisons were suffering "noxious idleness." New York reformers had succeeded in establishing a new kind of prison—the reformatory. In 1876 Zebulon Brockway, superintendent of Elmira Reformatory, devised a program of indeterminate sentences, progressive grades, parole, academic courses, and trade courses. Elmira became the model for an alternative to the industrial prison (McKelvey 1977).

Vocational training, academic education, and psychological intervention are advocated in Japanese juvenile training schools. Except for the limited provision of vocational training (as specified below), the rehabilitative purposes of the industrial prison are limited to "self-purification" and "self-discipline." When offenders are repentant, the Japanese favor leniency. Denied leniency by the prosecutors or judges, the adult prisoners appear to the public to be socially unworthy and, therefore, proper candidates for stern control.

Industrial labor, as opposed to penal labor, is expected to offer the opportunity for "self-purification." Unlike the Western concentration on legal responsibility, the Japanese emphasize the moral failures of offenders and see prison labor as an opportunity for moral redemption. The theme of "self-purification" is matched by the theme of "learning self-discipline" through prison labor. "Most prisoners have led a life of idleness; they did not work in society," I was told in an interview. "It is important that they learn to work. In a kind of control from outside, the inmates develop their self-discipline." The argument is especially salient in a society inhabited by "workaholics."

EARLY PRECEDENTS
IN JAPAN

Many elements of the industrial prison were present in Japan a century ago. In the Meiji Restoration, those sentenced to penal servitude were held in local confinement stations and performed labor for 12, 18, 24, 30, or 36 months. They were paid one-tenth of the wage of an ordinary worker; half of the daily income was held until completion of the sentence (Ch'en 1981). For its model, Japan drew on prison factories of the West, such as the central prisons of France that had modified Auburn's industrial prison and relied heavily on private contractors (O'Brien 1982).

During the Meiji Era, prison labor was directly involved in the economic development of Japan. In the late years of the nineteenth century, the Japanese prison was reportedly "a place of detention, of reformation, and of profitable work" (Griffiths n.d., 235). In the first workshop, a couple of hundred prisoners made machinery and steam boilers. Each warder, carrying only a sword, was in charge of fifteen men. The prisoners were working on contract orders, supervised by one skilled master and one representative of the contracting firm. In another shop, more than a hundred men with blocks of wood between their knees were carving all sorts of things, from simple trays and bowls to fragile and delicate long-legged storks. "There were also papermakers, weavers (who were making the fabric for prison clothing), fan-makers, lantern-makers and workers in baskets, mats, and nets. . . . In one of the shops jinrikishas were being made, in another umbrellas were being carved elaborately and in another every kind of pottery was being turned out. To the amazement of the visitors, they found sixty men, common thieves and burglars, making the exquisite cloisonné ware" (236–37).

The participation of prisons in the whole economy preceded the Meiji Restoration. Homeless paupers and, later, criminals were placed in workhouses where simple work was imposed, vocational skills taught, and some wages paid (Kyokai 1943; Hiramatsu 1972; Ooms 1985). During the Meiji Era, prisoners were employed in land reclamation and mining projects in Hokkaido, Japan's frontier at that time. Kabato Prison was opened in 1881 and Kushiro Prison in 1885. Beginning in 1882 Sorachi Prison provided labor for coal mines. Asahikawa-Abashiri highway traversing Hokkaido was constructed in 1886–91 (Yokoyama 1982, 3–4; Hiramatsu 1973, 35–36). The government began operating the Miike coal mines in Kyushu in 1873 with prisoners and free workers. The mines were privatized in 1888, and although 1,457 convicts were in the labor force of 1,932 in 1896, they made up only 138 of the 2,138 miners in 1908. The use of prisoners ended in 1933 (Hane 1982, 227).

Before the Old Prison Rules (1881) any private person could apply for use of the labor of prisoners, pick them up in the morning, and return them in the evening. Employers had the advantage of substandard wages in farming, construction, transportation of goods, or manufacturing. Trustworthy inmates and public tolerance were vital because the prisoners were not chained and guards made only periodic checks. Other groups of ten to fifteen prisoners would be chained in twos with their faces concealed by deep conic hats, with a guard and two assistants assigned to each group (Hiramatsu 1973, 37).

SUBCONTRACTING AND PRISON INDUSTRY

The extensive industrial activities of the prisons also are due to the great dependence of industries on small firms that account for a larger percentage of total enterprises in Japan than in other industrialized nations: "It was the small businesses which took the initiative in adopting and adapting the advanced technology of the West and making use of the native skills in order to speed the process of modernization" (Tadao 1979, 157–58). Subcontracting was introduced in the years preceding and during World War II, when manufacturers of military equipment shifted from producing everything themselves to relying on smaller firms because of lower wages, managerial skills, and the willingness to work longer hours (T. Nakamura 1981; Dore 1987).

Subcontracting links some small firms with a larger company. Beyond the primary contractor, secondary and tertiary subcontractors are not directly tied to the parent company. "It is not unusual to find several 'layers' of hierarchically organized subcontractors in a pyramid-like pattern, with each performing subcontracting operations for those at a higher level in the pyramid. Most commonly, the lower its stratum, the smaller the establishment" (Yoshino 1968, 155).[4]

When the economy is depressed, the parent companies have the option of canceling subcontracts while maintaining lifetime employment for their own people, of postponing payments on accounts, or of lowering the rate paid to subcontractors (Ishida 1971, 18; T. Nakamura 1981, 175). To obtain loans from banks for modernizing equipment, the small firms have difficulty unless sponsored by a parent company. Objecting to the negative evaluation, Friedman (1988) presents recent statistics showing that small firms do not insulate larger companies from adjustment costs, that the wage differentials narrowed greatly in the 1960s and 1970s, and that a large number of small firms have avoided permanent dependence by adopting flexible production strategies.

In keeping with the generalist approach of personnel management in Japan, the chiefs of industrial sections often assume their positions without specialized academic preparation or previous empirical experience. Sometimes a vocational instructor is promoted, but usually the chiefs are chosen from graduates of courses offered for persons in the rank of captain or above at the Training Institute for Correctional Personnel at Fuchu. Vocational instructors are required to have a trade school certificate from the Ministry of Labor.

All sectors of the staff have a keen interest in replacing any expiring subcontract because an active inmate

Table 5.1

Budget Income from Prison Industries and Contractors' Share of Revenue and Inmate Employment, 1990

| Prison Industries | Budget Income | | Contractors' Contribution | |
	Thousands of Dollars	Dollars per Man-day	Percent of Revenue	Percent of Labor
Metal Work	41,706.7	20.7	99.3	99.7
Assembly	(24,345.2)	(17.9)	(100.0)	(100.0)
Products	(17,706.5)	(26.3)	(98.4)	(99.0)
Western Tailoring	27,978.4	16.4	100.0	99.9
Woodcraft	15,455.7	23.1	98.7	99.0
Printing	10,454.1	25.3	99.8	99.8
Leather Work	7,734.2	17.8	100.0	100.0
Paper Knitting	5,293.4	4.3	99.9	99.9
Chemicals	2,139.3	18.3	100.0	100.0
Farm & Stock	1,802.2	27.8	3.5	9.5
Paper Bags	1,230.1	13.5	100.0	100.0
Auto Repairs	1,109.1	31.4	99.2	97.3
Ceramics	1,096.9	21.6	94.7	97.5
Spinning	684.8	15.6	100.0	100.0
Papermaking	544.0	42.5	69.3	28.8
Food Processing	160.9	15.3	88.8	95.7
Forestry	41.2	8.4	0.0	0.0
Total	117,429.2	17.0	96.1	98.8

Source: Research and Statistics Section (1991a).

Note: Table does not include miscellaneous jobs employing few inmates, jobs outside prison, vocational training, maintenance, building and repair, and other unclassifiable jobs.

labor force is of crucial importance in prison management. Some subcontracts come from other prisons that cannot fulfill them. Sometimes the headquarters of the correction region refers a contractor. Because an arrangement would be in its own interest, a local company may approach the prison. The correction fair, when prison-made goods are displayed for public sale, may awaken a company's interest. Newspaper advertisements and volunteers serving the prison also offer clues.

Assembly and production of metal products, Western clothing, and woodcraft (chiefly furniture) contributed 72 percent of income from prison industries in 1990 (see table 5.1). Printing is another prominent industry (8.9 percent of income). Leather products include shoes and such items as brief cases. Among the paper products, paper bags for retail stores are assembled in cells by inmates who are restricted from workshops, and by the physically handicapped and the elderly. Farming, animal raising, and forestry contribute modest income. Automobile repair restores vehicles for individuals or contractors.

Accrued revenue from prison industries in 1990 is listed in table 5.1 in descending order for the various products. The Correction Bureau also reports the number of man-days (its preference over "man-hours") devoted to each product category. The rank order for the products in terms of revenue per man-day often differs from their order in terms of total revenue. Papermaking ranked first in revenue per man-day because of the limited number of workers. Metal production, printing, and woodcraft did rather well in both rankings; other products required a larger labor force. Contractors provided 96.1 percent of the machinery, raw materials, and expert personnel, but their provision of such basic resources varied among the products. Their share was very significant for the products generating the greatest revenue: metal production and assembly, Western tailoring, woodcraft, and printing.

Declining prison admissions and predominance of unskilled inmates restrict the kinds of production that prisons can undertake. The Industrial Division in the headquarters of the Correction Bureau initiated a project that deviates from the usual emphasis on unskilled labor. The Ministry of Finance provided funds for labor-saving technology. A new factory building at Okayama Prison cost 151 million yen and the machinery 170 million yen. Beginning in 1990, a series of machines now makes metal shelving for a private company. The parts are placed on hooks of an endless belt and painted by automated equipment. Quality control is a reason Okayama was selected, because it has a reputation for efficient metalwork production.

MOTIVATING THE
INMATE WORKER

A couple of hundred Japanese prisoners in a shop concentrate on tasks without looking up to see the visitor. When I asked why inmates appear to be so diligent, an executive in prison industry summarized: "The Japanese people are workaholics; generally they like to work. Prisoners also are Japanese; they do not dislike work. Prison labor is an obligation; prisoners are prepared to work. Also, if they refuse to work they must undergo disciplinary punishment. If they do not work hard, there is less chance for parole. Also there is remuneration. Then too each work shop competes with other work shops. Each has a quota; if achieved the prisoners receive certain freedoms, such as watching television. A monetary award up to three thousand yen is earned by suggestions for improved production."[5]

Inmates receive a modest "remuneration" instead of "wage" because the reward is considered officially to be a privilege, not an economic right. The small amount is a real inducement in the prison.[6] Before April, the amounts of remuneration are set along a scale of ten grades. The amounts reflect the financial constraints on the Correction Bureau and the changes in average wages paid in regular factories. All inmates begin in the lowest "apprentice grade" and are promoted through the successive grades to the highest one. The position on the scale is dependent on the task skill, length of time in prison, and work attitudes. At a monthly meeting an inmate's position along the scale is decided. Committee membership usually consists of the factory manager, the industrial instructors, and the lieutenant serving as assistant chief of the industrial section.

The progressive stage system, a scheme for motivating inmates, was established by Ministry of Justice Ordinance No. 56 of 1944, Articles 16, 17, and 21.[7] The prisoner may be promoted from the lowest (fourth) to the highest (first) grade and granted privileges accordingly. Article 17 provides for exceptional merit: "The grade of treatment of a person who is strong in the sense of responsibility and promises to be fit for collective living may be advanced to a proper grade." A badge on the uniform indicates the grade. Promotion is for diligence in prison labor, general behavior, and sense of responsibility and volition. Eligibility for parole also is related to demonstrated good conduct, including workshop behavior.

The amount of remuneration that can be spent for the inmate's own use increases from one-fifth for the fourth grade to one-half for the first grade. The prisoners in second grade play sports or hold athletic meetings and, when in a single cell, are permitted to keep photographs of "lineal ascendants, spouse, and lineal descendants." First grade offers freedom from search of body and cell and permits a collective walk with other first graders and the use of the prison library. The Correction Bureau acknowledges that "Recently the progressive-grade system has been criticized to be less successful for the offender's rehabilitation than was originally expected," but expresses hope that, if the Prison Law is revised, "the meritorious aspects" can become part of a new treatment scheme (Correction Bureau 1990b, 33).

Close attention is paid to safety in the workshops; signs boast of the weeks and months passed without an industrial accident. At a rate of 130 yen to the dollar, compensation for injuries in work accidents in fiscal 1989 ranged from $731 to $29,800 (Research and Statistics Section 1991c, 38).

Prison workshops compete with one another to surpass their respective productivity quotas. The spirit of *gambare!*

(persevere, endure) engulfs every facet of society, Duke (1986, 122–23) declares: "Gambare is also a major component in developing a strong sense of competition, especially group competition. Regardless of the group's purposes or the ages of the participants, the goals must be pursued through a collective effort."

THREE KINDS OF
PRISON LABOR

When physically and mentally qualified for work, inmates are most likely to be assigned to industry. Maintenance duties in the kitchen, janitorial tasks, or repair of the physical plant or equipment are in the second position. A few persons are admitted to vocational training, sometimes to prepare them for jobs in prison industries. The correction regions and types of prisons differ in the percentage distributions of the three work assignments, but all have a high proportion of the inmates at work in industries. Table 5.2 represents only the major prisons, leaving out branch prisons and detention facilities.

Maintenance workers are evaluated generally as especially trustworthy because they can move rather freely about the prison. When a prison also houses the accused and suspects or houses a medical facility, more maintenance workers are needed. A disproportionate number of maintenance workers also may reflect an insufficient number of jobs in industries.

As table 5.2 indicates, the correction regions have varying proportions of industrial work assignments. The differences are partly explained by the kinds of prisons represented in a given region. In all regions there are at least some prisons in rural areas where the scale of industrialization is of low order. Among small and medium industries, productivity has increased at a greater rate for those

Table 5.2

Inmate Labor Assignments, by Region and Type of Prison, 1990

		Percentage of Work Assignments		
	No. of Work Assignments	Prison Industry	Vocational Training	Prison Maintenance
Correction Region				
Tokyo (13)	9,576	78.8	2.6	18.6
Osaka (8)	6,230	81.8	3.1	15.1
Nagoya (7)	4,342	84.3	1.2	14.5
Hiroshima (6)	2,513	76.2	5.6	18.2
Fukuoka (11)	5,533	77.8	2.7	19.5
Sendai (6)	2,744	78.8	3.1	18.1
Sapporo (7)	3,166	71.6	3.8	24.6
Takamatsu (4)	2,036	78.8	2.5	18.7
Total (62)	36,140	79.0	2.9	18.1
Type of Prison				
B Prisons (33)	22,842	81.3	0.8	17.9
A Prisons (10)	5,128	75.8	5.6	18.6
Juvenile Prisons (8)	3,468	65.0	14.7	20.3
L Prisons (6)	3,220	80.3	0.9	18.8
Women's Prisons (5)	1,482	84.6	2.1	13.3
Total (62)	36,140	79.0	2.9	18.1

Source: Data provided by CAPIC.

Note: Figures in parentheses are the number of primary prisons, excluding medical prisons.

located in the six largest cities (Caves and Uekusa 1976). Metropolitan prisons enjoy more companies in need of subcontractors. Class-B prisons are most numerous even in nonmetropolitan areas. For example, of Fukuoka's eleven prisons seven are class B, but they are comparatively small. Nevertheless, Fukuoka's class-B prisons make their contribution to the 60-percent share of all work assignments held by the class-B prisons generally. Class-A prisons have the advantage that their inmates are rated as lower custody risks. Class-L prisons hold persons with sentences of at least eight years; the lower turnover rate reduces the necessity to train newcomers to work tasks. Juvenile prisons are especially dedicated to vocational training.

RAISING THE SKILL
LEVEL OF INMATES

Vocational training in Japanese prisons comes in three modes. First, the training institutes, located at four juvenile prisons and three class-A prisons, carry out "intensive vocational training" of inmates recruited from other institutions. The Ministry of Labor offers evidence of instructional quality by awarding certificates to graduates of some courses. Second, special courses at particular prisons draw selected inmates from other prisons. Third, a prison conducts training for its own inmates.

In 1992 the male graduates of all vocational training were only 3 percent of the inmate population of the facilities carrying out the training. I have categorized the courses on the basis of whether they primarily served the policy objective of industrial efficiency or of preparing the inmate for postrelease employment; some courses (listed as "marginal jobs") serve both policies (see table 5.3).

As measured by the percentage of the inmates who graduated, prison-oriented training was dominant generally and for all four types of facilities. The training institutes had the highest percentage of graduates overall and in both prison-oriented and marginal occupations. They had an impressive number of graduates in welding, electric wiring, boiler operation, carpentry, plastering, and woodcraft. The mission of the institutes is to strengthen the competence of the labor force of youth and class-A prisons and to prepare the inmates for postrelease employment. Class-A

THE INDUSTRIAL PRISON

Table 5.3

Male Inmates Graduating from Vocational Training Courses or Awarded Ministry of Labor Certificates, by Type of Facility, 1992

Type of Facility	Type of Job Training			Total
	Prison-Oriented	Marginal	Post-Release	
	Vocational Training Graduates			
Training Institutes	238	182	18	438
% of Inmates	7.96	6.08	0.60	14.64
Youth Prisons	105	26	5	136
% of Inmates	3.87	0.96	0.18	5.01
Class-A Prisons	84	44	73	201
% of Inmates	1.85	0.97	1.60	4.42
Class-B prisons	112	60	25	197
% of Inmates	0.47	0.25	0.11	0.83
Total No.	539	312	121	972
% of All Inmates	1.58	0.91	0.36	2.85
	Ministry of Labor Certificates			
Training Institutes	72	118	34	224
% of Inmates	2.41	3.94	1.14	7.49
Youth Prisons	21	17	37	75
% of Inmates	0.77	0.63	1.36	2.76
Class-A Prisons	22	34	56	112
% of Inmates	0.48	0.75	1.23	2.46
Class-B Prisons	68	38	41	147
% of Inmates	0.29	0.16	0.17	0.62
Total No.	183	207	168	558
% of Inmates	0.54	0.61	0.49	1.64

Source: Research and Statistics Section (1993a).

Note: Totals exclude "unspecified jobs." Rates are computed from average daily population in 1992 for prisons of the given type.

prisons were preeminent in postrelease occupations, primarily construction machine operators and automobile driving. Training courses are primarily for the young and other persons considered most trustworthy. Class-B prisons have the greatest number of inmates, but their rates for training graduates are very low.

The certificates granted by the Ministry of Labor generate lower overall rates than the vocational training program and again reflect the superior performance of training institutes in producing graduates. Chiefly because of the training institutes, the marginal occupations draw the greatest number of certificates and postrelease occupations receive slightly greater attention at training institutes than is found for all facilities. Of the four types of facilities, youth and class-A prisons had slightly higher rates for postrelease certificates. The following courses had greater numbers of graduates: welding, 225; boiler operation, 105; carpentry, 86; electric wiring, 67; plastering, 66; and construction-machine operation, 60.

OPEN CAMPS AND
PRIVATE INDUSTRY

Five facilities qualify fully as open institutions: Ohi Shipbuilding Dockyard Camp, a branch of Matsuyama Prison on Khikoku Island; Arii Dockyard Camp in Onomichi on the Inland Sea of Seta; the Kagamihara Metal Industrial Camp near Gifu City; the Kitsuregawa School for Agriculture and Civil Engineering in Tochigi Prefecture; and Ichihara Prison for Traffic Offenders in Chiba Prefecture.

Ohi, Arii, and Kagamihara are the only open facilities with two characteristics: they are full-fledged open facilities and they were created and operate for employment by private companies in regular industrial work. The term "open" implies physical access to the inmates of conditions similar to those of the free community and their willingness to show self-responsibility in acting as free persons. Careful classification brings only the "cream" of inmates to open facilities. Two decades ago, Bixby (1971, 13) praised Ohi Camp as a prime example of "the collaboration of government and the private sector in preparing offenders to assume independent and law-abiding roles in the community."

A former prison officer (Mr. Arita), who was an employee of the rehabilitation aid hostel for released prisoners in Matsuyama, approached Hisao Tsubouchi with the idea that prisoners be employed in the Kurushima Dockyard. Tsubouchi was vice president of the Volunteer Council for Rehabilitation Aid Hostels of Ehime Prefecture and also president of the Kurushima Dockyard Company. As a prisoner of war he had decided that prisoners do not require strict supervision. In 1961 the Ohi Shipbuilding Dockyard Camp was established in a former employee dormitory.

In 1968 the Kurushima Company substituted at Ohi a three-story metal building for the wooden dormitory and in 1985 the present four-story building that is reminiscent of a college campus. Residents are organized into five groups with the leaders responsible for members at night. They march to work in groups. Within the spacious dockyard, the inmates are scattered about to engage in welding, drilling, and grinding the steel components for a ship. They mingle with free workers, distinguished from them only by a different color of protective helmet. The residents are recruited from class-A inmates; they are in prison for the first time with eighteen months to serve before release. The correction regions submit dossiers to meet assigned quotas of candidates; Matsuyama selects dossiers for further consideration. Ohi residents are trained in arc welding at Matsuyama Prison and have another month of training at the Ohi Camp.

The Arii Dockyard Camp is a subsidiary of Onomichi Branch Prison and occupies a two-story building with a large sports field adjacent; previously the building was quarters for shipyard employees. Traffic violators have been assigned there since 1968. The company contributes 125 yen towards the cost of each meal. The dining room also serves recreation purposes.

The Kagamihara Metal Industrial Camp is located in a residential suburb among small metal processing shops. Its one-story building merges with the other structures along the narrow streets of a crowded area. The camp residents walk to ten small workshops to operate machines for metal processing. The shops are among seventy organized into the Gifu Cooperative Metal Industry, a loose confederation sponsoring the camp. Residents are traffic offenders selected from prisons in the Nagoya Correction Region. They have less than two years to serve on their first prison sentence. They must be less than forty-five years of age, have no tattooing (considered to be the mark of dedicated criminals), and no mental or physical defects.

The three open camps, being dependent on employment of inmates by private companies, are very vulnerable to downturns in the general labor market. In 1992 the program at the Kagamihara Metal Processing Camp had been suspended because the private workshops faced a scarcity of subcontracts. The Ohi Shipbuilding Dockyard Camp and the Arii Dockyard had suffered from a recession for Japanese shipbuilding firms because of competition from third-world countries. When dockyard orders were obtained later, the discharged free workers were employed elsewhere; residents of the Ohi Camp were in demand. In 1988, when I visited the Arii camp, ship construction had ended and the twelve residents were cleaning canvas used to attract refuse in the harbor. During my 1992 visit the residents were cleaning rust from steel beams the Kosin-Sangyo corporation had sold to another company.

OIL SHOCKS AND
THE CRISIS FOR
PRISON LABOR

In 1973 and 1979–80 the oil producing nations of the Middle East sharply reduced exports as a means of raising the price of oil. Depending heavily on oil for its energy, Japan suffered huge increases in the cost of imports, inflation of domestic prices, unemployment, and interruption of the pace of economic growth (Beasley 1990). The loss of revenue was especially untimely because the fiscal budget of 1973 had initiated an unprecedented public investment in social services. Pension benefits of employees were almost doubled, insurance coverage of medical care for dependents increased, and free medical care introduced for the aged (Collick 1988). Increased taxes were politically impractical; deficit financing climbed from 11 percent of expenditures in 1974 to nearly 35 percent in 1979 (Wornoff 1986).

The budget for fiscal year 1974 limited expenditures but did not impose zero growth. To cover revenue shortfall the government issued "red national bonds" for construction of bridges and similar projects. In 1975 the Diet approved bonds that only met the shortage of revenue. Elimination of deficit financing became an ultimate objective. In July 1982 the Ministry of Finance (MOF) requested all ministries to reduce their requests for fiscal 1983 by 10 percent of the previous budget. The imposed ceilings gave the decisions to the ministries themselves (Campbell 1985). The MOF and the head of the Accounting Section of the Ministry of Justice noticed an item in the Correction Bureau's budget for four billion yen. The allocation for purchase of raw materials for prison industries equaled 10 percent of the total budget for the Ministry of Justice. The Ministry of Justice demanded that the budget item be eliminated but also negotiated for preservation of prison industries.

Elimination of the item, the head of the Accounting

Section told the MOF, would have profound adverse consequences for the Correction Bureau and the government in general. Unless raw materials were available, the bureau could not comply with the Prison Law's requirements for prison labor. The MOF would have a self-interest in the continued operation of prison industries because Article 27 of the Prison Law requires that all proceeds from prison labor "shall be vested in the national treasury" rather than be retained by the Correction Bureau.[8]

During consultations with officials experienced in prison industrial operations, the head of the Accounting Section was impressed with the possibilities of involving a private organization in the financing of raw materials. In usual practice, the proceeds of the sales would go into the national treasury without replenishing funds for further purchase of raw materials. A semiprivate organization would not be subject to ordinary accounting practice. Instead, it would furnish raw materials, sell the products, compensate the Correction Bureau for the contribution of inmate labor, and retain a portion of the proceeds for purchase of more raw materials.

The semiprivate organization would be able to purchase raw materials at least twice during a fiscal year; two billion yen a year—not four billion yen—would be sufficient. To introduce a semiprivate organization, funds would have to be provided for initial purchase of raw material. MOF agreed to provide a subsidy of two billion yen but insisted that it be spread over the years 1983–88—four hundred million yen a year for five years. Because there would be a shortage of 1.6 billion yen in 1983, MOF agreed to provide additional money for administrative and personnel expenses and interest to banks for borrowing the needed funds.

Taking Advantage of an Opportunity

The Correction Bureau personnel were reluctant initially because of doubts about the multiple use of funds in a fiscal year and, probably, about sharing authority with an outside party. They were forced to comply when told that, if they rejected the proposal, the budget item would be eliminated without a subsidy. There was insufficient time to create a completely new semiprivate organization and the Japanese Correctional Association (JCA) already existed. JCA presents awards for years of service, subsidizes research projects and several journals, maintains a library, lends financial aid to the Training Institute for Correctional Personnel, and offers other services to correctional personnel (Japanese Correctional Association brochure).

The JCA is an example of the *gaikaku dantai*, public corporations or extradepartmental groups that are incorporated as private associations, foundations, or unions at the initiation of the government bureaucracy. Each is an institutionalized private interest-group but is affiliated with a section of government in an intimate clientele relationship. They are staffed predominantly by retired government officials. In varying degrees, they rely on government funding (A. George 1988).[9]

The directors were reluctant that JCA become the proposed semiprivate organization. Membership dues were sufficient to support the association's own projects, and the large scale of the subsidized industrial activities raised the directors' doubt that JCA could manage them successfully. After a series of conferences with the Industrial Section in the Correction Bureau's headquarters, JCA agreed to add a special unit to its organization: the Correctional Association Prison Industry Cooperation (CAPIC).

CAPIC: Aims and Accomplishments

The head office of CAPIC is located in the JCA headquarters in Nakano, Tokyo. Divisional offices are in each headquarters of the correction regions and there are sixty-eight local branches at prisons with industrial activities. Subsidy payments, including loans to CAPIC, were 1,034 million yen in 1983, 930 million yen in 1984, 767 million yen in 1985, 210 million yen in 1986, and 189 million yen in 1987. Of the total sum of 3.13 billion yen, interest charges and administrative costs drew 1.13 billion yen.

Through an alliance with the Correction Bureau, CAPIC has set out to achieve major goals: "In the first place, it becomes possible to increase the opportunities of prisons receiving orders from outside through the flexible appropriation of funds for raw materials, without being bound by the budget, which serves the purpose of securing the stability of the value of work for inmates. Secondly, the introduction of corporate management systems makes it possible to strengthen the production control, time limits of delivery, costs, etc., and also to promote the development and research in new products and high value-added products" (Japanese Correctional Association, *Guide to CAPIC*, 2).

To create a more stable market, consumers are to be assured a dependable supply of quality products. A catalog of products has been issued, and CAPIC participates in a large-scale annual fair of the Correction Bureau in Tokyo. Retail stores operate in Tokyo and Nagoya and at some prisons. By introducing more sophisticated technology CAPIC hopes to increase productivity and economic return. CAPIC intends to employ 20 percent of the inmates. The national government contributes to the renovation of workshop equipment and sponsors training of workshop supervisors. CAPIC pays the secondary expenses for attending courses and seminars.

CAPIC reports considerable progress in accomplishing its goals, but the costs of administration and transportation of finished goods must be reduced.[10] Changes in markets and customer needs require constant monitoring. Nationwide operations involve an inventory of some four hundred products. For systematic management and planning, development of a data base and use of computers are necessary.

CAPIC uses three approaches in subcontracting. First, CAPIC furnishes the raw materials, the prison provides the labor, and CAPIC sells the products. Second, CAPIC obtains orders and provides the raw materials, and the prison makes the products. Third, CAPIC purchases raw materials from the contractor and relays them to the prison, and later CAPIC receives the finished products and sells them to the contractor. The first method is preferred as a means of stabilizing the market.

CAPIC has not increased its share of total contracts obtained, but its financial contribution has been enhanced. From 1985 to 1991, CAPIC reports, its share of net revenue rose from 24.8 percent to 32.4 percent, and its share of inmate man-days from 13.2 percent to 23.4 percent. Its sales increased from 4.17 billion yen in 1983 to 15.89 billion yen in 1991, a 381 percent gain. For fiscal year 1989–90, the customers were long-term contractors (46.4 percent), large-scale contractors (8.3 percent), government agencies (8.9 percent), the general public (23.5 percent), and annual fairs (12.9 percent).

Woodcraft (furniture making) contributes 35.5 percent of all CAPIC sales in 1991, tailoring 20 percent, metalwork 16.5 percent, printing 13.9 percent, leatherwork 6.9 percent, and ceramics 2.0 percent. CAPIC sales in fiscal year 1991–92 (16,363,266 yen) had increased 292 percent over sales in fiscal year 1983–84 (4,172,738 yen). (The Japanese fiscal year ends 31 March.) Between FY 1986–87 and FY 1991–92 leatherwork scored the largest gain in sales, an increase of 60.2 percent; and tailoring has done well, increasing by 57 percent. With high sales in FY 1991–92 woodcraft (38.9 percent increase) and metalwork (49.7 percent increase) made impressive gains. Ceramics kept pace with a 38.9 percent increase. As in other prison systems, printing is among the most profitable industries, but it scored only a 5.4 percent increase.

Gross profits were 3.9 percent of sales in FY 1983–84 and 10.0 percent of FY 1989–90 sales. However, operating costs also increased 337 percent. In the initial years net income was negative but became positive by 1987, reaching almost

$3.5 million in 1991. CAPIC has contributed a total of more than $2.5 million to various projects for the Correction Bureau in the 1985–91 period.

Yoshiho Yasuhara, then president of JCA, suggested that CAPIC create the Correctional Association Research Institute for Criminology. With a staff of fourteen, the institute is intended to fill the void of a private research center in the field of corrections and criminology. The institute has five divisions. General Affairs is responsible for the administrative support necessary for any organization. The Investigation Division negotiates with other research units in planning projects, publishes the *Bulletin of Correctional Research Institute for Criminology* that reports the institute's projects, and prepares teaching materials for the Correction Bureau's personnel training. The First Research Division examines the causes of crime, methods of prediction, trends, and crime prevention. The Second Research Division studies crime prevention, the effects of punitive and "protective" measures, and the efficiency of rehabilitation-oriented programs. The Third Research Division considers theories for therapeutic responses to offenders, the characteristics of criminals and delinquents, and the development of staff skills for treating offenders.

CAPIC's contribution to industrial activities is reported in table 5.4. Of all inmate workers, 22.9 percent were in CAPIC projects; the other projects were from subcontracts acquired by the prison personnel. Urbanized and industrialized areas showed the greatest success of prisons in soliciting subcontracts; for example, in one of the most metropolitan areas, the prisons of the Tokyo Correction Region were able to attract contracts with private companies without calling on the assistance of CAPIC. Of the inmates working in their industrial shops, 85.8 percent were fulfilling contracts the prison staffs or other Correction Bureau personnel had negotiated. In contrast, the Sapporo Correction Region is located on an island with less industrial de-

Table 5.4
CAPIC Employment in Prison Industries,
by Correction Region and Type of Prison, 1990

Correction Region	B	A	Juvenile	L	Women's	Total
			Type of Prison			
		Inmates Employed by CAPIC				
Tokyo	504	275	80	130	81	1,070
Osaka	792	100	90	—	39	1,021
Nagoya	564	158	—	211	69	1,002
Hiroshima	515	24	—	128	58	725
Fukuoka	631	116	57	113	4	921
Sendai	452	73	42	—	—	567
Sapporo	695	—	91	65	—	851
Takamatsu	156	120	—	116	—	392
Total	4,309	866	360	763	251	6,549
		CAPIC's Percentage of Prison Industry Employment				
Tokyo	11.9	20.0	7.3	25.6	24.3	14.2
Osaka	22.2	14.0	18.9	—	11.6	20.0
Nagoya	25.4	26.7	—	40.8	21.2	27.4
Hiroshima	39.9	20.9	—	31.2	57.4	37.8
Fukuoka	20.6	23.5	33.7	26.4	2.5	21.4
Sendai	28.2	28.2	13.9	—	—	26.2
Sapporo	37.6	—	42.3	32.3	—	37.5
Takamatsu	20.9	35.7	—	22.2	—	24.4
Total	23.2	22.3	16.0	29.5	20.0	22.9

Source: Data provided by CAPIC.

velopment, and its prisons placed a heavy reliance (37.5 percent of employed inmates) on contracts with CAPIC.

The correction regions differ in the distribution of the types of correctional institutions and in the varying dependence on CAPIC of those types. Sapporo had a comparatively high proportion of its class-B labor force at work for CAPIC. The region has a particularly high proportion of the class B among its prisons, and it also relies greatly on CAPIC for its single juvenile prison and single facility for prisoners serving longer sentences. The class-L prisons are popular for CAPIC in all the six regions where they are located, because inmates serving eight years or more will be available for longer periods after they have been trained in job skills. CAPIC especially benefits the single class-A prison in Takamatsu on the island of Shikoku and the Takamatsu Correction Region there. The Hiroshima Correction Region combines both urbanized areas and prefectures that depend on extractive industries; its class-B and women's facilities draw on CAPIC's resources. As an economically developed correction region, Nagoya is exceptional in that CAPIC is present only at Gifu, a class-L institution.

Twin towers of the headquarters of the Ministry of Justice in Tokyo.
(Courtesy of Ministry of Justice)

A wooden jail in Sendai typical of feudal domains in the Keicho Era, 1596–1615. (Courtesy of Museum of Miyagi Prison)

The original Miyagi Prison in Sendai, built in 1879, which duplicated a prison in Leuven, Belgium. (Courtesy of Museum of Miyagi Prison)

Products of the industrial prison, circa 1880: sandals, clothing, hemp rope, baskets, and wooden buckets. (Courtesy of Japanese Correctional Association Museum)

Furniture production at Fuchu Prison, Tokyo Correction Region. (Courtesy of Correction Bureau and Fuchu Prison)

Line of metal shelves entering automated painting stage at Okayama Prison, Hiroshima Correction Region. (Courtesy of Industrial Section, Headquarters, Correction Bureau and Okayama Prison)

Arc-welding instruction in the industrial workshop of Kanazawa Prison, Nagoya Correction Region. (Courtesy of Correction Bureau and Kanazawa Prison)

Inmates at Toyama Prison, Nagoya Correction Region, building a model of a mikoshi, a portable shrine carried through the neighborhood during a Shinto festival. (Courtesy of Correction Bureau and Toyama Prison)

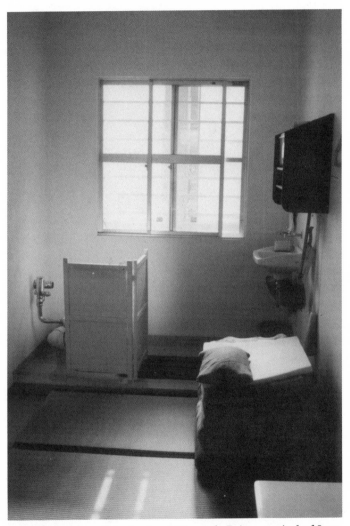

A single-person cell in Iwakuni Women's Prison typical of Japanese prisons. Toilet is shielded for privacy and sleeping futons are stored during the day. (Courtesy of Iwakuni Women's Prison)

Technique of sandbox diagnosis used at Tokyo Juvenile Classification Home. (Courtesy of Tokyo Juvenile Classification Home)

Naginata *exercise (ritual combat) at Haruna Juvenile Training School for Girls, Tokyo Correction Region. (Courtesy of Haruna Juvenile Training School)*

Bon *Dance Festival drummer plays a* taiko *(drum) for the dancers at Tama Juvenile Training School for Boys, Tokyo Correction Region. (Courtesy of Tama Juvenile Training School)*

Mother's Day visitation at Tama Juvenile Training School, Tokyo Correction Region. (Courtesy of Tama Juvenile Training School)

Wachukai Rehabilitation Aid Hostel in Osaka, the largest in Japan. The multistoried building, opened in 1987, cost 400 million yen and replaced a wooden building. (Courtesy of Wachukai Rehabilitation Aid Hostel)

Keiwayen Rehabilitation Aid Hostel in Tokyo. Typical of most hostels in size and construction, it is maintained by government subsidy and private funds. (Courtesy of Rehabilitation Bureau)

THE ORDERLY
PRISON

*G*riffiths (n.d., 229) declared that "Japan as an enlightened and progressive country has made strenuous efforts to establish 'as perfect a prison as possible; one which is in harmony with the advancement of science and the results of experience.' " He was describing the results of reforms begun in 1871 during the early Meiji Restoration and was comparing Japanese prisons then with what he had observed in India, Burma, China, Egypt, and Turkey. The reforms in Japan, he said, were hurried on by the great overcrowding of the small provincial prisons. There had been some system in earlier times, but "nothing has changed more completely than Japanese prisons" (231).

Griffiths praised the Japanese prisons in comparison with others in Asia that presented horrible conditions at that time. The early Meiji reforms were only the beginning, but they were considerable improvements over the Tokugawa policy toward criminals. "Throughout the whole Tokugawa period, criminal punishment was cruel, public, and exemplary" (Ooms 1985, 147). By observing the effects on criminals of decapitation, crucifixion, or bodily mutilation, the commoners were to be impressed by the bakufu authority and to learn discipline and respect for the social order. Parading the criminal through the streets and exposing the corpse of executed criminals also were prominent punishments. Later, bodily mutilations were sometimes replaced by tattooing. Bakufu penal laws were less stern in dealing with the crimes of the samurai than of commoners, except for gambling and robbery, considered flagrant violations of the samurai code (Duus 1969). Tokugawa villages punished some violators with monetary fines, required surrender of rice or sake, or demanded service as water guards, night watchmen, and storehouse guards (T. Sato 1990).

EARLY FORMS OF
PENAL CONFINEMENT

Penal institutions existed before the Meiji Restoration. The *roya*, a primitive predecessor to the contemporary prison, served primarily for pretrial detention, but penal confinement, executions, beatings, and tattooing for punishment also were carried out. The Tokugawa shogunate developed a second type, the *ninosoku-yoseba* ("Coolie Gathering Place" or "Stockade for Laborers") that was a forerunner, in some respects, for contemporary imprisonment. The *tame*, which dated back to 1687, originally received sick homeless persons under criminal investigation and homeless travelers who had fallen ill. The tame gradually became a sick ward for pretrial inmates (Hiramatsu 1973).

In the early Tokugawa period, individual assaults by unemployed samurai were fairly common. In the middle period, thievery by ordinary folk increased. In the seventeenth century, theft with arson increased. In the late period, there were numerous professional pickpockets (De Vos and Mizushima 1973).

Ogawa and Tomeoka ([1910] 1970) speculate that since there were criminals to be punished, there must have been places for confinement, although historical accounts first mention the ruler personally inspecting prisons in the year 483. In 701 the Department of Justice had a "prison office" with forty guards and twenty subguards. The Tokugawa shogunate placed prison affairs under the Commissioners of Temples and Shrines who would send constables to inspect the more than three hundred confinement facilities established by feudal lords.

The Tokugawa government operated a roya near Tokiwabashi from 1590 to 1592 and moved it to Kodemmacho (near Tokyo) sometime between 1596 and 1615 (Hiramatsu 1973). Destroyed by fire some sixteen times, it was rebuilt each time until it was closed in 1875. The prison building had five sections divided according to the social status of the inmates. Discipline was more lax for imprisoned samurai and priests who had commoner-inmates as personal attendants. All women were confined in one section. The prison held persons awaiting trial, but usually even defendants believed to be guilty were placed in custody of a relative or in a special inn. Persons found guilty were held pending execution (which was prompt without appeal) or exile to a distant island. A few individuals served lengthy imprisonment; women and minors under fifteen were confined for thirty to fifty days. Flogging was carried out in front of the prison and executions in the prison.

In the closed world of the prison, there existed a hierarchical structure of inmate roles broadly classified as "officials within prison," "prisoners with assignments," and "ordinary prisoners." The prisoner boss (*ronanushi*) and his deputy were appointed from confirmed criminals. The boss appointed other prisoners to be in charge of surveillance, food, clothing, and medicine, respectively. Discipline was enforced by flogging. "Prisoners with past records not only enjoyed privileges but even had a voice in intercession and mediation. Around the influential prisoner hovered those who owed their status solely to his favoritism" (Hiramatsu 1973, 6).

Some inmates were treated as "guests" when they gave presents to other prisoners or were already known to officials. No lamp or candle was allowed at night. Often, diseased prisoners were put to death in the darkness. Clothing and bedding had to be provided by relatives. "The inside of a prison was unclean, gloomy, and pestilent, just like those of Europe previous to the time of John Howard" (Ogawa and Tomeoka [1910] 1970, 308). The first full-fledged prisons seem to have been introduced in 1755 in the Kumamoto domain. To be reclaimed as useful persons, inmates performed labor, were taught skills, and given wages (Ooms 1985). Later, the bakufu adopted the idea as one way to manage protesters.

The appearance of ninosoku-yoseba stemmed from the efforts to control persons made homeless as a consequence of famine and changes in village life. The homeless included a minority with criminal propensities. One policy was to banish homeless persons to the island of Sado for hard labor; they were to be taught "a lesson." They were put to work dipping water from the silver and gold mines. Another policy was to establish a home for them in Edo; opened in 1780, it was terminated in 1786 (Hiramatsu 1973).

During the Kansei Reform begun in 1787, Matsudaira Sadanobu headed the Council of Elders and exercised power as adviser to the shogun. He asked concerned officials for recommendations for establishing an institution for homeless wanderers. Heizo Nobutame Hasegawa was responsible for investigation of instances of arson, theft, and robbery. He worked out the details for the ninosoku-yoseba and was ordered to establish it in 1790 on the small island of Ishikawajima at the mouth of the Smida River (Sansom 1963c; Takigawa 1972; Hiramatsu 1972).

The basic nature of the "Stockade for Laborers" is summarized by the instructions read to arriving inmates:

> You no longer are listed on your family register, and as innocent homeless you are to be sent to Sado. However, by "the Great Benevolence" you are now made workers and are allowed to pursue such skills as you may have

learned. You are enjoined to change heart, to come to your senses, and by hard work to try to earn enough capital to start a new life on your own. At the sign of repentance and reform, you will be released irrespective of the length of your sentence. In such event, this *yoseba* will provide you with an adequate plot of land if you are a farmer. You will be given a shop at the place of your birth if you happen to be from Edo. Otherwise, you will be provided with tools of a trade or granted appropriate allowances from the shogunate. (Hiramatsu 1973, 10)

The original Ishikawajima Workhouse for Criminals and Homeless Paupers was designed to resocialize homeless persons believed prone to becoming criminals. Initially, they were assigned to making lime, charcoal balls, or paper. They were paid to give them support after release, when they were expected to apply the skills learned (Takigawa 1972). In 1820 the workhouse began to house persons sentenced to forced labor, exiled from the Edo region, and scheduled to be turned over to guardians elsewhere (Kyokai 1943, vol. 1; Hiramatsu 1972). It was believed that the work would lead to postrelease employment and also serve punitive and deterrent functions. In the latter purpose, the workhouse became a model for penal establishments established by local feudal clans elsewhere in Japan (Hiramatsu 1972).

In 1870 the facility was renamed the Ishikawajima House of Correction and was turned over to the Keibusho, as the Ministry of Justice was then known. Afterwards it was turned over successively to the Shihosho (later the Ministry of Justice) and the Tokyo Metropolitan Government. In 1873 the institution was renamed Ishikawajima Choekijyo. In 1875 the Tokyo Metropolitan Police Agency assumed control. In 1895 it was moved to Nishi-Sugamo village and renamed "Sugamo Penitentiary Branch" in a new plant. The Ministry of Justice of the central government took it over in 1903. In 1935 it was moved to the Fuchu district of Tokyo and renamed Fuchu Prison, which exists today.

Appointed the equivalent of head of prisons in the Ministry of Criminal Affairs in 1870, Shigeya Ohara had been confined earlier, when he was thirty-one years of age, in Kodemmacho Prison. The experience had convinced him that penal reform was necessary. He improved sanitary conditions in the jails and abolished ronanushi, the custom of appointing certain inmates to oversee others. Ohara drafted the Kangoku soku ("prison rules" promulgated in 1872) that was distributed publicly as one of the policy documents in the Meiji period. He visited the British colonies in Hong Kong and Singapore to examine the prison and court systems of the West. He contributed significantly to the design of the prisons, along with Motohiro Onoda who had visited prisons in Belgium, France, and Prussia (Takigawa 1972; Hiramatsu 1973).

After drafting two penal codes that proved to be unsuitable, the Meiji regime asked Emile Gustave Boissonade to draft a new one on the French model. It was brought into force in 1882 but was replaced in 1907 by a code in the German model. It is still in force, although its abstract content has permitted interpretations consistent with new circumstances.

The Satsuma Rebellion of 1877 resulted in 27,000 prisoners and the hasty conversion of rice warehouses and stables into inadequate places of confinement. Rioting, arson, and escape were frequent. New prisons were completed in Tokyo and Miyagi (Hiramatsu 1973).[1] The Criminal Code of 1880 established a scheme of confinement facilities: *Ryuchijo*, attached to the courthouse or police station, detained accused persons; *kanso* confined unconvicted defendants; *chochijo* was intended for underage prisoners and for delinquency-prone youth; *hoekijo* was for adult convicts; and Tokyo Shuchikan, a prison in Tokyo, Miyagi Prison in Sendai, Kabato, Sorachi, and Kushiro Prisons in Hokkaido, and Miike Prison in Fukuoka were part of the *shuchikan*. The Prison Law (1881) specified the shuchikan would confine long-term and political prisoners serving more than five years (Ogawa and Tomeoka [1910] 1970).

Cell assignments separated individuals less than sixteen years of age from those over sixteen, first offenders from recidivists among those age sixteen to twenty, and first offenders from recidivists. A black mask was worn by unconvicted persons in pretrial detention when they left their cells, so they could not be recognized by accomplices. Names were not called; a number on white cloth was sewn to the coat. A confined mother could keep with her those children less than three years of age.

All persons were required to work, except those between twelve and sixteen years of age, over sixty, the ill, and the physically handicapped. When at labor outside the prison, they were chained in pairs and their faces covered with large straw hats. Selected inmates supervised the work. Earned money was accumulated until time of release, but withdrawals could be made for books, food, and remittances to relatives. Except for sake, tobacco, and other "injurious" items, presents could be received.

Good behavior showing moral change earned a prize medal and the privilege to write a letter and receive visitors every two months. Twenty-five sen were awarded the inmate who secretly informed about an escape attempt, who saved a life, or who had praiseworthy behavior in flood or fire. Punishment included prohibition of letter writing, confinement in a closed room, reduction in quantity of the daily ration, or confinement in a darkened room.

By 1900 there were 7 major prisons run by the central government, 47 prisons managed by prefectural governments, and 84 branch prisons. The major prisons followed French and German designs of the time. Prisoners were among the labor resources for the creation of an economic infrastructure, and thus set precedent for the extensive industrial activities in contemporary Japanese prisons.

PROBLEMS OF
MINIMAL CONFINEMENT

Prisons in contemporary Japan have not experienced disturbances since the years immediately after World War II when the prisons were crowded and resources were in short supply. Violence against other inmates is unusual and against staff even more rare. In 1991 there was 1 escape from a Japanese prison; the American maximum- and medium-security prisons of forty-one states and the federal government had 254 escapes. Japanese inmates suffered few casualties in 1991: 3 from suicide, 1 at the hands of other inmates, and none from accidental self-injuries. Equivalent deaths in American state and federal prisons were 89 from suicide, 55 at the hands of other inmates, and 35 from accidental self-injury (Research and Training Institute 1993, 84; Maguire, Pastore, and Flanagan 1993, 653–68).

The orderliness of Japanese prisons exists in spite of the assembling there of more and more convicted criminals who are less likely to be rehabilitated: those previously imprisoned, older than average for persons apprehended by the police, identified with the yakuza, or otherwise classified as possessing "advanced criminal tendencies."

Official leniency is suggested by the history of the males entering prison for the first time in 1990. Of the 7,463 males, 59.8 percent had received a suspended sentence after an earlier appearance before a court, usually for a crime other than the one for which they had recently been imprisoned. Also, 13.6 percent had experienced juvenile training school (Research and Statistics Section 1993a, 86–87).

By granting leniency for earlier offenses, the prosecutors and judges allowed time to pass, and the repeat offenders to age, before the ultimate decision for imprisonment was made. The mean age of male admissions consistently has exceeded 30 years and has risen from an average of 31.9 in 1970 to 39.8 in 1992 (see table 6.1). Increasing age, per se, does not make for more violent behavior, but the chances

Table 6.1
Age of Males Entering Prison, 1970–92

Age at Admission	1970 %	1975 %	1980 %	1985 %	1990 %	1992 %
16 to 24	27.1	15.9	10.8	12.4	12.6	11.8
25 to 29	24.5	23.8	16.3	12.5	14.5	14.7
30 to 39	31.3	36.1	41.6	36.0	25.4	24.2
40 to 49	12.3	17.8	23.1	26.3	29.5	29.9
50 to 59	3.7	5.0	6.5	10.6	14.1	15.0
60 and Over	1.1	1.4	1.7	2.2	3.9	4.4
Total	100.0	100.0	100.0	100.0	100.0	100.0
Mean Age	31.89	34.30	36.46	38.07	39.34	39.84

Sources: Research and Statistics Section, *Annual Report of Statistics on Correction* for given years.

for abandonment of criminal ways decline. The age categories differed greatly in the effect of time on their share of total male admissions. The younger group assumed smaller shares as the years unfolded; the percentage decline was 56.5 percent for age group 16–24, 40 percent for age group 25–29, and 22.7 percent for age group 30–39. The older groups took up the slack; their percentage increases from 1970 to 1992 were 143.1 percent for age group 40–49, 305.4 percent for age group 50–59; and 300 percent for age group 60 years and more (Research and Statistics Section 1971; 1993a).

The trend toward more advanced age of prisoners mirrors the aging of Japanese society. Male longevity has grown from 42.6 years in 1946 to 75.9 in 1989, female longevity from 51.1 to 81.8 years over the same period. Governmental and private agencies face the necessity to invest in ways to meet the needs of an expanding elderly population. Although prisoners over sixty years of age continue to be few, their escalating rate of growth foreshadows greater medical costs and fewer able-bodied persons for prison labor. Probation, parole, and aftercare services will face difficulties because many elderly offenders lack family linkages and employability.

The enigma of recidivism lies in the difficulty of separating the faults of the particular serial offender, lack of tolerance of the community, and the failures of criminal justice agencies. The increase in the share of recidivists among males entering prison is a case in point. The combination of personal faults and community factors is suggested by the experiences of released prisoners. Of the 28,630 men released in 1981, 57.7 percent were back by 1990. Of the 406 released women, 46.5 percent were returned by 1990. Most returns were in the second year after release; thereafter, the number dropped progressively (Research and Statistics Section 1991a, 156).

Previous imprisonment is among the criteria used by public prosecutors and sentencing judges as they decide whether or not official leniency is appropriate. To attribute the trend to those decisions alone would be premature; but the decisions (presumably consistent with appropriate criteria) contributed to the increased representation of former inmates in prison admissions over the years. The percentage share of "first-termers" among male admissions decreased from 47.4 percent in 1970 to 35.9 percent in 1992 and, concurrently, the percentage share of those in prison for at least the fourth time rose from 25.4 to 35.5 percent (see table 6.2). The trends are summarized by the rise of the mean number of prison admissions for all males from 2.82 to 3.53.

The trend for greater recidivism is intimately related to the trend for more advanced average age of inmates entering prison. Once defendants were sent to prison they were more likely to be sent there again. To demonstrate the interaction between age of incoming inmates and repetitive imprisonment, the percentage distributions of prison admissions were standardized to eliminate the effect of age.

Table 6.2
Previous Exposure to Penal Incarceration of Males Entering Prison, 1970–92

No. of Admissions	1970	1975	1980	1985	1990	1992
	Percentage of Male Admissions					
1	47.4	42.5	40.9	38.9	37.1	35.9
2	16.8	17.9	18.2	18.3	16.7	16.5
3	10.4	11.5	12.3	12.4	11.8	12.1
4 or more	25.4	28.1	28.6	30.4	34.4	35.5
Total	100.0	100.0	100.0	100.0	100.0	100.0
Mean No. of Admissions	2.82	3.02	3.06	3.19	3.44	3.53
Mean Standardized by Age[a]	2.82	2.65	2.47	2.43	2.48	2.55
	Percentage of Yakuza Male Admissions					
1	33.0	31.4	29.7	26.5	27.6	25.3
2	25.4	23.1	22.1	21.0	19.4	18.9
3	14.6	16.8	16.4	17.7	15.3	15.9
4 or more	27.0	28.7	31.8	34.8	37.7	39.9
Total	100.0	100.0	100.0	100.0	100.0	100.0
Mean No. of Yakuza Admissions	2.89	2.98	3.12	3.34	3.45	3.57
Mean No. of Non-Yakuza Admissions	2.80	3.04	2.80	3.14	3.43	3.52

Source: Research and Statistics Section, *Annual Report of Statistics on Corrections* for given years.

[a]To control for the effect of increasing age of inmates admitted over the years, the percentage distribution of inmates by age group was standardized for subsequent years on the basis of 1970 data.

For each of the subsequent years, the total number of male admissions were redistributed according to the percentage distribution by age of all men entering prison in 1970. With all the years having identical percentage distributions by age, the estimated number of men in each age cell for the given year was multiplied by the actual rate that year of previous imprisonments for men of that age.

The means, standardized by age, are presented in table 6.2 and show that, with the age differences removed, the mean numbers of exposures to penal incarceration are considerably reduced. In other words, by delaying the referral of serial offenders to prison, the procuracy and judiciary increased the average age of incoming prisoners. Their policy of leniency for the "worthy" defendants was reversed when a former prisoner was again apprehended. Then the defendants previously sent to prison became increasingly represented among incoming inmates over the years.

The yakuza (the Mafia of Japan) as inmates usually resist official persuasion that they abandon criminal ways. The great majority cling to a criminal subculture. They raise security problems by trying to continue intergang conflicts, by preferring to be with members of their gang, by striving to recruit nongang inmates, and by trying to manipulate the staff to gain advantages. The gangsters have taken larger and larger shares of the prison population. The yakuza are especially unlikely to be in prison for the first time; that tendency has become stronger with the years. As table 6.2 also shows, they have exceeded the nonyakuza males in average exposures to incarceration.

As pursuers of illicit profits, the criminal organizations generate their own menu of crimes. Their imprisoned members have been especially involved in violence against persons and offenses lumped here as "societal violence": extortion, transgression of the law against violence, possession of "firearms and swords" (a centuries-old prohibition), and possession of explosives. Traffic in illicit drugs has drawn many of them to prison, along with drug abusers. The gangsters' share of these crimes is large and has increased considerably over the years. Although the overall number of admissions is small for violations of the law against prostitution and prohibited practices in gambling and lotteries, the yakuza are overrepresented among the men entering prison for those violations. Sex, traffic, and property offenses are more characteristic of the nonyakuza.

According to official judgments, as the years pass the prisons are receiving more and more criminals who will not respond to official efforts to prevent their future crimes. During reception, inmates are classified on the basis of whether they exhibit "advanced criminal tendencies" (class B) or do not (class A). Four general criteria distinguish the former: Previous incarceration more than twice in a juvenile training school or a child-care institution as a delinquent, or imprisonment within the previous five years, or commission of serious crimes after release from previous imprisonment, although more than five years had passed; association with a criminal group as a core member or a marginal member for more than one year; modus operandi of present offense suggesting habitual or intentional criminal acts; and habits and attitudes indicating a criminal lifestyle or persistent departures from rectitude, such as narcotic abuse, alcohol addiction, or vagrancy.

According to the four criteria, the class-B men were 64 percent of all male prisoners in 1975 and they continued to hold that percentage share through 1990. The yakuza held an imposing 21-percent share of the class-B inmates in 1975 and progressively increased their share to 32 percent by 1990. By some class-B criteria, the yakuza would be the most likely to be classified as exhibiting "advanced criminal tendencies." In 1985 that classification applied to 85 percent of the gangster inmates, and in the 1980s increased to 92 percent (Research and Statistics Section 1984, 120; 1987, 70; 1992, 70).

ENVIRONMENT OF CONSTRAINT

Domiciliary institutions, including prisons, differ in purposes: hospitals strive to overcome the ailments of their patients and prolong their lives; the military post prepares its residents to protect the nation from foreign aggressors. The prison would safeguard citizens from the aggressors within their own ranks and ultimately reduce the crime threat. The residents of domiciliary establishments live with one another in a specific place around-the-clock within a scheme of activities imposed upon them. Goffman (1961, 5–6) calls this arrangement the "total institution" and notes that it stands in sharp relief from the basic social arrangement in modern society "where the individual tends to sleep, play, and work in different places, with different coparticipants, under different authorities, and without an overall rational plan." Prisoners sleep and work in the same place and with the same persons. All inmates are supposed to be treated the same and are required to do the same thing together. Their daily activities are tightly scheduled according to a master plan; the first phase leads to another at a prearranged time. The scheduling is imposed from above and reinforced by a code of rules.

A small number of supervisors can manage a large number of subordinates. "When persons are moved in blocks, they can be supervised by personnel whose chief activity is not guidance or periodic inspection (as in many employer-employee relations) but rather surveillance—a seeing to it that everyone does what he has been clearly told is required of him, under conditions where one person's infraction is likely to stand out in relief against the visible, constantly examined compliance of others" (Goffman 1961, 6–7).

New inmates are greeted by an ongoing system of regimentation that envelops them in routinized activities. Daily activities are tightly scheduled with the prison labor taking up most of the daylight hours of weekdays. They march to the workshops after breakfast in the cell and begin work at

7:20 A.M. In midmorning there is a fifteen-minute tea break in the workshop. Lunch is also there at noon, and work resumes at 12:40. After tea break in midafternoon, work ends at 4:30 for the march to the cell for the 5:00 P.M. dinner there. Lights are out at 9:00 P.M.

In the bizarre environment of forced confinement, the routinization of daily events may be considered a strategy for managing time. The strategy certainly serves the prison administration by controlling inmates, but it also serves the interests of the prisoners (Galtung 1961). Regularity promotes predictability and reduces tensions about the future. Especially for inmates with a long sentence, time becomes a problem. The present cannot be measured against the anticipated pleasures of weekend events of one's own choice. If the present is meaningless, the prison routines become the benchmarks of time for the course of life, especially if mental and physical deterioration is feared.

The management of prisoners in Japan also can be assessed in terms of disciplining of bodily movements. Foucault (1977) illustrates the control of bodily movement by the example of military drill. In recruit training, the apprentice-soldiers are taught to conform their physical gestures to a predetermined scheme. In marching, the feet are pushed ahead in steps of specified length and in coordination with fellow marchers. The training and participation in marching deprive soldiers of the spontaneity of self-induced physical movements; they are pressed into habitual conformity. Instruction in marching is part of the orientation of new Japanese prisoners. Groups are moved about the prison, arms swinging in the British style, with an inmate monitor shouting orders and prison officers trailing along.

MULTIPLE ROLES OF JAPANESE OFFICERS

Because they play crucial roles in the daily affairs of the correctional institutions, the systematic recruitment and in-service training of Japanese prison officers, as sketched in chapter 4, are fundamental advantages for the Correction Bureau. Prison officers are in the most direct and continuous contact with inmates and are able to observe their unique qualities and problems. They are especially influential in shaping inmates' impressions of the prison's power over them and what is expected of them.

In relationships with inmates, Japanese officers are expected to carry out concurrently three roles: the security monitor, the moral educator, and the lay counselor. Shikita (1972, 19), former director general of the Correction Bureau, outlines general features of the roles:

> The Ministry of Justice, by directives, requires guards to be thoroughly familiar with the backgrounds of all prisoners assigned to them. . . . A guard . . . is expected to know the inmate's moods and to be in a position to readily detect any symptoms of worry, concern, or unusual behavior on the part of the inmate. He is expected to counsel the inmate when these appear. . . . Although some prisoners try to reject their guard because of the authority that he carries, the majority regard him as an older brother or father figure, and readily accept his guidance and advice, at last on an emotional level.

Standing in sharp contrast to the American principle that correctional personnel should maintain social distance from prisoners or risk manipulation by connivers, the Japanese officer is expected officially to be "an older brother or father figure" for prisoners in keeping with the oyabun-kobun relationship and its supporting principles of giri (see chapter 2). Traditions press the officers to feel concern for the inmates' interests and long-term welfare. The subordinate kobun status leads most inmates to accept, without loss of dignity and self-respect, dependency on the officers in the oyabun status of the paternalistic superior.

The policy of strict enforcement of official rules lends priority to the security-monitor role; officers are instructed to report the most trivial violations. Surveillance is supplemented by shakedowns of inmates and their possessions. Body searches are routine whenever the inmates leave cells, enter the factory or other parts of the prison, and depart the locations. When meeting a visitor, they are searched leaving the cell or workshop, entering the visiting room, and again leaving the room. Multiperson cells are searched when the occupants are absent; single-person cells may be searched with the inmate present.

The discovery and punishment of rule violators is at the core of custody for security. The officer carries an electronic device for alerting the security section. The security section of each prison has its own code; for example, three short buzzes announce a prisoner is being brought to the section. A long buzz indicates an emergency, and the entire security section responds. The officer in charge takes the inmate to the security section for holding in a single-person cell during investigation. Accused inmates usually work in a single-person cell without denial of privileges. The inmates write their own versions of the rule-violation incidents.

Each officer has a particular jurisdiction for conduct reports. Workshop officers are responsible only during working hours. Thereafter, the cell-block staff relays information on inmate conduct to the workshop officer who prepares conduct reports. The reports go to a committee for that section of the prison. The committee's reports go to the committee for the whole prison for progressive-stage promotions and parole recommendations.

Prison Law, Article 60, lists the range of punishments: reprimand; suspension of good treatment, such as remuneration, for three months or less or its discontinuation; prohibition of reading books or seeing pictures of family members during three months or less; suspension of work for ten days or less; suspension of using self-furnished clothing and bedding for fifteen days or less; suspension of self-supply of food for fifteen days or less; suspension of physical exercise for five days or less; reduction of food for seven days or less; and solitary confinement in a one-person cell with regular meals.

Persons in punishment are required to sit in the traditional position most comfortable for the individual: *seiza*, sitting erect on knees, or *agura*, sitting with crossed legs. Physical exercise for inmates in solitary confinement is usually conducted under conditions of physical isolation from one another. If the punishee shows "clear signs of reformation," the punishment may be remitted.

The emphasis on security measures is consistent with the tendency of the Japanese to reject those offenders found wanting by the procuracy and judiciary. In Japan's consensual society there is strong agreement on rules of behavior and general rejection of the socially unworthy. Japanese believe each person has an innate capacity for self-correction. The residual cases left after the diversionary processing tend to be stereotyped as meriting close surveillance.

As domiciliary institutions, prisons become responsible for meeting the ordinary physiological needs of inmates: proper nutrition, clothing, sleeping arrangements, shelter from the weather, protection from disease and aggression of other persons, and care after natural and manmade disasters. Officers are intermediaries between inmates in need of services and those staff members directly responsible for the particular service. Also, the officers are most visible in inmates' evaluation of the prison's responsiveness to their legitimate needs.

In arguing that the combination of industrial labor and stern discipline promotes the rehabilitation of inmates, the ideology of adult prison presents the premises of "correctional training": enforced compliance to a circumscribed behavioral script that is expected to become ingrained habit (see chapter 3). Here the three roles of the prison officers are combined to encourage compliance to the prison's expectations. By being knowledgeable in disciplinary measures, the officers are expected to bring the security-monitor role to that purpose. Compliance is supposed to be promoted by positive inducements as well as the threats of punishment. The officer roles of moral educator and lay counselor operate within the Japanese oyabun-kobun relationships and the support of the positive inducements.

VALUE ORIENTATIONS
TOWARD RULE VIOLATIONS

The body of rules express Japanese values and are a barometer of the prison administration's approach to managing prisoners. The infractions represent the divergence between, first, what inmates believe are their self-interests and justifiable needs in the prison environment and, second, the official perceptions of what is best for the prison and inmates. In my research reported below, rule violations were categorized according to the value orientations of the officials of Japanese prisons.

Annual statistics published by the Ministry of Justice include tabulations of rule violations, but some 30 percent of the rule violations are reported as "others." To obtain the details on the unclassified infractions for 1990, officials from nine class-B men's prisons, five class-A men's prisons, and five women's prisons were asked to list in detail all rule violations. The infraction percentage rate for all the prisons in the sample is 65.6 (see table 6.3). A rate of 63.2 for all institutions holding convicted prisoners in 1990 is reported by the Ministry of Justice (Research and Statistics Section 1991a). The sample did not include the prisons in these classifications: J, for juveniles; Y, for young adults under twenty-six years of age; and L, for those serving sentences over eight years of length. Those types of prisons usually have lower infraction rates. The infractions in the sample survey were tentatively grouped according to the classes listed in table 6.3. Japanese security officials were asked to evaluate the placing of each of the reported rule violations

Table 6.3
Rule Violations in Three Types of Prisons, 1990

Infractions	B-Prisons		A-Prisons		Women's Prisons	
	No.	Rate	No.	Rate	No.	Rate
Antiprison Threats	753	10.51	114	5.56	98	6.52
a. Custody	(9)	(0.12)	(1)	(0.05)	(8)	(0.53)
b. Penal Law	(744)	(10.39)	(113)	(5.51)	(90)	(5.98)
Antistaff Threats	1,845	25.76	141	6.87	147	9.77
a. Confrontation	(996)	(13.91)	(76)	(3.70)	(48)	(3.19)
b. Inimical Threats	(849)	(11.85)	(65)	(3.17)	(99)	(6.58)
Inmate Cohesion	585	8.17	83	4.05	216	14.36
a. Criminal Signs	(147)	(2.05)	(24)	(1.17)	(31)	(2.06)
b. Inmate Interaction	(438)	(6.12)	(59)	(2.88)	(185)	(12.30)
Prison Industry	971	13.56	138	6.73	59	3.92
a. Sabotage	(286)	(3.99)	(37)	(1.80)	(9)	(.60)
b. Shirking	(685)	(9.56)	(101)	(4.92)	(50)	(3.32)
Contravening Acts	459	6.41	65	3.17	85	5.65
a. Targeting Prison	(123)	(1.72)	(20)	(0.98)	(75)	(4.99)
b. Anticivility	(336)	(4.69)	(45)	(2.19)	(10)	(0.66)
Inmate Relations	1,016	14.19	138	6.73	120	7.98
a. Conflict-Inciting	(755)	(10.54)	(88)	(4.29)	(70)	(4.65)
b. Estrangement	(261)	(3.64)	(50)	(2.44)	(50)	(3.32)
Total	5,629	78.59	679	3.11	725	48.20
No. of Inmates	7,162		2,051		1,504	

Source: Sample survey of 14 men's prisons and 5 women's prisons conducted by author.

Note: Number of inmates represents average daily population in 1990 of the prisons in the sample. Rate is the number of infractions per 100 inmates.

within the typology. The classes are represented below in the order of priority assigned by the officials.

First priority was assigned to violations of the penal code and escapes as direct challenges to custody. I consider these violations to be "antiprison" because the target is confinement itself. Of the crimes covered by the penal code, certain ones are most relevant to management of prisoners: murder or bodily injury of staff or other inmates and obstructing an official from performance of his duty. Escapes are included under "custody" in table 6.3; only one escape occurred, that of a male prisoner in A-class. From the Japanese perspective, violation of "custody" involves unattended walking or being in forbidden places and jeopardizing health by certain techniques for obtaining release from prison. Techniques are suicide attempts, swallowing an object, and refusing to take a meal or a medical diet or to see a physician. The Japanese inflate the rate of "antiprison threats" by including those techniques among rule violations.

Second priority is accorded "antistaff" violations of rules that are designed to preserve staff authority. Direct challenges (confrontation) are illustrated by refusing an order, obstructing an officer's performance of duty, refusing to be taken somewhere by an officer, and disrespect to an officer. Implied challenges to staff authority ("inimical threats") are unauthorized actions either in communication, or in the manufacture, trade, use, processing, abuse, or possession of articles. Other violations are having a concealed article or product, giving a false report, introducing tobacco (smoking is totally prohibited in Japanese prisons), being impolite to an officer, unauthorized eating, abusing paint thinner, and engaging in social manipulation. Some infractions occur infrequently: making persistent demands for cell transfer, failing to return a tool, and placing another inmate's number on clothing.

In third priority are infractions suggesting "intimate cohesion" that are conceived to conflict with the official belief that Japanese prisoners will not affiliate with one another in opposition to the keepers. Enforcement of rules is a means of preventing the development of major group linkages among inmates. Rule violations called "criminal signs" are considered evidence of yakuza membership or of dedicated opposition to the keepers: a certain style of haircut, shaven head, improvised dress, tattooing, and a ring around the penis. Organizing "bad company" and gambling also suggest dedicated criminality. Infractions called "inmate interaction" are transfer or exchange of unauthorized articles and openly greeting arriving inmates. Not regarded to be as serious a challenge as "criminal signs," these infractions are still treated as evidence of inmate cohesion.

Fourth priority is assigned to violations of rules designed to promote disciplined effort in the workshops. Some violations are perceived as sabotaging productivity: refusing to work, failure to observe instructions, making substandard products, damaging products, leaving the designated seat without permission, and leaving a tool unattended. Other violations are seen as shirking: looking aside, unauthorized talking, discarding an article, and violating safety rules.

Fifth priority is given to "contravening acts" that violate respect for one another's interests in a physically circumscribed "community," rather than involving the dominance of the keepers over the kept. "Contravention" lingers between the extremes of open conflict and willingness to accept fully the expectations of officials. In that middle ground, "targeting the prison" refers to interference with smooth prison operations: hindering the operations, destruction of portions of a building or its equipment, clogging a toilet, spoiling a cell, dumping food, or throwing food seasoning. The word "civility" carries the expectation that "civilized" persons will practice the etiquette of politeness that makes for good neighbors. "Anticivility" is exhibited in unauthorized conduct: washing of self or clothing at an unauthorized place, using water or using a locker without permission, engaging in physical exercises in a cell, violating the daily schedule, improperly using books and writing letters, and watching television without approval.

Security officials give the lowest priority to violations in relationships among inmates that are minor irritations in circumscribed space. "Conflict-inciting" incidents are regarded more seriously: quarreling between inmates, practicing intimidation, instigating inmate misconduct, slandering inmates, extorting food, stealing, and conducting an indecent act. "Estrangement" refers to behavior irritating to other inmates: being rude to an inmate, engaging in annoying or embarrassing conduct, being noisy, playing tricks on others, and performing an unsanitary act such as urinating in an inappropriate location.

Differential Violating by Inmate Groups

The sample produced a percentage rate of 65.6 infractions when the sexes were combined (see table 6.3). The rate is similar to the rate of 63.2 percent reported in official statistics for all convicted. Class-B males exceed class-A males in rates for respective infractions and for all violations. The official choice of certain individuals as appropriate members of class B is confirmed.

Each major category in table 6.3 has two subcategories, identified as either *a* or *b*. The Japanese officials considered type-*a* infractions to be more serious than type-*b* infractions. Usually type-*b* subcategories held the greater number of incidents; however, the violations mostly were comparatively minor.

In "antiprison threats," the officials considered "custody" violations to be the most serious because of escapes or behavior believed to be associated with escape. Class-A prisons had the single escape; class-B prisons and women's prisons presented rule violations for behavior believed to suggest an intention to escape: being in a forbidden area or trying to injure one's own well-being or health. The latter kind of incidents included a suicide attempt or refusing medical assistance; I consider the Japanese interpretation to stretch excessively the scope of "custody." The murders and assaults, listed as "penal law," merit greater concern. Here class-B prisons exceeded both class-A and women's prisons in rates, especially in murders.

Class-B prisons also had the higher rates for "antistaff threats," especially for the more grave "confrontations" that were mostly refusals of an order. Women's prisons had an unusually high rate (although lower than class-B prisons) for "inimical threats" that largely were prohibited communications among inmates. Female inmates appeared to be especially prone to band together to ease the travail of penal confinement. The possibility is given credence by the unusual number of female rule-violations for forbidden exchange of articles; the female rate for "inmate interaction," an aspect of "inmate cohesion," was exceptionally high. For "criminal signs," tattooing was the only infraction of women and most frequent among the men, while only class-B men had yakuza haircuts and dress.

Japanese inmates are prepared to accept, at least tacitly, the behavioral standards of the industrial prison.[2] Moreover, the Japanese prisons adopt certain inducements for buttressing the work ethic (see chapter 5). In addition to the positive inducements, the code of punishable offenses includes violations of rules peculiar to prison workshops (see table 6.3). Refusing to work is the exclusive "sabotage" infraction of women and class-A men. Class-B males also had a few other versions of sabotage: making shoddy and damaged products. Shirking—the set of violations posing less direct threat to productivity—draws the greatest attention of rule enforcers; of all kinds of violations, shirking is especially common for women, primarily violation of safety rules and unauthorized talking. Otherwise, their total work-related infraction rate would be even less significant. Except for ignoring safety rules, men had definitely higher specific rates. Only males were reported for looking aside while working.[3]

Women had the highest rate for the "targeting prison" subcategory of "contravening acts" due to violations lumped together as destruction of the building or equipment. The conduct could be seen as expressions of rebellion, but it is also possible that the cell walls or the equipment within them had been modified to suit the inmates' convenience. In "contravening acts," males were more inclined toward "anticivility," especially the class-B inmates who were very active in inappropriate washing of clothing and hair and violating the daily schedule.

In "inmate relations," the "conflict-inciting" incidents drew greatest official concern: Class-B males had the highest rate but class-A males and women also had rates exceeding those for less-serious "estrangement." Quarrels among inmates were the dominant form of conflict incitement, but class-B males also were active in instigating inmate misconduct and slandering inmates. Rudeness to fellow inmates and being noisy were the predominate kinds of estrangement.

DISTINCTIVE ASPECTS OF DETENTION WORK

Detention facilities hold three kinds of inmates: suspects being held for investigation, the accused awaiting trial, and the convicted either awaiting transfer to a regular prison or assigned to tasks at the detention facility. The detention environment makes for special conditions for the work of employees. Rapid turnover of the inmates, their diversity, and their uncertainty about their immediate future affect the work situations. The newcomers are strangers and the staff does not know what to expect. Reception tasks in detention houses are rapid and repetitive; individuals usually move in and out of the detention centers before the staff is able to learn much about their probable conduct. Escorting the accused and suspects to and from the court is time-consuming.

The detainees necessitate distinctive management. Suspects and accused persons are considered innocent until convicted and must be separated from the convicted. Their diversity is yet to be probed by the classification procedures: traffic offenders and murderers, stable and mentally troubled persons, depressed and aggressive personalities, and the confused first offender and the experienced gangster. Tokyo Detention House has received a former prime minister accused of pocketing a bribe, the president of a private company involved in another scandal, and the central figure in the notorious killing of four little girls.

The Correction Bureau maintains temporary detention units adjacent to the courts that hold accused persons during trial proceedings. For example, Correction Bureau buses transport them from the Tokyo Detention House to the district court building in the center of the metropolis. The buses appear ordinary, except for two horizontal bars across the windows and window shades that prevent public observation of the passengers. Prison officers sit on one side of the aisle and handcuffed defendants on the other side.

Through a long hallway, the Tokyo defendants go to or from the basement parking area. They go by elevator to the single-person and congregate cells on an upper floor. The cells have a toilet and cots for sitting. One cell has a one-way mirror for observation. Women occupy a wing; their toilets are shielded for privacy. At the end of the basement hallway, a control room has television monitoring of the cells and the parking area. An account board notes the cell location of inmates and the courtroom for their appearance. Another board shows the assignments of prison officers. Controls are available to override the passenger operation of elevators if an incident occurs on them, but the staff told me that the only emergency had been the fainting of a defendant. Adjacent to the control room separated by a glass panel, a room is available for prison officers awaiting performance of their duties.

In pretrial detention, the possibility of rule violations is enhanced by the unfamiliarity of some inmates with incarceration and uncertainty about what the future holds. The suspects and accused persons held in detention facilities in 1990 had an infraction rate of 28.77 percent (Research and Statistics Section 1991a, 244–45). Detainee-violators tend to be especially involved in aggression against staff, illegal communication, and destruction of buildings or equipment. Although only at a modest rate, the detainees exceeded regular prisoners in targeting prison officers as representatives of the criminal justice system. The rate for illegal communication is only slightly greater than the rate for convicted persons.

Managing "Problem People"

In spite of general orderliness, Japanese wardens report that some types of prisoners raise difficulties: the violence-prone, homosexual, suicidal, litigious, mentally ill, politically extreme, gang-involved, and escape-prone. The types were not necessarily as "troublesome" quantitatively and qualitatively as similar prisoners encountered by many American wardens. The Japanese warden is expected to manage the "problem people" in the prison population. Occasionally an individual is transferred to another institution when relationships with other inmates raise very grave possibilities. Transfers within a correction region require approval of the headquarters of the correction region and acceptance of the inmate by the other warden. Central headquarters in Tokyo must approve interregional transfers.

Officials are on the alert for persons likely to be aggressive against staff or inmates. The yakuza inmates are dispersed among the industrial shops and cells with the intention of dampening prospects for intergang conflicts and intragang solidarity. Gang bosses and members who present particular custodial difficulties are limited to labor within single-person cells. When gangs are not at war with one another in the community, members of several gangs may be placed together, but the staff is alert for development of undesirable associations. Inmates and staff are cautioned not to reveal gang identifications. The yakuza are urged to abandon gang activities, but the efforts are seldom successful.

Homosexuality is believed to threaten the well-being of inmates through unwelcome physical attacks and the institutional order through triad conflicts. The brief sentences of many inmates reduce the chance of such events. The policy is to hold identified homosexuals in single-person cells at night and employ them in janitorial duties as a group during the day.

Suicide attempts are most likely to occur during the stay at detention centers and usually are made because of emotional turmoil stemming from family problems. People respond variously to being tried and to facing the prospect of penal confinement. The detention period aggravates any frustrations. A small number of the accused engage in self-injuries by swallowing objects or slashing themselves. One woman drank shampoo when her frustration was aggravated by the theft of her clothing by a "friend."

"Sometimes a person in detention becomes violent," the director of security at a detention house told me. "They may refuse to eat. Probably all think about escape, and some think about suicide. Officers are concerned about both possibilities. Behavior may be very good or very problematic for the few confronting the possibility of a death penalty, but extreme behavior is not limited to those accused of a serious crime."

Officials believe that recidivists are better prepared to handle imprisonment emotionally because they have had previous experience and know how to avoid threatening incidents. When inmates are in a state of crisis, they are placed in a protective "padded" cell for television monitoring from the security office. When the perceived suicidal tendency eases, they are transferred to a regular cell and assigned ordinary work duties. Other kinds of mentally disturbed individuals are placed temporarily in single cells or the hospital ward. The physicians decide whether transfer to Hachiojo Medical Prison is necessary. When assessed there as being in remission, they are returned to the regular prison for appropriate work assignments.

From 1967 to 1980, Japan suffered violence, first by left- and right-wing political extremists and then by terrorists known as Japan's United Red Army Faction. The "New Left" among university students drew international attention in the 1960s through violent confrontations with the police in opposition to the expansion of Haneda International Airport near Tokyo and anti-American demonstrations. With the political failure of the movement, a small minority emerged as the Red Army Faction with a very militant and international orientation. In 1972 the nation watched a nine-day battle of five members with the police in a summer resort in the Japan Alps. In the same year, three other members killed twenty-six and wounded seventy at the Tel Aviv, Israel, airport. The public largely rejected the Red Army Faction, and even left-wing groups dissociated themselves (Kuriyama 1973).

"Litigious Inmates": Patterns and Reactions

In the list of "difficult" prisoners, Japanese wardens join their American colleagues in adding the "litigious inmate" who files complaints repetitively as a means of exploiting the grievance system for purposes other than obtaining remedies to abuses.[4] Americans are alert to the possibility that special-interest groups will seize upon inmate grievances, whether well founded or not, as an opportunity to condemn the prison and its staff in general. Japanese officials are less vulnerable to pressure-group politics, and any tendency of Japanese inmates to express openly their dissatisfaction is inhibited by the cultural heritage. When prisoners file a grievance, Japanese officials are inclined to perceive them as moving away from the reciprocal duties of the subordinate to respect the authority of the superior and to be accusing the superior of failure to take care of the subordinate's needs.

Opportunities to openly express grievances release a variety of motivations: "It is inevitable that some prisoners will complain about their treatment. They may be disturbed or their perceptions disoriented. They may be out to make as much trouble and create as many difficulties as possible. They may even have a genuine grievance. It would be an unusual prison system that generated no legitimate complaints among inmates" (Zellick 1982, 21).

Repetitive filing of grievances stirs suspicion of the inmates' sincerity. In 1990, the 1,395 inmates making official complaints averaged 3.97 submissions (see table 6.4). Of the 142 petitions submitted to the Minister of Justice in 1985 from the Tokyo Detention Center, one inmate filed 35 and another inmate 23 petitions (Shinkai 1992). In other words, 2 of the 1,500 inmates at the detention center made 41 percent of the complaints. Shinkai describes two kinds of litigious inmates: the persistent and the left-wing types. The persistent type may repeat the same allegation in spite of decisions in previous cases, will bring up an incident occurring several years previously, or will cite petty matters ("officer's footsteps are too noisy at night"). The left-wing type uses the grievance system in trying to undermine the political establishment. Since the 1970s, that type has become rare.

Since 1908 prisoners have been permitted to write an uncensored letter to the Minister of Justice or to express a grievance to an official inspecting the prison. According to Yanagimoto (1970), the expression of grievances became

Table 6.4

Inmate Grievances, by Type of Filing, 1965–90

Type of Filing	1965	1975	1980	1985	1990
Petition to Justice Minister	124	240	658	757	689
Civil Suits	31	66	145	175	66
Criminal Complaints	89	314	707	469	276
Law-Related Organizations	29	238	398	390	364
Total	273	858	1,908	1,791	1,395
	Rate per 1,000 Inmates				
Petition to Justice Minister	1.95	5.25	13.01	13.67	14.28
Civil Suits	.49	1.44	2.87	3.17	1.37
Criminal Complaints	1.40	6.87	13.97	8.49	5.72
Law-Related Organizations	.46	5.21	7.87	7.06	7.54
Total	4.29	18.78	37.71	32.41	28.92

Sources: Research and Statistics Section (1990b); Research and Training Institute (1990); 1990 data supplied by Security Section, Correction Bureau.

more active after 1960, and third parties have intervened increasingly in the affairs of the Correction Bureau. Filings increased between 1965 and 1980, but have declined since then in number of grievances and number of inmates making formal complaints, although more inmates have become involved in multiple filings. Table 6.4 documents the increasing volume of grievances and the tapering off since 1980. The rate of grievances per 1,000 inmates was 4.29 in 1965 and rose to 37.71 in 1980; thereafter the rate dropped to 32.41 in 1985 and 28.92 in 1990.

Four routes are followed in filing grievances. First, the Prison Law, Article 7, authorizes "If an inmate is dissatisfied with an action of the prison, he may petition to the competent Minister or an official visiting the prison for inspection, in accordance with the provisions of Ministry of Justice Ordinance." For a petition to the Minister of Justice, the inmate will seal the written statement in an envelope, which prison officials are forbidden to open, and the warden immediately forwards it to the minister. The ordinance, Articles 4–9, requires the warden to grant interviews to inmates who ask to make complaints about their treatment in prison or their personal affairs. When the inmate requests the interview in advance, the inmate's name is entered in an interview record book. After the interview, the warden writes a response to the inmate in the same record book.

When planning to file a grievance with an official inspecting the prison's operations, the inmate will notify the warden in advance, who then enters the name in the petition record book. The inmate may present the grievance to the inspector either orally or in writing. No other prison official will be present when the inspector interviews the inmate, except in case an official's presence is deemed necessary. Either the inspector will make the decision and enter it in the petition record book or request the Minister of Justice to make the decision. The warden promptly notifies the inmate what the decision is.

The second procedure allows the inmate to file a suit under civil law. Third, an accusation or complaint may be directed to the police or public prosecutor. The Code of Criminal Procedure, Article 366, requires the warden or a deputy to write the application for an appeal of the sentence if the accused person is unable to prepare the statement. Fourth, a court, bar association, or legal affairs bureau may be asked to deal with an alleged violation of human rights, to commit a case for trial, or to preserve evidence.

Petitions to the Minister of Justice have been most numerous and have assumed an increasing share of grievances over the years. Complaints to the police or public prosecutor were very numerous until 1980 but declined thereafter. Civil suits continue to be of minor quantitative importance. Appeals to law-related organizations have gained importance over the years, although they remain short of the rates of petitions to the Minister of Justice. The appeals frequently claim "human rights" violations; but the topics of grievances indicate the tendency was secondary to the practical concerns attending penal confinement.

The four routes for submitting complaints in 1990 were roughly similar in the general topics covered but different in emphasis. Relations with the staff were universally of greatest concern but especially for criminal complaints and petitions. Petitions focused on the basic elements of life in prison: clothing, bedding, food, room appliances (lights, radios, and toilets), washing clothing, and bathing. Civil suits primarily questioned correspondence and visiting regulations, punishment of rule violators, security procedures, and educational opportunities. Appeals to law-related organizations dealt especially with medical treatment, handling of correspondence, and visiting.

THE JUVENILE
JUSTICE
SYSTEM

 $\mathcal{T}$ he juvenile criminal justice system of Japan shows the same pattern of official tolerance we have reported for the processing of adult offenders but also presents its own noteworthy features. Today it is composed of the family courts, juvenile classification homes (JCHs), and juvenile training schools (JTSs), all products of the latest of four stages in the history of the handling of juvenile offenders in Japan.

TRACING TREATMENT
OF JUVENILES

Traditions imported from China were very influential in the first stage, extending from A.D. 668 to 1341.[1] The Japanese developed their own regulations in the second stage (1526 to 1862). The policies of the Imagawa and Takeda clans were especially influential in shaping the Tokugawa approach from 1723 to 1862. Of the four Tokugawa regulations, the 1742 version was most important. In the third stage (1868 to 1933) English and French laws regarding juvenile justice were followed. Because of the Allied Occupation after World War II, American influences were prominent in the fourth stage that brought basic changes in juvenile law in 1947 and 1948 and introduced the contemporary juvenile justice system of Japan.

As early as A.D. 668, juveniles were treated differently than adult offenders; juvenile delinquents received corporal punishment rather than being confined except for detention. Persons less than seven years of age were assumed to be free of culpability; those aged eight to sixteen years had limited culpability and were not subjected to torture in order to force a confession. Persons eight to ten years of age could be sentenced to death only with imperial approval. When persons ten years or younger committed a felony, they were confined without pillories or manacles. Use of fetters was prohibited when the offender was sixteen years of age or younger. Punishments for adults could be waived for juveniles, women, and the elderly with a sum of money set for expiation of the damage to the victim and redemption of the offender.[2]

The maximum age was raised to seventeen years, and the death penalty for all criminals was suspended from A.D. 818 to 1156 by custom, not by formal regulation. According to Soejima (1974), a judge asked a number of persons whether seventeen years would be the proper maximum for treating offenders as juveniles; they agreed, and the practice was adopted by the court. The maximum age was lowered again to sixteen years in the period 1185–1333. During the period ending in 1590, when civil warfare was constant, the clans ignored any formal policy and differed in degree of severity in treating juvenile offenders. The regulations of the Imagawa Clan (Imagawa Kana Mokuroku of 1526) specified that parents should stop quarrels among children. When the parent and child were involved in a quarrel, both would be punished. Punishment would be withheld if a juvenile less than fifteen years of age killed a friend unintentionally. In 1723 a municipal ordinance in Edo (now Tokyo) specified that an arsonist less than fifteen years old should be exiled and one over sixteen should be burned at the stake.

Juvenile thieves were sentenced to punishments one degree less severe than for adults. Juvenile thieves would be whipped but less than fifty times. In 1742 homeless juvenile thieves could be placed under the supervision of the Chief of Outcasts who would supervise them in rag picking and similar work. When a juvenile was sentenced to death, the sentence might be commuted to exile on an island. Juvenile murderers or arsonists would be placed in the care of a relative until age fifteen years and then sent to the island. The relative might induce the juvenile to escape just before reaching that age. The relative would be ordered to find the juvenile within thirty days. When the "search" was futile, two extensions of thirty days and then one year would be granted. If found, the juvenile would have the severity of the sentence raised from exile to death, but such juveniles were seldom apprehended. If caught, they were executed.

During the Meiji Period, four types of penal law existed: Karikeiritsu (proposed in 1868 but not enacted), Shinritsu-kouryo (1870), Kaiteiritsurei (1873), and the "old" Penal Code (1880). Imprisonment with forced labor replaced whipping, caning, and exile. The age limit for juveniles was set at fifteen years, and crimes punishable by imprisonment could be expiated by payment of money. For accidental homicide or injury of another, if the juvenile could not make the payment, a sentence to a reform prison would be ordered. The fines were graded according to the length of the prison sentence; twenty-five sen for a ten-day sentence to thirty-five yen for a life sentence.

In 1881 a kind of reformatory (chochijo) separated juveniles from adults, provided some education, but came to be regarded as violating progressive concepts. Increasing demands for education led to new institutions operated by private persons and groups: Mrs. Yukie Ikegami in Osaka (1884), Shinkyo Takase in Tokyo (1885), Chiba Buddhist Association in Chiba (1886), Seikai Chiwa in Okayama (1888), Sakuzo Yamaoka in Mie (1897), and Chaplain Kosuke Tomeoka in Tokyo (1899). The Reformatory Law of 1900 substituted educational discipline for punishment; the principle of individualized treatment, then being advocated for American and European prisons, was influential. Several arguments had been advanced: The increasing number of juvenile delinquents called for ways to reform them; the reform prison had failed, and the civil law did not provide a proper substitute; and a new kind of institution with a capacity for fifty boys should be set up in each prefecture.

Two models of juvenile institutions emerged late in the last century. The original juvenile prison opened in 1872 and closed in 1907, but another institution for juveniles (the first model) was established in 1881. That model has persisted to the present day as juvenile institutions operated by social service agencies. Today these facilities receive more juvenile offenders than the second model that was authorized by the Reformatory Law of 1900 to be part of the then Prison Bureau. When that bureau was moved from the Ministry of Home Affairs to the Ministry of Justice, the Juvenile Training School Law of 1922 (now known as the "old Juvenile Law") led to the training schools in the Correction Bureau today.

During the debate culminating in the "old Juvenile Law," the juvenile courts of the West, especially those of the United States, stimulated an interest in a similar system. The new law created the Juvenile Inquiry and Determination Office (Shonen Shimpansho), which was a predecessor of the family court later established in 1948. The office was an administrative entity under the Ministry of Justice, rather than a court in a strict sense (Supreme Court 1989). It received juveniles up to age eighteen who were not prosecuted in criminal courts. It had wide discretion in selecting among dispositions appropriate to the given juvenile (Rehabilitation Bureau 1990). The nine kinds of "protective treatment" were: an admonition; a schoolmaster's warning; an oath written by the juvenile promising to engage in proper conduct; custody by a guardian; custody by a temple, church, or hostel; probation; commitment to a private reformatory; admission to a training school; or hospitalization.

Juveniles less than sixteen years of age were excused from life sentences and the death penalty. The principle of indeterminate sentences was introduced because a short stay was considered insufficient for education and training. Under the Reformatory Law of 1922, the government established two juvenile training schools in 1923, Naniwa in Osaka Prefecture and Tama in Tokyo. In addition, private organizations operated a number of juvenile institutions.

The Reformatory Law was abolished in 1933. The Law for Training and Education of Juvenile Delinquents set the minimum age at fourteen and called for child observation committees. On 15 August 1945, the war ended when Japan surrendered unconditionally; during the occupation the juvenile justice system was particularly influenced by American practices. In 1947 the Juvenile Law and the Training School Law were replaced with new laws. The maximum age of juveniles was set at nineteen years. The family court replaced the juvenile inquiry agency. Alternative dispositions were identified: homes for child education and training, probation, and training schools. Juvenile classification homes (JCHs) were established and placed within the Correction Bureau. Means of appeal from dispositional decisions were provided. The privately operated institutions were abolished.

In tracing the history of JCHs during an interview, Kazuo Sato, superintendent of the Tokyo Juvenile Classification Home, identified a precedent in the years 1924–28 when Shimpansho, a branch office of the contemporary reformatories, diagnosed juveniles, but it did not detain them in a residential facility before 1928. The detention unit was subject to the authority of the prison system, thereby setting a precedent for an unorthodox arrangement: the later placing of a service for the courts (the juvenile classification home) under the authority of a prison system (the Correction Bureau). In 1933 Japanese law first mentioned diagnosis when the Juvenile Teaching and Protective Law called for diagnosis of neglected and delinquent children in child education and training schools, but World War II interrupted the full introduction of the services.

After the war the question was debated whether or not the JCHs should be established. Dr. Katsuro Narita (who had been in Shimpan Sho's medical section), Dr. Masao Otsu, and Professor Taro Ogawa were influential in framing the new juvenile law and insisted the homes become part of the juvenile justice system.[3] Louis Burdett, who was on the staff of the Correction Division of the General Headquarters during the Allied Occupation, suggested the model of juvenile detention homes in the United States. Since they were given the detention function, Sato hypothesized, the JCHs were placed within the Correction Bureau.

PARTNERS IN THE JUVENILE JUSTICE SYSTEM

An unusual facet of Japan's juvenile justice system is the placement of JCHs in the Correction Bureau: a partnership of judicial agencies (the family court) and executive agencies (the Correction Bureau). The partnership departs from the respective ideologies usual for the courts and the correctional agencies. The partnership is grounded in thought patterns usually associated with the field of social welfare. "Without doubt the most unusual development in the Japanese court system is the new family court," Burks (1964, 171) asserted thirty years ago. "For one thing, it functions as much as a social welfare institution as it does a court." Unlike usual judicial tribunals, the family court uses the casework method and staff investigators trained in sociology and psychology as nonlegal personnel.

The family court deals with juvenile delinquents as an aspect of its major function in conciliating a variety of family disputes. Tamiguchi (1984, 36) asserts that "In that sense, family court conciliation has constituted a useful tool of conflict dissolution in a changing society." New family laws contributed to the withdrawal of "paternal or joint family authority" in settling disputes. The family courts implement the new laws and also ease the adjustment of the Japanese to the conditions of nuclear families.

The JCHs are models for further introduction of diagnostic services in presentence deliberations of Japanese courts. District court judges rely on public prosecutors or defense attorneys for information about the defendants when deliberating the situation for sentencing. Then too, the family courts could make greater use of JCHs, especially for some of the juveniles whose cases are dismissed.

Place and Nature of Family Court

The family courts are located near district courts and some summary courts. They have jurisdiction in family disputes in such matters as declaration of incompetence, permission for adopting a minor, appointing or terminating guardianship, probate of wills, family support, and partition of an estate. Of interest here is the family court's involvement with juvenile delinquents under twenty years of age and with adults accused of damaging the welfare of juveniles (Supreme Court n.d., 31–32).

The Juvenile Law is concerned with three classes of juveniles. First, there are the "delinquents," aged fourteen through nineteen, accused of breaking the penal code or special laws. Next are the "child offenders," less than fourteen, who are not subject to prosecution under criminal law. Child guidance centers are responsible for receiving the child offenders and for treating physical or mental handicaps. When there is high risk of repetitive offenses likely to injure citizens, the child guidance centers may turn to the family court for compulsory referral to a child education and training home. Finally, there are the "predelinquents," less than twenty years of age, who have not been apprehended for offenses but are believed to be susceptible to future offenses.

The term "predelinquent" conveys the idea that, before any violation of the law has occurred, certain symptoms indicate that the boy or girl will move inexorably toward delinquency and possibly crime. The government assumes the responsibilities of a parent worried about the long-term welfare of children, but instead of employing the measures of a caring parent, brings criminal sanctions to bear on the problem. In accepting predelinquents the juvenile justice system broadens its net to take in juveniles not charged with lawbreaking. Prediction that the juvenile is likely to become a delinquent raises the risk of assuming that outcome is inevitable in spite of the many personal and social factors involved in anyone's future conduct. Applying the force of the law to the young may stigmatize them as though they, too, had broken the law.

Predelinquents before the family court increasingly have been female over the years, from 42 percent in 1970 to 60 percent in 1987. The predelinquents of both sexes, for the most part, were runaways from home or had been accused of being promiscuous or, increasingly, of being associates of questionable persons. School truancy, "unwholesome" amusements, and "nocturnal habits" were of minor importance. Over the years fewer and fewer predelinquents were adjudicated by the family courts: 5,096 in 1951 and 2,558 in 1987. During the same period, the dispositions of predelinquents swung from juvenile training schools (from 22 down to 15 percent) toward probation (from 14 to 32 percent). Referrals to other childcare agencies were infrequent, changing from 8 to 7 percent in the same period. Dismissals of the predelinquent cases remained the most common disposition, their share declining from 56 to 46 percent of all predelinquent dispositions (Shikita and Tsuchiya 1990, 276).

Referrals to the family courts follow several routes.[4] Infrequently, the police refer directly to the court the predelinquents and minors accused of offenses punishable by a fine or lesser penalty. Otherwise, the police send the case to the public prosecutor who relays it to the family court. When the offense occurs elsewhere, the case is transferred to the family court in the juvenile's place of residence. Occasionally, the court's investigator will bring the youngster before the family court under special circumstances, such as the recent location of a juvenile who had disappeared. A parent, guardian, or other person responsible for the juvenile may make a referral, but since such persons are likely to be reluctant to do so, the investigator can act for them. Finally, the child guidance center may send juveniles to the family court if they run away or are unmanageable.

At intake, the family court's investigator studies the facts of the offense, the young person's character and environment, and the risk to the community. In most cases the judge requests the investigator's recommendation. The juvenile and parents are asked to come to the court's hearing room for an interview. Sometimes the young person is reluctant to talk with the parents present. If the parents agree, only the juvenile is interviewed, because previous to the juvenile's appearance before the judge, the parents' approval is indispensable.

The written report of the court's investigator is submitted to the judge who may dismiss the case without a hearing after considering its contents. A legal paper informs the juvenile about the decision. When a hearing occurs, fact-finding and disposition occur simultaneously. The persons present in an informal setting are the juvenile, parents, sometimes other relatives, the probation officer, perhaps a caseworker from a child guidance center, and sometimes the juvenile's employer. Public prosecutors do not attend.

The family court may employ "tentative probation" as a kind of deferred disposition. Wanting more time for decisions, the judge may ask the investigator to supervise the juvenile for the time being. The officer may require a written report on an assigned book or the drawing of pictures for diagnosis. In Tokyo the youngster may be placed in a nonsecure childcare facility called "Small House" and an employer paid for supervision. Regular probation is usually for two years or until age twenty is attained; tentative probation is for about six months. Tentative probation, unlike regular probation, is not a final disposition; it does not involve voluntary probation officers and is solely for diagnostic purposes.

As the gatekeeper to the juvenile justice system, the family court diverts a few older serious offenders to the public prosecutor for possible adjudication under the criminal law, grants probation, sends some young people to juvenile training schools, and returns most to families. Of all juveniles, only 9 percent in 1951 and 2.1 percent in 1990 went to training schools (see table 7.1). When choosing to send juveniles to a training school, the judge decides the appropriate type of school: primary, middle, special, or medical school.

When a very serious crime is committed by a youth under sixteen years of age, the family court's options include referral to a training school, not to a juvenile prison among the adult facilities. Two general situations call for referrals to the public prosecutor for processing the youth as an adult criminal. First, youths older than twenty years are not in the jurisdiction of the family court. Second, the nature of the offense, the circumstances within which it happened, and the personal characteristics of the offender may lead the family court to believe that referral to the public prosecutor is appropriate.[5] If the public prosecutor refers the case to district court for trial, the youth faces the possibility of being sent to one of eight juvenile prisons (distinct from juvenile training schools) receiving adults less than twenty-six years of age and emphasizing vocational training. As shown by table 7.1, referrals to the public prosecutor comprise a small and declining share of family court dispositions. Over the years, fewer youths under twenty have entered juvenile prisons, from 2,259 in 1945, to 736 in 1965, to

Table 7.1
Family Court Dispositions, 1951–90

	1951	1961	1971	1981	1990
Disposition	%	%	%	%	%
Referred to Public					
Prosecutor	5.6	3.4	1.6	0.6	0.5
Deserves Criminal					
Disposition	(5.6)	(2.8)	(1.3)	(0.4)	(0.3)
Over Age Limit	—	(0.6)	(0.4)	(0.2)	(0.2)
Probation	18.8	13.7	9.8	7.5	7.3
Various Agencies[a]	0.9	0.7	0.3	0.2	0.2
Dismissed	65.7	76.4	85.7	89.5	89.9
After Hearing	(25.9)	(23.2)	(25.6)	(19.0)	(17.5)
Without Hearing	(39.8)	(53.2)	(60.1)	(70.4)	(72.4)
Juvenile Training					
School	9.0	5.8	2.6	2.2	2.1
Total	100.0	100.0	100.0	100.0	100.0
No. of Cases	134,966	138,143	112,340	188,541	169,714

Sources: Shikita and Tsuchiya (1990); Research and Training Institute (1992).

[a]Includes Child Guidance Centers, Centers of the Prefectural Government, Child Education and Training Homes, and Homes for Dependent Children.

63 in 1990 (Shikita and Tsuchiya 1990, 311; Research and Training Institute 1992, 165).

Juvenile probation has occupied a significant but declining place among dispositions. A few referrals are to treatment centers outside the scope of the juvenile justice system; 57 child education and training schools receive children who have been evaluated as predelinquents or child offenders. Prefectural governors are authorized to send children to these institutions with the consent of parents or guardians, or to one of the 534 homes for dependent children responsible for children without parents or guardians, subjected to abuse, or otherwise needing protective care. The family court may dismiss a case because the delinquent act is petty, the guardian is expected to provide proper supervision, the offense was the first by the juvenile, and so on. Dismissals were 65.7 percent of all dispositions in 1951 and 89.9 percent in 1990.

Organization of Juvenile Classification Homes

Juvenile classification homes were established as part of the 1949 reorganization of the juvenile justice system. The fifty-three homes, including one branch home, collectively had 1,211 staff members in 1990: 121 executive and administrative officers, 227 classification specialists, 726 instructors (line personnel), and 137 other functionaries (Correction Bureau 1990b, 65–66). Staffing varies with the size of the facility. As the largest in Japan, the Tokyo Juvenile Classification Home has a superintendent and deputy superintendent; a chief and fifteen administrative personnel in the general affairs section; a chief, two physicians, a psychiatrist, three nurses, and a clerk in the medical care section; and a principal specialist, four chief specialists, twenty psychologists, and thirty other functionaries in the classification, observation, and treatment (COT) coordination unit.

The position "Chief Specialist in Planning and Arrangements" was introduced in 1988 as a means of improving coordination between classification functions and observation of daily behavior of inmates by staff members in direct contact with them. Information about individual inmates is shared at case conferences and flows to the chief specialist. The psychologists conduct diagnostic interviews, administer psychometric tests, and prepare reports. The observation subsection supervises inmates during meals, physical exercises, visits to the medical care section, and visits by family and others. The "planning" part of the job title refers to scheduling staff work;

"arrangements" involve scheduling of the juveniles' daily activities.

Upon receiving a juvenile case, the family court has the option of sending the young person to the JCH for detention within twenty-four hours in either of two circumstances. First, Articles 11 and 26 of Juvenile Law permit the family court to issue a summons to the juvenile or the juvenile's guardians when necessary for investigation. If the summons is disobeyed "without good reason," the family court may issue a warrant of detention. Second, Articles 12 and 26 permit a family court warrant against the juvenile when "necessary for the welfare of a juvenile who is in urgent need of protection."

Detention of juveniles is unusual but is most likely to occur in police lockups or the detention centers of the Correction Bureau. For example, in 1989 the police lockups or detention centers held 7,142 male juveniles and 614 female juveniles, whereas the JCHs detained 977 juvenile males and 126 females (Research and Training Institute 1990, 245). Those figures exclude traffic offenders.

Several explanations may be offered for the greater number of juvenile detentions in police stations or adult detention centers. The very serious offenses are less common than minor offenses but can result in detention previous to referral to the family court. District or summary court judges have the option to select the JCH for detention, but they tend to prefer otherwise for several reasons: The offender may be in the older age range for juveniles and resemble adult offenders in criminal history or lifestyle; the police may prefer to interview suspects in their stations where physical evidence and witnesses are more readily available; or the JCHs may be located a considerable distance from the police station and time-consuming travel would be required for interviews.

When receiving the juvenile, the family court may employ detention in the JCH as a temporary measure for seven days (Juvenile Law, Article 26-2). Of 1990 JCH admissions,

Table 7.2
Juvenile Training School Admissions and
Age-Specific Rates by Sex, 1950–90

| Year | Admissions | Girls (%) | Age-Specific Rates[a] | |
			Boys	Girls
1950	6,867	10.6	117.3	8.3
1955	8,604	9.3	146.2	15.2
1960	8,992	9.2	149.9	15.4
1965	7,874	9.3	109.5	11.5
1970	3,965	7.7	67.9	5.8
1975	2,549	7.3	48.8	3.9
1980	4,720	11.0	84.6	10.9
1985	6,029	12.5	93.9	14.1
1990	4,234	11.0	62.1	8.0

Source: Shikita and Tsuchiya (1990); Research and Statistics Section (1991b).
[a]The number of admissions per 100,000 of the general population in a given age group (here, 14 to 20 years of age).

only 8.4 percent were for protective detention during investigation of the case and 1 percent for runaways from juvenile training schools or juvenile parole violators (Research and Statistics Section 1991b, 2). Processing of detainees is limited to a medical checkup and preliminary interview, and access is limited to family members, concerned employers or teachers, attorneys, and police investigators.

CHANGES IN THE
TRAINING SCHOOLS' INTAKE

The juvenile justice system has followed the policy of limiting its reliance on training schools as a means of dealing with juvenile delinquency. Table 7.2 shows the consequence for the training schools; the number of young people entering the JTSs declined from 1950 to 1975, but then experienced an upsurge. The age-specific rates shown for both sexes underscore the impressive reduction in admissions over the years. For the years 1950–75, the girls assumed decreasing shares of the admissions.

From 1980 until 1990 the number of admissions, the age-specific rates, and the percentage of female admissions increased dramatically. What accounts for the sharp rise in admissions? For both sexes larceny continued to be a major offense while drug offenses assumed unprecedented numbers, as did traffic offenses for boys.

Greater official concern was focused on the drug abuse and traffic acrobatics of the *bosozoku* (youthful automobile or motorcycle gangs). In 1975 admissions of boys, 19 were for stimulant drugs, 63 for road-traffic laws, and none for chemical agents (such as paint thinner). In 1985 admissions had risen to 312 for stimulant drugs, 397 for traffic violations, and 208 for chemical agents. The lower rate for 1990 can be explained largely by reduction of stimulant-drug admissions to 101 and a sharp decline in larceny admissions. Meanwhile, admissions of girls showed a similar trend but the distribution of offenses differed. Stimulant-drug admissions rose from 4 in 1975 to 214 in 1985 and dropped to 92 in 1990. Chemical-agent admissions had a similar trend but, along with traffic violations, were of very minor importance in actual numbers. Predelinquent admissions were instrumental in the changes for girls: 84 in 1975, 237 in 1985, and 158 in 1990 (Research and Statistics Section 1988, 98–99; 1991b, 98–99).

Rationale of Training Schools

Advocates of the training schools frequently express a commitment to the "wholesome rearing of juveniles" and speak of "protective measures" instead of punishment and deterrence. The JTS philosophy is challenged when a young inmate fails to live up to the official rules. Typically, the personnel say they regard rule violations as evidence of latent personal difficulties. For example, a boy at Tama Juvenile Training School had eleven infractions. The staff suspected that he was troubled by inability to sustain good relationships with his peers and broke the rules in order to be placed in a solitary room. He spent 250 days in this fashion and established a record by staying 729 days at Tama. The decision was to place him in a small group and thereby teach him gradually how to relate to other persons.

In specifying disciplinary measures, Article 8 of the Juvenile Training School Law places greater emphasis on the juveniles' needs over efforts to control them. Three measures are specified: reprimand, confinement in a "sanitary solitary room" for up to twenty days, or reduction of marks awarded for meritorious conduct. Each month the dormitory instructors rate conduct ranging from A to E. A grade of C is minimal for gaining marks under the progressive-stage system.

Escapes are called "walkaways" to avoid the heavy emphasis on breaking custodial confinement. For the eleven years 1980 through 1990, the average number of walkaways per year was 17.4 for boys and 1.2 for girls (Research and Statistics Section 1990b; 1991b). Such incidents are more frequent than the rare escape from Japanese prisons for adults, but returning juveniles receive only administrative sanctions; prosecution in court occurs only for any crimes committed while a walkaway.

Among the rule violations, attacks on other inmates in quarrels take up a good portion; yakuza-style tattooing and eyebrow clipping are among the infractions. Most incidents are minor: loud talking, saying "evil things" about others, failure to turn off lights, and so on. Betting is a unique violation in training schools. Tissue paper is issued to all inmates; through successful betting on sports events, an inmate will accumulate tissue paper as a symbol of superiority.

Intake classification takes two weeks in single-person

rooms in the newcomer's dormitory. The staff probes the possible problems of inmates and tries to determine their best fit into the school's activities. Interviews are based on information from the JCH and the family court's investigator. The JCH is responsible for diagnosis and guidelines for the individual's treatment regimen. The JCH psychologist is summoned if the regimen needs revision or the youngster needs to go to another training school. By the end of the second week, the dossier prepared by the school's classification section goes to the treatment committee for framing the inmate's treatment plan, including assignment to a regular dormitory.

The treatment committee (*syogu shinsakai*) meets once a week to consider punishments and rewards for inmates, promotions in the progressive-stage system, room and program assignments, schedule of events for the month, recommendations for inmates to be transferred to another school, and recommendations on release into the community. The committee usually is chaired by the superintendent; the members are the deputy superintendent, the principal specialist of the education section, the chiefs of subsections of the education section (classification, planning, and coordination, intermediate-stage education, and prerelease stage), and dormitory supervisors. The planning and coordination unit receives all information about the inmates and relays it to interested parties. The unit also plans duty assignments of the staff, including vacation schedules and replacements for sick personnel. Sometimes the several sections do not agree on recommendations; the unit negotiates concurrence and relays the reports to the treatment committee. The recommendations of the treatment committee go to the superintendent for final decision.

The dormitory supervisors, called "instructors" officially, have several functions in keeping with the generalist approach of Japanese personnel administration. They supervise the inmates in the dormitory, are responsible for direct and continual contacts with three or four juveniles, prepare the basic reports on the conduct of those juveniles that end up before the treatment committee, organize and conduct the living guidance courses, and carry out the afternoon group-discussion sessions of inmates.

Organizational Scheme for Programming

Article 2 of the Juvenile Training School Law specifies four types of training schools. Primary and middle schools receive persons who are not "seriously defective mentally or physically." Primary institutions are for juveniles fourteen or more years of age but generally less than sixteen. The middle schools receive adolescents generally from sixteen through nineteen years of age. The advanced (or special) schools deal with persons who have no serious mental or physical defects but have "advanced criminal tendencies" and generally are in ages sixteen to twenty-three years. Medical schools are directed to treat those juvenile inmates, regardless of age, who have serious mental or physical disabilities and ailments.

The differentiation assumes the allocation of inmates to programs should recognize age, presence of "serious mental or physical defects," and evidence of "criminal tendencies." If a training school receives only a given category of inmates, the programmatic activities can be selectively directed in keeping with the particular variables of inmates. The variables are crude and constitute only the beginning of individualization of treatment.

Juvenile Training School Law, Article 11, specifies that inmates be released when they become twenty years of age but also makes exceptions. When the inmate is "considerably defective physically or mentally or his criminal tendency has not been corrected," the superintendent may ask for the court to order that the individual be held beyond the age of twenty but not beyond twenty-three. In 1990, 641 males and 47 females were held beyond age twenty. Subsection 5 states: "If the court finds, upon the application of the

JTS superintendent, that it is improper, for public welfare, to release the inmate who has become twenty-three years of age from the juvenile training school because he is mentally defective to a remarkable degree, it shall make a ruling which orders his continued custody in the medical juvenile training school for a fixed period not over the twenty-sixth year of his age." In 1990, Subsection 5 authorized the holding of 212 boys and 24 girls beyond the age of twenty-six (Research and Statistics Section 1991b, 194).

In June 1977, the Minister of Justice announced a new agenda for the management of juvenile training schools: differentiation of short-term and long-term programs, smooth passage of juveniles from the schools to aftercare agencies, treatment and length of stay in the schools according to the needs of the given juvenile, similar individualization in fitting clearly defined goals and varied treatment modalities of each school to the juveniles in its charge, and a dialogue and integrated effort among correctional agencies, other private and public organizations, and private citizens (Correction Bureau 1990b, 51). A long-term program and two short-term programs were created.[6]

Lasting for up to two years, the long-term program was designed for juveniles assessed as having relatively advanced delinquent tendencies and being difficult to resocialize in a shorter length of time. The five courses are living guidance, vocational training, academic education, special education, and medical care. The programs are discussed in detail below.

The first short-term program was a general program for juveniles without "advanced criminal tendencies" and amenable to short-term intervention for four to six months. The second was directed specifically to juveniles violating road laws including motor homicide or inflicting injuries.

In September 1991, the scheme of short-term programs was changed. A general short-term program replaced the program for traffic offenders, and a special short-term program was begun for inmates suited for open treatment. The duration of the general short-term program is usually for four or five months; the maximum is six months. Three courses are offered: academic education for those not completing compulsory schooling, vocational guidance for employment after release, and career guidance in postrelease planning. Recommendations of the juvenile classification homes assist the family courts in deciding which young people should be admitted to the short-term programs. For the period September 1991 through August 1992, short-term programs in twenty-two training schools received 305 juveniles. The number of referrals have been increasing.

The new short-term program for open treatment is designed for extramural vocational or academic education. The juveniles attend schools in the outside community, usually for three months, or four months at a maximum, while staying with their families on weekdays. Saturdays and Sundays are spent at the training school. The juvenile with a regular job usually commutes every day between the workplace and the training school and spends weekends in the training school. As a rare exception, if the work is near home, the juvenile stays with family on weekday evenings and at the training school on weekends.[7] This program is an extension of the day leaves and overnight leaves granted to preserve positive relationships in the community. In 1990, 88 percent of the boys and 94 percent of the girls were granted one or more day leaves. Overnight leaves were less common: 10.4 percent of the boys and 13.6 percent of the girls received them (Research and Statistics Section 1991b, 170, 172).

Effect of the Small Population

If the organizational scheme of training schools is to operate efficiently, a sufficient number of inmates must be available for each of the following subgroups. First, the eight correction regions divide the national population into eight subgroups. Second, each regional subgroup is further divided into four groups for primary, middle, special, and medical schools, respectively. Finally, the thirty-two sub-groups are doubled by the segregation of the sexes.

One of the key advantages of the juvenile justice system is that relatively few young persons end up in training schools, but the low rate of confinement has the disadvantage of providing too few inmates for effective implementation of a promising organizational scheme. Training schools have greater capacity (sometimes called "bed space") than the number of inmates present. With the medical training schools removed, about 65 percent of the capacity was utilized in 1990, using the year-end population as the unit of measurement. (The medical facilities receive both sexes and can adjust their capacity to meet changes in the number of patients according to sex).

The utilization of capacity varies among the correction regions according to sex of the inmates (see table 7.3). The Tokyo region has the largest capacity and the highest utilization rates for boys but still falls short of full utilization. Sendai, Fukuoka, and Takamatsu have the lowest rates for boys, although Takamatsu has an especially low capacity. In all regions the capacity of girls' schools is far short of that for boys, but Sapporo is the only region in which the girls' utilization rate is almost equal to the capacity. Tokyo and Fukuoka have greater capacity than Sapporo but lower—although respectable—rates.

To test the effectiveness of the organizational scheme, the distribution of inmates by sex was related to the type of school (primary, middle, special, and medical) according to "single function" or "multiple functions" (see table 7.4). On 31 December 1990, the training school population was 3,111 males and 418 females. A "single function" school receives only inmates classified as appropriate for that type of school; a "multiple functions" school receives two or more categories of inmates. Mixing two or more categories of inmates obstructs matching the type of school with certain qualities of inmates.

Table 7.3

*Capacity and Utilization of Juvenile Training Schools,
by Correction Region and Sex, 1990*

| | Boys | | Girls | |
Correction Region	Capacity	Used (%)	Capacity	Used (%)
Tokyo[a]	1,402	72.4	178	79.2
Osaka[b]	708	70.1	97	57.7
Nagoya	493	69.0	—	—
Hiroshima	246	62.6	51	27.4
Fukuoka	842	53.0	100	79.0
Sendai	381	55.1	60	35.0
Sapporo	306	68.0	60	93.3
Takamatsu	176	58.5	50	40.0
Total	4,554	65.3	596	64.9

Sources: Data on capacity from the Central Office (Tokyo), Correction Bureau; Research and Statistics Section (1991b).

Note: Utilization (used) is calculated from year-end population.

[a]Kanto Medical Training School excluded; its capacity is 140. 1990 year-end population was 59 boys and 21 girls; percentage of capacity used was 57.1.

[b]Kyoto Medical Training School excluded; its capacity is 144. 1990 year-end population was 80 boys and 10 girls; percentage of capacity used was 62.5.

Table 7.4 demonstrates that multifunctionality is dominant. All girls are assigned to schools serving more than one function in the scheme of primary, middle, or special schools. The organizational scheme suffers from an insufficiency of boys as well; only 143 boys in Tokyo are in primary schools exclusively and 761 boys are in middle schools only. The single-function middle schools (receiving only "middle-type" boys) are in the Tokyo, Osaka, Fukuoka, and Sendai regions. Medical schools inevitably are multifunctional; patients come from other schools regardless of the scheme for differentiating among schools. The

Table 7.4
Inmate Population of Juvenile Training Schools,
by Type of School and Sex, 1990

Type of School	Males		Females	
	No.	%	No.	%
Primary Schools	444	14.3	96	23.0
Single Function	(143)	(4.6)	(—)	(—)
Multiple Functions	(301)	(9.7)	(96)	(23.0)
Middle Schools	2,360	75.9	280	67.0
Single Function	(761)	(24.5)	(—)	(—)
Multiple Functions	(1,599)	(51.4)	(280)	(67.0)
Special Schools	166	5.3	11	2.6
Multiple Functions	(166)	(5.3)	(11)	(2.6)
Medical Schools	145	4.5	31	7.4
Multiple Functions	(145)	(4.5)	(31)	(7.4)
Total	3,111	100.0	418	100.0
Single Function	(904)	(29.1)	(—)	(—)
Multiple Funtions	(2,207)	(70.9)	(418)	(100.0)

Source: Research and Statistics Section (1991b).

special school is a myth; the few special juveniles are in schools that also receive middle-type juveniles.

Superintendents report that when several types of juveniles are present they are assigned to separate dormitories and programs with more staff provided. Special inmates are too few to occupy fully one of the four dormitories of a training school. The even fewer special girls particularly raise questions about the feasibility of a separate staff for them. Interregional transfer is a possible solution.

The number of training school inmates first increased by 932 and later dropped by 912 between 1985 and 1990. That fluctuation within a decade has brought about elimination of seven training schools and the slicing of the total staff by 100 employees. Between 1980 and 1985, the ratio of inmates to employees rose from 1.36 to 1.79, but it dropped back to 1.42 by 1990. Instructors provide a variety of "line staff" functions in the generalist personnel model. As a result of reductions in force, their representation and that of the few but vital medical specialists assumed greater relative shares of the reduced total staff. The reductions were directed mainly to the service personnel such as automobile drivers.

Living Guidance Course

The term "living guidance" covers a variety of approaches taken to move persons who are "socially deviant or immature" toward "disciplined social life." The Correction Bureau explains: "Living guidance is conducted for juveniles to improve their way of thinking and attitude toward social life, through such methods as group activities, counseling, lectures, and psychotherapy" (Research and Training Institute 1990, 58). The majority of inmates are assigned to living guidance courses according to three conceptions of social deviancy or immaturity. The G1 group needs "therapeutic guidance individually because of excessive deviance of their personality." The G2 group focuses on juveniles "who are uncontrollable because of their lower intelligence or immature personality." The G3 group consists of those inmates who are neither G1 or G2.

Purposes depend on the method chosen: to motivate inmates to abide by social rules and laws, to provide a setting for positive relationships, to deal with the personal problems contributing to the delinquencies, or to teach social manners and personal hygiene. For all purposes, relationships with instructors are a kind of community.

In the educational approach, particular problems of inmates are the topic, such as: drug abuse, especially paint thinner; family difficulties; traffic violations, especially those of the bosozoku; and antisocial associations. Specific staff members are assigned responsibility for lectures, selecting audiovisual materials, obtaining voluntary experts, and leading group discussions. Considerable preparation must be made; staff members usually are not expert on the topics.

In afternoon discussion groups, a half dozen or so inmates meet in a dormitory with one or two staff members present. The inmates are expected to talk freely; sometimes the inmates choose the topic and determine the course of interaction; sometimes the staff makes the choice. Usually, the inmates are expected to comment on one another's conduct. One method is to put one of the students in the "hot seat," subject to criticism by the peers. The quality of psychological intervention varies considerably, and the particular approach taken differs among the training schools. Systemwide formal training in group methods is lacking and, as for living guidance in general, the specifics of implementation are left to the particular training school.

As goals for individual and group discussions, juveniles are expected to accept, as their own, eight purposes of their experience. Any discrepancy between actual conduct and the eight purposes become a topic for comment in counseling or group sessions. The individual is required to set three personnel goals, such as "I will get along well with other inmates," "I will complete this or that course," or "I will write my regrets to the persons I hurt." Personal goals are modified during the school career.

The other five goals are set by regulation: (1) norm orientation, or behavior consistent with social standards; (2) basic living customs, or acquisition of skills necessary for normal social life; (3) learning attitude, or willing participation in programs; (4) interpersonal relationships, or attitudes toward guardians, staff, and inmates; and (5) life planning, or preparing for the future in the community.[8]

MEDICAL JUVENILE
TRAINING SCHOOLS

Two medical juvenile training schools in Japan—Kanto for eastern Japan and Kyoto for western Japan—are hospitals for the physically ill and seriously mentally disturbed juvenile inmates. The two hospitals also receive retarded individuals with behavioral problems. Otherwise, Kanagawa, Miyagawa, and Nakatsu Training Schools accommodate retarded and emotionally disturbed juveniles.

Special education courses are organized in two versions: H1 for the mentally retarded or other inmates needing the same treatment and H2 for those with emotional immaturity needing "special therapeutic treatment." In 1990 Kanagawa, Miyagawa, and Nakatsu delivered the H1 course to seventy males and the H2 course to eighty-six males. Meanwhile, Haruna, Katano, Chikushi, Aoba, and Marugame Juvenile Training Schools served fourteen females with the H1 course and six females with the H2 course. Kanto and Kyoto Medical Juvenile Schools provide the "medical care" courses: P1 for the physically ill or pregnant; P2 for the physically handicapped, including the blind, deaf, or mute; M1 for the psychotic or those with considerable psychotic tendencies; and M2 for the psychopathic or those with considerable psychopathic tendencies.

Established in 1950, Kanto has experienced changes in its types of patients. Immediately after World War II, Kanto was crowded with abandoned juveniles who lacked nutrition and suffered infectious and sexual diseases. By the mid-1960s the admissions were characterized by mental disorders. In the mid-1970s the physiological and mental effects of paint-thinner and stimulant-drug abuse were apparent. Many patients had been in mental hospitals of the Ministry of Health and Welfare where they threatened nurses, rejected medical treatment, and otherwise defied hospital procedures.

Diagnoses are a crucial responsibility, the Kanto superintendent declared. A great variety of medical experts is required. For example, a juvenile may have the symptoms of a cramp accompanied by fainting; inquiry must determine whether the symptoms are due to drugs or epilepsy. Sometimes treatment requires a battery of experts.

He cited the case of an eighteen-year-old girl who had poured oil over her father and burned him to death. Examination disclosed that beatings had so compressed her teeth that she could not open the back of her mouth. Because skin disease had disfigured her, a home for dependent children had refused her while accepting her brothers and sisters, and she had been forced to remain with the alcoholic father who beat her. She had developed hostility toward all persons. A Kanto dentist persuaded the hospital of Yamagata University in northern Japan to accept her as a model for medical students. Her skin disease was rare: a special team of dermatologists, mouth specialists, a psychiatrist, and others was formed. Kindness and medical care changed her attitude; she sent gifts, such as a bottle of pickles, to the Kanto dentist. Upon release from JTS she would go to the "House of Wheat" operated by the Roman Catholic Church in Tokyo.

Dormitory assignments are on the unit basis, not according to treatment stages. In one dormitory, male juveniles with grave problems are on the first floor and must stay in a single-person room day and night. Others with physical problems are on the second floor; those with mental difficulties on the third floor. Newcomers and short-termers are on the fourth floor. Five staff members are assigned to each floor. Girls are allocated to rooms in a separate wing.

For individuals at Kanto for less than one year, the superintendent is authorized to ask the regional parole board to release them. To extend a stay beyond one year, the superintendent asks the family court for permission. If there is a possibility of patients doing any harm to others, the family court can order holding them in the medical school until age twenty-six; otherwise, release at age twenty is mandatory. When a patient posing a threat to others has to be discharged, the Medical Sanitorium Law requires the superintendent of the medical school to notify the prefectural governor for possible confinement in a regular mental hospital.

Kanagawa Medical Juvenile Training School is for those males between ages fourteen and nineteen who are mentally handicapped (IQ score under 69) or emotionally disturbed. Most boys come directly from the family court. Theft is a common offense, but not violent acts, because the boys usually are physically weak. Frequently, they have been scolded by parents, police, and other people and they are depressed. They may commit arson or sexually attack young children they can control. Even in sexual attack, few have experienced sexual intercourse.

The hour of rising is 6:30 A.M. After breakfast there is drill practice and a morning meeting in the dormitory. At 9:00 the boys gather for calisthenics before work, lessons, or therapy. From 6:00 to 8:00 P.M. a teacher lectures, after which they practice self-learning and have an evening meeting. From 8:00 to 8:50 they watch television. Lights go out at 9:00 P.M.

The dormitory has six sections: three are for the intermediate stage; another two for newcomers, solitary inmates, and those receiving special education; and the final section for prerelease inmates. Each section has a staff office. Visiting families who come a distance may stay overnight in a house. The treatment and education ward has rooms for therapy, work-therapy, and lessons during the intermediate stage.

A new inmate receives a medical examination, an EEG, an ECG, and a dental examination. The staff includes two doctors, one pharmacist, and one nurse. The medical section has a medical examination room, pharmacy, x-ray examination room, psychiatric examination room, and EEG examination room. Once a month a dentist visits the school as a volunteer.

The maximum enrollment is eighty and the authorized staff size is forty-eight. The average stay is thirteen months. Programs include Japanese language, mathematics, and physical training to promote health and physical well-being. The inmates are guided and encouraged to develop basic living habits through therapy and work-therapy. There are several treatment modalities. Psychodrama takes place in a room that has a three-step semicircular stage. By acting out situations related to their problems, inmates are encouraged to develop healthy emotional responses. Psychomotor therapy (described at Kanagawa as "kinezi-therapy") attempts to produce a smooth interaction of mental and physical activity. Group counseling involves seven or eight boys sitting around a round table and speaking freely about some theme. Each boy receives counseling from other inmates. The therapy is intended to release them from a defensive attitude caused by anxiety, fear, and distrust. Individual counseling is important, but the primary purpose of group counseling at Kanagawa is to teach the inmates to express themselves.

Shopping training involves giving juveniles money, say 1,500 yen, each month to spend for daily needs such as a toothbrush, toothpaste, tissues, and the like. They learn to buy and calculate expenses and can book unspent money for the next month. Work therapy consists of four courses in ceramics, woodcraft, agriculture-gardening, and a corrugated-paper box factory.

Junior high school courses are aimed at the younger boys who are becoming more prevalent among the juvenile delinquents in Japan. The school endeavors to have the inmates complete compulsory education. Physical training consists of running, gymnastics, baseball, soccer, and swimming in a 25-meter pool. Among the club activities are music, painting, paper-patch picture-making, English conversation, calligraphy, table tennis, volleyball, and softball.

PROGRAMS IN
VOCATIONAL PREPARATION

Two juvenile training schools—Naniwa in Osaka Prefecture and Tohoku in Miyagi Prefecture—specialize in vocational training of selected boys. Ibaragi, Hitoyoshi, and Hokkai have courses for operating heavy construction machinery. Tama Juvenile Training School offers sophisticated vocational guidance with a staff of vocational instructors and workshops for carpentry, metalworking, word processing, printing by computer, and lathe machinery. Other training schools for boys and all of those for girls limit themselves to "vocational guidance" intended to encourage the juveniles to seek employment after release, to cultivate sound work habits, and to prepare them for seeking jobs.

In 1990 releases, 19.6 percent of the boys received certificates for vocational activities, as did 30 percent of the girls. Of the 159 certificates granted girls, 76 were for the abacus, 13 for bookkeeping, and 2 for the Japanese typewriter. Of the 795 certificates awarded boys, 404 were for welding, 115 for handling dangerous materials, 121 for operating special motor vehicles, 10 for operating construction machinery, and 20 for installing electric wiring (Research and Statistics Section 1991b, 180–81).

Tohoku Juvenile Training School receives selected boys from eastern Japan. The headquarters of the Sendai Correction Region specifies quotas for the courses. The JCHs select candidates according to these criteria: ages seventeen through nineteen years, completion of nine years of schooling, no physical defects or personality deviations, IQ score of 80 or more, desire for vocational training, and aptitude for a relevant vocation. The courses are in electricity, carpentry, automobile mechanics, plumbing, and welding.

Each has a well-equipped workshop and two vocational instructors with certificates of a college who have also passed an NPA examination for JTS instructors.

Of the forty-six on the Tohoku staff, thirty-two men supervise the five dormitories, and each is directly responsible for four or five boys. One dormitory is for the reception period and another for prerelease. In the intermediate stage, the students are assigned to one of three dormitories according to the course taken. Tohoku graduates may obtain vocational licenses by satisfying examinations of the Ministry of Labor. Tohoku has instruction in handling explosive materials.

Serving western Japan, Naniwa Juvenile Training School offers vocational courses in electrical work, laundry, gas and electrical welding, metal-processing machinery, and carpentry. Juveniles completing the laundry course can seek a license to operate laundry machinery by passing a prefectural government examination. Regardless of the course taken, Naniwa boys take a week-long course in computer-assisted design. Those taking the electrical work course can take an examination for a license in using fire-prevention equipment. Naniwa offers instruction in handling explosive materials or their storage.

Now conducting a course in operation of heavy construction machinery, Ibaragi originated in 1932 as a farm operated by a private corporation with parolees as employees. The government purchased the farm in 1949 and erected new buildings then, except those now occupied as staff residences. The obsolete plant was scheduled for total reconstruction by March 1992. Of the 125 boys, 100 work the farm of 150,000 square meters. The instructors for the dormitories allocated to the farm workers are qualified in agriculture. For instruction in heavy machinery, a variety of machinery provides practical experience in the three-month course three times a year. The twenty-five in the course are housed in one dormitory in which every staff member has a certificate in operating the machinery. The headquarters of the Tokyo Correction Region recruits students from the Tokyo, Sendai, and Nagoya Correction Regions. The students must be at least eighteen years of age, have had no serious traffic violation, and be motivated to work in construction.

PROGRAMS IN ACADEMIC EDUCATION

Among the juveniles admitted to training schools in 1990, 316 of the boys (8.3 percent) and 98 of the girls (21.1 percent) had not satisfied the nine years of compulsory schooling (Research and Statistics Section 1991b, 142–43). Nineteen schools deliver academic education; all nine girls' schools are included. Kitsuregawa in the Tokyo Correction Region and Fukuoka in the Fukuoka Correction Region provide senior high school courses; Akagi in the Tokyo Correction Region and Uji in the Osaka Correction Region specialize in junior high school courses. The students at the four specialized schools are selected from other training schools.

When returned to the community in 1990, 259 boys and 83 girls had received junior high school certificates from the schools in their home communities. The accomplishment can be measured against the 316 boys and 98 girls who entered the juvenile facilities that year without completing the nine years of schooling. Upon leaving the training schools in 1990, another 90 boys and 39 girls reentered junior high schools in their home communities. Moreover, 41 boys and 6 girls reenrolled in senior high schools (Research and Statistics Section 1991b, 128–29, 188).

Named after a nearby mountain, Akagi Training School was established in 1940 by a public prosecutor as a private reformatory.[9] After enactment of the Juvenile Law it was taken over by the Ministry of Justice and provided academic education for boys fourteen years or older. The average stay is eleven months but can be extended if behavior is unsatisfactory. When I visited the school in October 1990, a fifth of the boys present were in the eighth grade and the remainder in the ninth grade. At entry the inmates are tested for competence in the Japanese language, mathematics, and English. Results are used for assignment to one of three groups: A for competence only through the fifth grade, B for the sixth and seventh grades, and C for the eighth grade. All courses for the boy are at the same grade level. When a pupil is less advanced in a subject, supplementary instruction is conducted in the dormitory.

If a boy at Akagi completes nine years of schooling there, they take a vocational course in gas welding and handling dangerous chemicals. The year is divided into the first semester beginning in April and the second semester starting in September. In the prerelease phase all boys engage in farming, gardening, laundry work, or kitchen work as a kind of vocational guidance.

Like in Akagi, the courses in Uji are similar to those in regular junior high schools: Japanese language, English, mathematics, social science, the natural sciences, music, fine arts, and physical exercise. The teachers of the academic courses on the staff have teaching certificates and conduct some of the living guidance courses. Volunteer teachers from the community supplement the regular staff, especially in music. Instruction in mathematics and English is one-on-one, and the other subjects are taught in groups even when the students are at different grade levels. The daily schedule supplements academic education with activities found in all training schools: living guidance courses according to the boy's particular personal problem, vocational guidance, club activities, and physical training.

Special Schools for "Problem Juveniles"

Like juvenile training schools generally, admissions have declined in recent years for the schools serving concurrently as special and middle institutions. While inspecting the Kurihana Juvenile Training School, one of those receiving boys classified as special, I was told that a positive prognosis could not be given for even those boys sent there as middle-school types, but special inmates were described as especially experienced with juvenile training schools and often associated with the yakuza and drug abuse, largely with paint thinner. They are highly likely to come from broken families and to lack social-psychological support from parents.

During the five years previous to 1990, 41 percent of the arriving juveniles in the middle group were in a training school for the first time, as were 7 percent of the special group. For all 1990 admissions, 80 percent of the boys were in training school for the first time (Research and Statistics Section 1991b, 111). For the last five years previous to 1990, a third of the admitted boys at the school had been members of yakuza gangs and 22 percent had been marginal associates. Tattooing is considered evidence of self-identification with the yakuza. For the five years, 23 percent had heavy tattooing on the arms, shoulders, and back; 7 percent had medium amounts of tattooing, and 13 percent a small amount.

The staff at Haruna, a training school for girls receiving the special type, agree that these girls are not alone in being underprivileged and recidivists, but they differ from middle-school girls in important respects. First, their offenses are more akin to that of mature criminals. Second, having experienced training schools previously, they pretend to be in conformity with staff expectations but are convinced that behavioral change is unnecessary. For example, a girl was in a training school for the third time; in her most recent offense, she had drugged a man so she could rob him while he was unconscious. Her divorced parents had disowned her, a brother had raped her, and she had attempted suicide once. She differed from the usual Japanese juvenile inmate by refusing to confront her personal problems while raising a front of participation in the staff efforts to assist her.

Kurihana recognizes that the special-school inmates raise peculiar difficulties for the usual approaches of Japanese training schools. Previous experience with training school insulates these inmates from their usual methods and they require greater management and control. Special-class inmates seem to have become more passive, but the school staff is more familiar with aggressive personalities.

When arriving at Kurihana, the inmates are screened roughly into two groups according to the general differentiation for living guidance courses: G1 versus G2 and G3. The latter group receives regular modes of treatment. For the special-class inmates (G1) three major approaches have been adopted. First, the inmates engage in self-introspection about personal problems for a half hour each day and then are interviewed by the instructor. Second, the inmates draft essays on personal problems with more specific topics than usual in the diagnostic use of essays. The instructor returns the essays repetitively and asks for more details. Gradually, the inmates are moved toward recognizing the roots of their behavioral difficulties and perhaps undertake solutions. Third, lifeboat instruction teaches "the importance of life," taking advantage of the facility's location on Tokyo Bay at Yokohama.

Years ago, the Shinko Juvenile Training School in Hiroshima, now closed, taught juvenile delinquents to be fishermen or prepared them for other seafaring occupations. At Kurihana the training for and use of the lifeboat has great appeal for juveniles. The course is intended to motivate the juveniles to accept responsibility for other persons, similar to the lifeboat crew's dedication to save persons from drowning. Throughout their stay at Kurihana, the inmates follow three phases of instruction in addition to instruction in the use of the lifeboat: signaling with flags, knot tying, and first-aid training leading to a Red Cross certificate.[10] The three approaches are supplemented by five vocational guidance courses: printing (for middle-type inmates), ceramics, gas welding, carpentry, and gardening. Sandbox therapy is being tried as a nonverbal technique for persons who do not communicate well with other individuals.

8

COMMUNITY-BASED CORRECTIONS: JAPANESE VERSION

Through probation, parole, and aftercare, the Rehabilitation Bureau completes the continuum of criminal justice reactions to crime and delinquency begun with the apprehension of suspects. Most persons removed from the community ultimately return there. If granted probation, the removal is rather brief; if imprisoned, the parolee may have been away for years.

In seeking affiliation with the "community," correctional agencies usually are trying to obtain participation of private citizens in their affairs; the objective may be the greater effectiveness of the agency's administration without significant change in established practice. Alternatively, through the active participation of private citizens, the agency strives to bring communal forces to bear on crime and criminality in unprecedented ways. To that end, the agency reassesses familiar practices and is prepared to experiment with new and promising strategies.

HISTORY OF COMMUNITY CORRECTIONS

The name of the Rehabilitation Bureau stresses the importance of "rehabilitation" as a goal. The term covers a variety of conceptions of how to deal with criminality, and its interpretation has changed over time. Along with illness and plagues, offenses in ancient Japan were considered blemishes that should be cleansed by religious rituals. Noda (1976, 21–22) explains that the notion of *tsumi* corresponds to the modern word "sin": "The priest said prayers for purification and sometimes there was a washing of the bodies of condemned persons." When a crime aroused the gods' displeasure, the "filth attached to one's person as a result of a transgression" was to be cleansed by priestly invocation or immersing oneself in water (Ishii 1980, 10–11).

The belief that severe physical punishment and the death penalty would be deterrents also permeated early efforts to turn individuals away from further criminality. Whipping and caning were common methods to press them to accept "proper" behavioral standards. Hanging and beheading were to be object lessons. Exile from the family and village was a formidable sanction in an age of limited physical mobility and conveyed a simple message that community forces would manage criminality at minimum cost to governments. Ostracism set the deviant adrift, and acceptance was crucial to reintegration within local life.

Awareness surfaced that something beyond the forced atonement of prisoners was necessary. Perhaps there was humanitarian concern for the plight of discharged inmates without resources or a desire to encourage them to become effective members of the labor force. Official forgiveness existed as early as the eighth century, when the emperor granted amnesty and clothing to a burglar (Satoh 1989). However, forgiveness is only the beginning of an institutionalized commitment to readmitting the offenders to the social-psychological and structural elements of community.

Even more than institutional corrections, community strategies in modern form emerged later in Japan than in most Western societies. Postrelease problems of prisoners drew the earliest concern. Conditional release from prisons was first specified officially in the Penal Code of 1881 that authorized police surveillance after three-quarters of a prison sentence had been served. The Penal Code of 1907 reduced the requirement to one-third, but parole was granted only on a limited scale. Before World War II, parole held a minor place in releases from prison, 3.7 percent in 1930 and 12.7 in 1940, but thereafter assumed more importance: 55.1 percent in 1950, 68.4 percent in 1960, 61.8 percent in 1970, and 51.8 percent in 1980 (Shikita and Tsuchiya 1990, 371-72). Japanese prisons were greatly overcrowded during the socioeconomic crisis at the end of the war; parole was seized upon for speeding the exit of prisoners.

The first modern noninstitutional approach to corrections in Japan emerged with the "old" Juvenile Law in 1923. The juvenile tribunal could send a juvenile to a reform school, conditionally release a reform school inmate, or place the juvenile in the community under supervision. For lack of financial resources, the law was not implemented throughout Japan.

Today probation is connected with the Law for Suspension of Execution of Sentences, introduced in 1905, but it does not provide for the supervision that is a crucial element of probation. Adult probation was introduced in combination with the suspension of sentences as a part of the revision of the penal code in 1953 and 1954. The Law for Probationary Supervision of Persons under Suspension of Execution of Sentence was enacted and probation of adult offenders came into practice in 1954 (Kouhashi 1985; Nishikawa 1990). The juvenile tribunal was abolished in 1949 when the new Juvenile Law (Article 24) and the Offenders Rehabilitation Law established the family court, the juvenile parole board, and the juvenile probation office. According to Article 33 of the Offenders Rehabilitation Law, the juvenile probation office was responsible for supervision of juveniles granted probation by the court or parole from prisons or training schools.

Now Article 24 of the Juvenile Law authorizes the family court to place the juvenile under the supervision of the probation office. According to the law (Article 2) the family court has jurisdiction over any juvenile who is alleged to have committed an offense, including any juvenile under 14 years of age who is alleged to have violated any criminal law or ordinance. Also the family court has jurisdiction over any juvenile (predelinquent) who is prone to commit an offense or violate a criminal law or ordinance in view of his or her character or environment. The reasons for including predelinquents are habitual rejection of a guardian's control, staying away from home without good reason, association with a person of criminal propensity or of immoral character or with places of evil reputation, and propensity to commit acts harmful to his or her own moral character or to that of others (Nishikawa 1990; Hyotani 1985; Shiono 1969).

Scope of Community-Oriented Corrections

Correctional agencies in any democracy have reasons to extend their attention to the community beyond their organizational and jurisdictional boundaries. First, citizens, especially politically influential persons, can promote correctional programs. Lauen (1990, 24) speaks of "community-managed corrections" that would involve citizens in the development, governance, and monitoring of community-oriented programs. Local citizens would have an active role in policy making. However, one of the usual ideas of community-based corrections is that citizens play an advisory role in support of agency-determined goals and means of implementation. The second and most prevalent role of citizens is direct service; volunteers potentially perform a variety of functions in administration and in direct contacts with probationers and parolees. Third, ideally, citizens and their groups are agents of change toward improvement of agency policies and practices.

Advocates of community-based corrections make a number of claims that innovations in policy and practice will revolutionize the field. Duffee (1990, 8) doubts that new ideas are exclusive to probation and parole: "Persons interested in innovation can probably learn as much about innovations in maximum security prisons as from innovation in parole or probation work, and may do well to study or practice both at the same time."

Japan provides a special setting for the relationships between the community and corrections.[1] The diversionary decisions of the procuracy and judiciary rest on a faith that, first, the offender is capable of self-correction and, second, the capability will be supplemented by relationships with sundry groups making up the offender's community. The bulk of offenders are diverted from prisons and training schools. In the judgment of public prosecutors or judges, they do not require the stern sanction of imprisonment; the community orientation deals to the correctional institutions the least promising offenders.

The judges also send to the probation offices the least promising among the individuals granted suspension of a prison sentence; in the West, probationers are supposed to be the best prospects among defendants convicted in court. The Japanese judges regard probation as a kind of punishment, imposing the inconvenience of official supervision. When there are extenuating circumstances, they are inclined to suspend the prison sentence and return the person to the community *without* supervision; supervision is ordered for persons (granted suspension of the current prison sentence) who had committed offenses while under suspension without supervision for a previous crime.

The linkages between corrections and the community

in Japan are marked by the government's long-term preference to leave to the private sector many of the functions handled by government in other industrialized societies. As a corollary, the governmental bureaucracy has been kept at a comparatively small size. The preference can be traced to the Meiji Restoration; the regime initiated direct governmental involvement in industrialization but by 1900 turned to private entrepreneurs. Much has been left to the private sector in social welfare, health care, regulation of labor, higher education, and research and development (Pempel 1982). In regard to social services, the government has clung to what Watanuki (1986) has called a "Japanese-type welfare society." The politicians typically have been obscure in discussing the delivery of social services, but their central idea is that three social institutions (family, community, and the employing enterprise) would assume major responsibilities and that the government would spend relatively little for pensions and health insurance.

The Japanese government is among the smallest in the industrialized world; its employees were reported as only 9 percent of the labor force, compared with 14 to 20 percent in Western nations. The National Personnel Authorization Law of 1969 fixed the total number of national officials at 506,571. Then the Cabinet required each ministry and major agency to reduce personnel by 5 percent over a three-year period.[2] Many local governments tried to fill the void by expanding activities in social welfare, environmental protection, education, transportation, and health care (Pempel 1982).

The Correction Bureau relies on the direct services of volunteer chaplains, vocational instructors, and a limited number of counselors, but the Rehabilitation Bureau is preeminent in this regard. The voluntary probation officers (VPOs) and private associations that operate hostels are primary examples of turning governmental functions over to the private sector. The industrial prison flourishes because of an advantageous linkage with private enterprises. The linkage also has provided the opportunity for several open camps that moderately resemble the free community.

Both the Rehabilitation Bureau and the Correction Bureau are well aware of the necessity to cultivate influential groups in the community. VPOs are considered major intermediaries. The rehabilitation aid hostels have drawn objections. For example, a child day-care center is adjacent to the Korakukai Hostel in Tokyo; some neighbors object to "criminals" residing next to young children. Persons living near the Sinkou Kai Hostel in Tokyo have complained about the men pounding on the door for admission when returning late from a local bar. The bar owner has telephoned the hostel about unpaid bar bills.

Juvenile classification homes orient neighbors and offer them diagnostic services upon request. Detention houses must be located near courts in the middle of metropolises. The oppressive appearance of walled facilities draw complaints. Suzuki (1983) notes the new Nagoya Detention House, opened in 1983, was designed to minimize such complaints. Its twelve-story high-rise structure resembles nearby office buildings; in a green area around the detention house, tennis courts are available to the public.

POLITICS AND
CORRECTIONS IN JAPAN

"Politics" refers to the competition among special-interest groups for influence over how resources are allocated and choices made among alternative courses of action. To obtain resources and ideological support, correctional agencies are among the special-interest groups that present themselves as indispensable instruments for attaining the high ideals of their society. Otherwise, the Correction and Rehabilitation Bureaus are less involved than their American counterparts in the competition among interest groups.

Crime and the policies of the bureaus rank low on the public's scale of priorities among major issues. The low ranking reflects the low crime rate; the insulation of the bureaus from intensive political pressure also stems from the Tokugawa heritage. Politics tends to be seen as the special preserve of government officials and not of particular concern for ordinary citizens. "The ruler was, by definition, virtuous and knew better than anyone else what was good for the people. Since the ruler's job was to rule, there was no need for the citizen to be concerned about the affairs of government which are the concern of the ruler and his officials" (Yanaga 1956, 17–18). Peasants did protest some actions of feudal lords but, seldom violent, they expressed serious grievances as violations of their status within the feudal social system (Keirstead 1990). Even their protests acknowledged their subordination in a "political game" dominated by the shogun and daimyo.

That history has marked Japanese politics with the notion of a shared community, general acceptance of the inequality of persons according to their position in the social structure, and the interdependence of politics and ethics (Leiserson 1973). The political community draws on the notions that the Japanese are of one race with a single language, that they share common customs, that their history was marked by isolation from other peoples and the rule of the imperial family for centuries, and that earlier dominance of rice growing and fishing has instilled a sense of mutuality in their relationships.

Organized economic interests—primarily big business and agriculture—have enjoyed "an astonishing level of access to policy making," but noneconomic interests have had little incentive to amass "the staff or other organizational resources needed to play a role of policy making" (Pharr 1990, xi–xii). Criminal justice issues are unlikely to surface. If they do, the Ministry of Justice would frame any legislation, just as the overwhelming majority of bills passed by the national Diet are framed by the affected agencies (Muramatsu and Krauss 1984).

"FRATERNAL COMMUNITY": LINK TO THE PAST

The term "community" has been interpreted in a number of not necessarily compatible definitions: pattern of land use, residents' identification of self with a locality, a sense of solidarity derived from sharing a common culture and social experiences, a sense of personal significance gained through communal membership, or the member benefits delivered as services by schools, hospitals, government bureaus, employing enterprises, and other units of the community's organization. Two interpretations provide a framework for discussion: "fraternal community" or "interdependent community."

In what we identify as fraternal community, attention is focused on the local community and its capacity for binding its residents in a kind of intimacy—a sense of communion—because they trust one another, share common beliefs, and can depend on the cooperation of fellow residents. In the idealized fraternal community, members develop a strong identification with one another by sharing each other's fate over a long period of time. Social solidarity is favored by the small number of residents, their cultural homogeneity, and the relative absence of changes in their way of life. The homogeneity and traits of residents lend uniformity to behavior. Most residents engage in similar kinds of work and social activities. Few strangers challenge the residents' conviction that they alone know "the right way."

As in other industrialized societies, Japan has a history of fraternal community and its discipline maintaining social order and stability. The effects of fraternal community, as outlined above, are exaggerated because dissension, conflict, and dissatisfactions have always existed, but the concept helps explain the objectives of community-based corrections.

Fraternal community is reasonably descriptive of the feudal villages that obtained community solidarity by the effects of rice agriculture and the village autonomy incidentally given by the Tokugawa system of social control. The cultural history made contributions that persist today to a degree: Confucian ethics, hierarchical social structure, and emphasis on social harmony and duty. Self-discipline is rewarded by the personal benefits of prestige, knowing one's place in the societal scheme, and holding the respect of others by observing ethical standards.

In the Tokugawa system of rule, the samurai were forced to live in a castle town and serve as salaried bureaucrats or surrender their aristocratic status. "While the physical distance of the *samurai* from the farming land enhanced their bureaucratic character," Tonomura (1992, 169) says, "it also restricted them from direct intervention in village affairs. With minimal involvement of the urban bureaucrats, the primary producers paid taxes and kept the local peace and order." The village's headman, appointed by the government from among the local people, represented them in contacts with the government and also was held responsible for the village in satisfying the tax assessment calculated in units of rice, overseeing the registration of members of households, and disseminating the rulers' orders. Local officials were able to oversee conduct of residents because of the information provided by the household registration: name, sex, occupation, birth, marriage, divorce, death, and movements of household members.

Masland (1946, 356) claims that although the system of neighborhood associations "was used principally as a political tool, it did nevertheless develop as an autonomous body of neighborhood families for the handling of community problems." Villagers obtained a sense of community solidarity because the Tokugawa system of social control accorded autonomy to the feudal villagers as long as the political purposes were served, but the rural hamlet exerted heavy social pressure for conformity. Ostracism by vote of the residents had great force because of an emphasis on harmony among residents and because agricultural production demanded the neighbors' cooperation (R. Smith 1961; Steiner 1965).

In an action that proved relevant to community-based criminal justice, Hideyoshi Toyotomi ordered in 1597 that the peasants form five-householder groups (the *gonin-gumi*). The head of each group had to make certain that the peasants lived frugal lives, worked hard, and paid taxes (Braibanti 1948). In ancient Japan the arrangement had either imposed criminal liability on the offender's relatives (*enza*) or on unrelated persons in the same office (*renza*). Later the responsibility had been extended to the neighbors (Ishii 1980).[3]

The Meiji regime officially abolished the gonin-gumi, hoping to substitute reverence for the emperor for loyalty to the immediate neighborhood (Braibanti 1948). Nevertheless, the groups survived through weddings, funerals, festivals, harvesting, and care of the sick. In 1940 the Home Ministry revived the neighborhood organization as *chonai-kai* for many wartime functions: registration of residents, census studies, administration of rationing, selling bonds, collecting scrap metal and taxes, air-raid defense, dissemination of government information and instructions, welcoming returning soldiers, and working with the police. The chonaikai had become a tool of centralized government, rather than reflecting neighborliness (Masland 1946). The rural *buraku-kai* were based on traditional communal units. In cities the chonaikai (district or block associations) were composed of four hundred to six hundred households. Legislation in 1943 authorized local governments to control the associations. Their wartime functions recalled the services of feudal villages demanded by the Tokugawa dictatorship (Masland 1946; Shihgetoh 1943).

"Interdependent Community" and Urbanism

Fraternal community is based on similarities among its residents and their activities, but urbanism necessitates a social order based on differences among residents. Because large populations are built up chiefly through migration, cities have a mixture of people with differing backgrounds and beliefs; the urbanites have more contacts with strangers and experience competing claims about the "right way" to behave. The city has many occupations and specialized residential areas. High population density erodes personal identity, favors anonymity, and weakens a feeling of belonging to a group of persons who care for one another. Flesh-and-blood persons are treated as inanimate objects because a large volume of customers, medical patients, employees, and similar groups must be handled in delivering services quickly.

Urban life undermines the fraternal community, but urbanites depend on a high level of order in the relationships among organizations to deliver food, manufacture and sell clothing, provide transportation, deliver education and health care, and safeguard them from fire, criminals, and illness. Individuals will police their own conduct, but the moral unity of the fraternal community is not available. Instead, achievement of a high level of public order in the interdependent community depends on the capacity of the social structure to deliver promised benefits.

The interdependent community extends beyond the local confines of the fraternal community to take in entire sections of a nation and even the nation as a whole. As elsewhere, changes accompanying urbanization have weakened the influence of the local areas. Nevertheless, the cultural heritage lingers in the social psychology of contemporary Japanese to an extent remarkable among economically advanced societies. Keiichi (1978) describes a "hierarchical community" that, in keeping with the vertical dimension of oyabun and kobun roles, severely curtails the private life of members; fixed, inclusive, and family-like relationships encompass the total personality.

"Americans tend to underline the voluntary aspects of association membership. Japanese are more aware of its compulsory facets—of the moral pressure of the *waku*" comments Plath (1964, 141). The social control system (the waku) gives priority to the interests of the group over self-interests when persons participate in community groups. As Dore (1958, 254) says, the acts of giri "spring from a sense of obligation rather than from spontaneous inclination." (The Tokugawa system of controlling villages lingers in contemporary attitudes.) Japanese are more likely than Americans to cooperate with the authorities. Lacking the "widespread alienation and tradition of righteous indignation" of Americans, Plath (1964, 141–42) continues, they have less sympathy for criminals. Americans sometimes find that they have been "volunteered" for participation in PTAs and charities, and some Japanese find active membership in community groups to be exciting, "but there is no doubt that Japanese have tended to be more accepting than Americans of government surveillance and control of organizations." That tendency has the cultural roots traced in chapter 2 but also draws partially from the gonin-gumi imposed by the Tokugawa rulers.

Services to the military dictatorship persuaded the Allied-occupation authorities to disband the chonaikai. Many Japanese viewed the community associations with apathy and sometimes with covert hostility (Steiner 1965). Voluntarism has to cope with the Japanese tendency to avoid strangers and the separation of the general population into the social clusters of employing firms, villages, and so on (Azumi 1974).

Social changes have failed to eliminate the chonaikai but have modified their nature. The distinction between two interpretations of "community" become especially relevant: the bonds of mutuality among local residents versus the structure of relationships among them derived artificially from influential organizations outside the locality. The chonaikai hovers between, on the one hand, a membership group expressing a sense of communal fellowship independent of direct government control and, on the other, a semiofficial component of government. "The chonaikai is unquestionably the neighborhood's most important and visible organization," Bestor (1985, 127) declares. "In some senses it acts as a semi-official local government, providing services to residents both at local initiative and at the behest of the municipal authorities." They are multifunctional in contrast to the specialized functions of government agencies. Households, not individuals, are members; membership is taken for granted rather than being a conscious or clearly compulsory act (Hachiro Nakamura 1968).

Ishida (1983, 16–17) asserts that voluntary associations emerged only with the end of World War II, because previously "all groups were subordinated to the emperor system" and then were in practice "more or less dependent on government." He explains that since political parties and labor unions had failed to deal with pollution and other postwar local issues, "the citizens felt that they had no organization that could support them and so they started a voluntary organization to tackle the problem." The postwar version of the chonaikai in urban fringe areas often has opposed local governments by voicing claims of citizens that their rights have been violated (Aoyagi 1983). Since protest groups concentrate on local issues, the correction agencies—operating on the national level—are not usually a target. One possible exception would be opposition to the location of a prison or other penal facility.

The conclusion of a number of studies is that present-day political activity in localities shows self-conscious purpose in responding to forces beyond the local community (Ben-Ari 1991). First, localities differ in their emphasis on particular issues, depending on the mix of subgroups within the local population. Participation in local affairs has become selective. Second, although they show some concern about local issues, male employees divert their time and loyalty to the workplace and workmates. Third, rural hamlets and urban neighborhoods have been integrated into the larger administrative districts. In spite of greater dependence on organizations external to the locality, self-conscious reactions against those forces exist in a selective way. Fourth, like urbanites in other societies, contemporary Japanese are likely to withdraw from active participation in community affairs when their economic, social, and emotional investments in the affairs fail to reward them.[4]

Voluntary Groups and Corrections

In the interdependent community, voluntary associations recruit selectively from segments of the population. Organizations expressing dutiful support of governmental agencies attract older citizens. In his study of neighborhood associations in Fuchu, Allinson (1979) found that well-educated and white-collar persons, who often came from urban backgrounds, were inclined to resist the associations; they remember their wartime services and regard them as troublesome intrusions on their private lives. Long-term residents of the area and older retirees from commercial and professional occupations were the core of the associations. Among newcomers and the young, low-status workers with rural backgrounds were most likely to join.

The Correction and Rehabilitation Bureaus are nationwide entities unlikely to benefit from a locality-based issue. The Rehabilitation Bureau endeavors to localize the VPO program; the Volunteer Probation Officer Law speaks of "rehabilitation areas" differentiated by "circumstances in the community." Voluntary organization operate the rehabilitation aid hostels. Volunteers for the bureaus tend to be older persons, including many retired persons, who step forward as individuals. The Big Brothers and Sisters movement is exceptional in drawing younger persons.

Japanese Rehabilitation Aid Association. Founded in 1939, this association provides support, chiefly financial, to the VPOs, hostels, the Women's Association for Rehabilitation Aid, and the Big Brothers and Sisters Association. The latter two organizations also have offices in the modern building in Tokyo owned by the Japanese Rehabilitation Aid Association. For income, the association rents two floors to a private corporation. One primary aim is to provide 700 million yen for reconstruction of hostels; 500 million yen had been obtained from private businesses by 1992. The association pays for rental of halls, printing of course materials, and other resources for VPO training. In addition, a primary course in counseling is conducted. A monthly magazine, *Kosei-hogo* (Rehabilitation), is published for members of volunteer organizations. The association encourages research through grants on topics of major interest to the Rehabilitation Bureau. The association also publishes the quarterly journal, *Hanzai-yobo* (Rehabilitation and Prevention), that carries case histories and descriptions of research for probation office staffs.

Volunteer Probation Officers Association. The group carries out training and is a communication conduit among members and probation offices. The branch in each probation area is affiliated with one of the fifty prefectural federations, which, in turn, compose eight regional and one national federations. VPO member contributions meet the association's expenses.

Big Brothers and Sisters Movement. Initiated by college students in Kyoto in 1947, the movement spread throughout Japan among students, workers, and others eighteen to thirty years of age. They work with juveniles referred by probation offices, family courts, child guidance centers, and the police. Sports, camping, and hiking are the most popular activities. Some branches help juvenile traffic offenders on probation. The national federation sponsors an annual conference.

Women's Association For Rehabilitation Aid. In the role of mothers, the members visit juvenile institutions, prepare meals at rehabilitation aid hostels, give aid to inmates in correctional institutions and their families, and participate in crime prevention. Women VPOs are the core of the membership.

National League of Voluntary Prison Visitors. The league endeavors to prevent repetition of crimes by visits to penal institutions and juvenile training schools for counseling and smoothing the return to the free community. Other services are vocational training, recreational activities, and assistance in family relations. Prison visitors are appointed for two-year terms.

National League of Chaplains. The league sponsors training for chaplains serving correctional institutions when the warden asks for them. Chaplains are volunteers because the Constitution of Japan requires the separation of state and religion. Inmate attendance of any religious services is optional.

Juvenile Friends Association. The association was formed by the Tokyo Family Court to assist juveniles on tentative probation. Clothing and other necessities, when needed, are provided to juveniles in probation homes, new places of employment, or their own residences. Women members prepare meals at probation homes and organize recreation to express the goodwill of "ordinary persons."

Volunteer Probation Officers

"Without about 48,000 volunteer probation officers who are actively engaged in the offenders rehabilitation service across the country," declares the former director general of the Rehabilitation Bureau, "we have only 1,000 probation officers in 50 probation offices, to take care of about 100,000 persons placed under probation or parole" (Satoh 1989, 17).

The Rehabilitation Bureau's heavy reliance on unsalaried volunteer probation officers (VPOs) is a preeminent example of community-based corrections in Japan and remarkable for international criminal justice.[5] The emphasis is consistent with the Japanese belief that criminals are capable of self-rehabilitation; the belief implies the sufficiency of guidance by average persons willing to devote their time and energy to helping others. The bureau's explanation of the origin of the strategy is as follows:

> At the time of reorganizing the Japanese community-based treatment system in and around 1949 there was an argument that our probation and parole services should also be established thoroughly on the basis of a professional service as in many countries. Nevertheless, the new organization turned out in the form of a combined service of professional staff and volunteer workers. It is true that the shortage of funds at that time precluded the realization of overall professionalization. But the even greater reason making a determination to maintain volunteers obviously lays in the fact that the trust of the authorities in the potential of volunteer workers was so overwhelming. (Rehabilitation Bureau 1990, 13)

The Volunteer Probation Officer Law defines the mission: "to contribute to the welfare of the individual and the public by helping persons who have committed criminal offenses to improve and be rehabilitated and at the same time by leading public opinion for the prevention of offenses and by cleaning up the community, in the spirit of social service" (UNAFEI n.d., 287–89).[6] The maximum number of VPOs for all Japan is set at 52,500 and they are allocated by the Minister of Justice in "rehabilitation areas" fixed according to the population, economic characteristics, crime rates, and "other circumstances in the community."

The minister appoints VPOs for two-year terms, subject to reappointment (or delegates the function to the chair of the regional parole board) according to these criteria: Having the confidence and popular approval of the community in character and conduct, enthusiasm and time for the work, financial stability, and being healthy and active. Persons are unqualified if adjudicated as incompetent, sentenced to prison, or guilty of organizing or being a member of any organization advocating the overthrow of the Constitution of Japan or the government by force and violence. No salary or allowance is paid, but expenses in performing duties are paid "within the limit of the budget."

VPOs receive three kinds of training by the probation office of the given area: initial orientation of recruits, periodic refresher training, and special sessions bringing together experienced VPOs for study of a selected topic. Initial orientation lasting one day introduces recruits to such rudimentary subjects as basic laws and regulations, agency procedures, report writing, and interviewing. Advance training deals with case conferences, role-playing, casework, and so on. VPO associations have their own training at periodic meetings.

The Investigation and Research Section in the headquarters of the Rehabilitation Bureau prepares and distributes three training booklets for VPO training. The first volume is for initial orientation to these topics: instruction in how to write a letter or report, supervision and interviewing techniques, confidentiality of information, development of a treatment plan, guidance and material aid, supervision of classes of offenders (such as traffic, drug, and mentally disordered offenders), crime prevention, pardons, and environmental adjustment of released inmates.[7] The second volume is for refresher training on these topics: criminal policies, history of the rehabilitation system, and organization of the system. The third volume deals with conditions of supervision, management of traffic offenders, procedures for granting parole, methods of interviewing, client relationships at work, and supervision of paint-thinner and glue-sniffing offenders.

Individuals' Involvement in Corrections

In addition to the VPO program, a number of voluntary associations benefit the correctional agencies by the willingness of some citizens to devote some leisure time to community service. Wagatsuma and De Vos (1984, 29) explain that "although for Westerners the word 'paternalism' often has a negative connotation, for the Japanese paternalism is deeply expressive behavior—giving to others the nurturance that one had in one's own childhood." In their research in Arakawa Ward, Tokyo, they attributed in part the drop of delinquency rates in the 1960s to voluntary associations, a variety of organizations composed of and maintained by individuals who volunteer their services for various social purposes. Several voluntary organizations, described earlier in this chapter, are dedicated to serving the Rehabilitation and Correction Bureaus. The Rehabilitation Bureau recruits and assigns VPOs as individuals, but the individuals become members of a local voluntary probation officer association. The membership enjoys the fellowship based on common experiences and collegial relationships. Through the VPO associations the probation offices carry out refresher and advanced training of the VPOs and extend the Rehabilitation Bureau's appreciation at annual meetings.

According to Hashimoto (1983, 184), "VPOs are invariably persons of high social standards and belong to the middle or upper strata of society. Relatively few are social workers, school teachers, or practicing lawyers, but many are religious professionals or workers in agriculture and fishing who are influential persons in small towns and villages.

In attracting members, the VPOs and other voluntary organizations are selective rather than drawing on all segments of the population. The heavy representation of persons from "the middle or upper strata of society" suggests performance of the oyabun role in hierarchical community. The VPOs tend to be advanced in age and their average age rises as the years pass. The traditional sense of duty seems to press them to serve, rather than only a quest for personal advantages.

In responding to my inquiry during an interview in Yokohama about why he chose to become a VPO, a man said he responded to the expectations of his family and community: "My father owns a Japanese restaurant, a Western restaurant, a Chinese restaurant, and an Italian restaurant, and I manage the family business. Twenty-two years ago the prefectural government sent me for almost a month to see youth programs in Soviet Russia, England, Germany, Switzerland, and Italy. The government decided to build a youth hostel. The officials said to me: 'You spent the government's money to go abroad; now you should do voluntary probation work.' My family expected me to do something without pay. I had no reason to say 'no,' so I said: 'Okay! I will do that.' "

At a training session for VPOs in Sendai, many respondents mentioned the support of family members. A man explained that family members made possible his long service. When he is away, they receive the probationers in his home. Another man said that in many difficult cases he wondered whether or not he should keep trying, but his wife has always given him support. Another businessman draws enthusiasm from being part of a community movement; he mentioned being impressed by people marching in the annual nationwide crime prevention campaign (Movement for a Brighter Society) sponsored by the Ministry of Justice.

Priests were especially influential in the early history of services for prisoners. That tradition persists; a Zen priest explained that his senior priest had persuaded him to join the movement. Now with his own temple, he has been a VPO for twenty-seven years. A Shinto priest had been a soldier and was happy to return alive because many did not. On his return, he found many were jobless and there was much crime; he wanted to help. After conversations with a VPO in the neighborhood, he decided forty-one years ago to assume responsibility.

Community-oriented programs are favorable settings for recruiting VPOs. Two persons had contacts with VPOs through the Parent-Teacher Association. A former winemaker had been the president of a PTA at his daughter's elementary school; the previous president, a priest involved in VPO work, invited him to participate. A housewife who had been a VPO for thirty-six years explained that a PTA colleague recruited her. An official of an agricultural assistance association wondered what to do after retirement.

Why did veteran VPOs continue service for many years? Several respondents reported that they had gained new respect for their clients and special satisfactions from their work. A woman told me: "Being a VPO gives me a very good opportunity to develop my total personality by studying other human beings. A girl who inhaled paint thinner was called by the family court. Probationers are reluctant to go, but she went because of me. Her attitude made me feel richly rewarded." Another woman wrote me a letter in which she recalled the beginning of her work and her increasing confidence over the years:

> About a quarter century ago, I and my family were in Pittsburgh for two years; the Americans were very kind, including members of the Pittsburgh Council of International Visitors. After coming back to Japan, I wanted to do volunteer work as in the U.S. My friend, an expert VPO, asked me to serve. I was afraid, but the probationers are no different than other Japanese. I think of them as ordinary people; we talk about the normal things of life. Unless asked, I do not give them

advice because a judge or probation officer has told them what they do or not do. At first, I usually say: "Let's try our best together." I have had over thirty cases in ten years. One-third were young offenders: thieves, violent offenders, prostitutes, and paint-thinner sniffers. The adults were swindlers, users and sellers of drugs, prostitutes, and a murderer paroled from a life sentence. Two are back in prison; I write them once a month.

Volunteers: Pros and Cons

The community produces offenders, Angata (1990) argues, and through their participation in treatment, citizens represent the community in relationships with offenders. "As members of the community where the offenders live, the VPOs' knowledge of every facet of local life enables them to take the most suitable approach to the particular setting. They find themselves in a more advantageous position in bringing about changes in the public's attitude toward offenders. They can obtain cooperation from the community's residents and mobilize social resources" (Hashimoto 1983, 185).

The nonofficial status of VPOs is considered advantageous (Hashimoto 1983). They know the local community and are persistent residents, whereas professional probation officers (PPOs) are more apt to be transferred to other probation offices. VPOs are more acceptable to offenders and the offenders' families because of their nonsalaried status and their contrast to governmental authority. Not bound strictly by regulations and working hours, they are more flexible in service delivery than rule-bound PPOs. Responsibilities of PPOs end with termination of supervision; personal ties of VPOs and offenders can continue. When VPOs express warm concern, the clients are apt to gain a favorable self-image and be more willing to accept the community's behavioral standards. When the VPOs also belong to other organizations affiliated with governmental bureaus, they can mobilize resources (such as public assistance for the needy) for probationers and parolees (Angata 1990).

Private persons and criminal justice personnel were the major actors in the establishment of hostels. Today, many of the 470 salaried members of the staffs have retired after service in probation or parole. Their experience is an asset, and the hostels supplement their pensions. "The average age of staff is rather high, and the average pay is rather low," according to Udo (1990, 5). He provides 1989 data that show, first, the average pay of sixty-four hostel directors was less than the average for clerical staff and, second, the average age of directors and chief guidance workers exceeded sixty years, the age of retirement.

Since 1960, urbanization has accelerated the trend towards nuclear families and has extended the discrepancy between claimed support of community organizations and actual participation in their activities (Buendia 1989). The high average age of volunteers stands in sharp contrast with the youth of most probationers and parolees. The proportion of VPOs over sixty years of age has gone from 29 percent in 1953 to 65 percent in 1990. Differences in social-class status also is a barrier to easy communication, but class and subcultural differences are smaller in Japan than elsewhere, claims Shiono (1969). He contends that VPOs from minorities and lower-income groups are needed less, and in oriental cultures the young respect grandfather figures. His view is not held universally.

Competent VPOs who are in touch with the clients' changing needs are especially difficult to recruit for high-delinquency areas. Hashimoto (1983, 186–87) describes the problem: "Even if VPOs are recruited, they are not able to maintain good relationships with probationers because of the lack of daily contact in the community." Value conflicts may obstruct constructive communication because urban life favors conflicts of political and economic interests. The PPO may not be reliably informed on the client's situation. "When two probationers show the same progress, one may be discharged from probation based on the favorable reports of a lenient VPO, whereas the other may remain under the further supervision of a strict VPO."

Police officials and ward officials who work with volunteers in corrections find merits but also see liabilities (Wagatsuma and De Vos 1984). Levels of intelligence, ability, personal maturity, and education vary. Some VPOs are very out of touch with the changing concerns of youth and some are too old-fashioned to adopt the approaches of professionals. VPOs may spend little time with their charges or ignore them at critical times because of their own pressing business activities, illnesses, or trips.

Two decades ago, Tomita (1971) complained that Japanese probation and parole services suffer from "overlaicisation," meaning they were too much under the direction of, or open to, laymen. He listed several recommendations: PPOs should be more numerous and their training should be strengthened, it should be made clear that VPOs are not replacements for PPOs, and ex-offenders should not be automatically barred from voluntary service. The special abilities of given volunteers should determine their task assignments. Recruits should represent all social strata, particularly the younger ages.

Article 20, The Offenders Rehabilitation Law, states: "The volunteer probation officer provided for in the Volunteer Probation Office Law shall assist the professional probation officer and make up for inadequacies of the latter's work. . . . " Instead of assisting the PPO, the VPO performs treatment, Angata (1990, 9) contends: "We are short of professional probation officers, and there is little prospect of a rapid increase of professional probation officers because of the presence of the VPO system." Taking a different tack, Shiono (1969) argues that complete professionalism was never intended; many problems are due to excessive reliance on volunteers, not due to the VPO system.

REHABILITATION AID HOSTELS

In meeting the reentry crisis, the family is the primary buffering agency for many released prisoners; for those without family support or other resources, rehabilitation aid hostels cushion the shock for four classes of persons in addition to parolees and discharged prisoners: those sentenced to prison, but for whom an unserved portion of the sentence has been excused due to illness or other exceptional circumstances; those granted suspension of a prison sentence, but for whom the suspension is not yet final; those receiving a suspension of sentence without probation; and those not prosecuted because prosecution was found unnecessary.

The Law for Aftercare of Discharged Offenders, Article 5, lists the obligations of "any person other than Government or local government wishing to operate rehabilitation aid services" and the general criteria to be applied by the Minister of Justice. Article 6 authorizes the chief of the probation office to commission hostels to commence rehabilitation and emergency aid. The hostels are required to submit to the Minister of Justice a written account of activities. Article 14 requires operators of hostels, when planning to seek financial contributions, to submit to the minister a statement describing the effort and how the contributions will be used. Article 12 specifies a government grant, "within the limits of the budget," to the hostels for clerical services, improvement of physical plants, and the "commissioning of rehabilitation aid."

A postrelease facility for juveniles was established in Osaka in 1884 and one for released adult prisoners in 1888 in Shizuoka (Hyotani 1985). Meizen Kimbara was a philanthropist troubled by the suicide of a released prisoner who had been rejected by his family. Kimbara was prominent in establishing the Shizuoka Hostel and in founding the Shizuoka Prefecture Ex-Prisoners' Aid Corporation, which was a predecessor for contemporary private organizations engaged in prisoner aftercare. Charity-minded and religious groups opened halfway houses in subsequent years; two more in 1891, twenty-six by 1900, sixty-one by 1910, more than one hundred in 1920, and eight hundred by 1927 (Udo 1990, 2–3; Shikita and Tsuchiya 1990, 224).

Buddhist and Christian groups, plus the Salvation Army (their members frequently serving as voluntary prison chaplains) and some prison personnel, were especially active. Lack of sufficient resources had motivated the government to request voluntary organizations to provide assistance and moral support for ex-offenders (Satoh 1989). In 1907 the government began to supplement private sources of financial support (Udo 1990).

In 1913 the chief public prosecutor in Fukui Prefecture had a major role in organizing private citizens, largely Buddhist priests, to assist discharged offenders. By 1917 there were 140 private organizations (Hyotani 1985, 2). The Judicial Rehabilitation Service Law (1939) required private organizations to be licensed. The law called for governmental subsidies, but World War II interfered (Udo 1990; Shikita and Tsuchiya 1990). The 1950 Law for Aftercare of Discharged Offenders was substituted.

The history of Shiga Kozenkai in Shiga Prefecture begins in 1897 when the warden and chaplain of Zeze Prison (now Shiga Prison) rented a house for discharged prisoners. In 1898 the warden, governor of the prefecture, and chief public prosecutor of Shiga initiated a hostel; in 1901 a nongovernmental foundation assumed responsibility. The hostel came within the national system in 1950. In July 1980, a two-story concrete building, costing 113 million yen, was occupied and named Kofu Ryo (Light and Wind Dormitory).

Wachukai Hostel in Osaka was established in 1912 by the Federation of Buddhist Temples to serve the many prisoners granted amnesty at the death of Emperor Meiji. Its facilities were destroyed in 1945 in an air raid. A house offered makeshift quarters until two three-story buildings were constructed in 1960 and 1971. The hostel now occupies a nine-story brick building costing about 400 million yen in 1987; it has sixty-eight rooms for eighty-two residents, offices, counseling rooms, a kitchen, and dining hall. The earlier buildings have twenty-eight rooms, living quarters for staff, and a garage.

Miyagi Tokakai in Sendai was intended to serve Miyagi Prison, which had confined warriors who had fought the Meiji movement. Discharged prisoners without a home were quartered within the prison. In 1911, contributions of judges, public prosecutors, the bar association, and the Miyagi warden financed the purchase of farmland. A new two-story building was opened in 1969. In 1990 an addition expanded the capacity to thirty with two persons per sleeping room. The staff has five members, most of whom had been probation officers. Residents go to the employment security office to seek jobs. The hostel staff approach employers to obtain jobs in construction.

Korakukai Rehabilitation Aid Hostel in Itabashi-ku, Tokyo, was established in 1946 by the warden of Fuchu Prison in a residence he owned. In 1953 a rehabilitation aid association was created, and in 1968 a three-story building and warehouse were constructed. Private firms rent the warehouse and a parking lot. The facility has a capacity of twenty and a staff of four. The building has an office, a recreation room, a laundry (but the residents prefer a nearby coin laundry), a small kitchen for residents' use, a larger kitchen, a meeting room, and bathrooms.

Sinkou Kai (New Beginning House) is in Tokyo's Toshima Ward. Tsutumi Miyamoto, a newspaper reporter and voluntary prison chaplain, donated the land and financed the construction in 1952. He died in 1970; his widow is the chief guidance worker today.

Bombing during World War II and later economic difficulties forced a reduction in the number of hostels from 150 in 1958 to 98 in 1988 (Udo 1990; Shikita and Tsuchiya

1990). Ninety-six hostels were operating in 1990; thirty-four are in the Kanto Region (Tokyo). Eighty-four of the hostels are for males, only seven are for females, and five serve both sexes. Most (68) serve both adults and youths: 61 of the 84 hostels for males only, five of the seven for females only, and two of the five for both sexes.

The hostels expect their residents to find their place in the community with modest counseling and staff intervention with other agencies. The assumption is that the residents do not have serious psychological difficulties and can handle the reentry crisis without profound assistance. In that way, the hostels resemble those of the West that provide only basic support.[8]

"The halfway house has to deal with offenders who are more seriously deprived than other offenders in one way or other," according to the Rehabilitation Bureau (1990, 19). Udo (1990, 6) notes a "lack of well-qualified staff members to provide the probationers and parolees with appropriate treatment." Hyotani (1985, 33) comments: "Adequate care must be given to appropriate training of its [the rehabilitation aid association's] employees and their condition of work including their monthly salary."

The number of residents has declined considerably; the average daily population of all hostels was 3,120 in 1960 and 1,405 in 1988. The average per hostel dropped from 76 in 1960 to 58 in 1988, in spite of the reduction of the number of hostels from 158 to 98 and their authorized capacity from 4,122 to 2,400 (Udo 1990, 9). The trends reflect a budgetary crisis. Table 8.1 shows that only half of the average revenue comes from the government's subsidy. According to the Rehabilitation Bureau, "The difficulty in administering the service is being aggravated by the shortage of funds generally seen among most halfway houses. Hostels which run some profit-making businesses are in a relatively advantageous position, but they are the exception" (Rehabilitation Bureau 1990, 19).[9]

Wachukai in Osaka, the largest hostel in Japan, is among

Table 8.1
Budget of Rehabilitation Aid Hostels, 1989

Expenditure	%	Revenue	%
Personnel	37.7	National Subsidy[a]	48.7
Aid Services	25.0	Workshops	20.4
Workshop Expenses	14.3	Donations	9.3
Depreciation	2.1	Property Dividends	5.5
Construction and Repairs	5.6	Residents' Contributions[b]	6.7
Office Expenses	9.6	Local Government Subsidies	2.7
		Member Fees	1.1
		Other	5.6
Total Expenditures	94.3	Total Revenues	100.0

Source: Data provided by Rehabilitation Bureau.

Note: 1989 budget, 2,897,326,672 yen; at 130 yen per $ (U.S.), $22,287,128.

[a]Reimbursement and subsidy from the probation offices and family courts for entrusted services, office expenses, construction, and repairs.

[b]Residents' payments for lodging and board when their stay exceeded the period of service authorized by the probation office.

the exceptions: some thirty companies contribute about eight million yen a year. Korakukai, in Itabashi-ku in Tokyo, rents a storage warehouse and a paved parking lot to private companies. Miyagi Tokakai in Sendai leased part of its land in 1983 for construction of an apartment building; the lease payments are income. Keiwayen in Nakano Ward, Tokyo, rents a parking lot for four million yen annually.

CONTINUED EFFORTS TO REVISE PENAL LAW

New approaches are facilitated when the proposals fit into established relationships with some part of the society's institutional network. The next chapter considers innovation by the Rehabilitation Bureau. Here we note such efforts by the Correction Bureau, especially the long-term effort—futile to date—to make the penal law consistent with today's conditions.

Japanese prisons enjoy a very active industrial program through a relationship with private industry. A limited number of open camps, resembling the conditions of the free community in some respects, have been established through that relationship. Japan experienced a major economic crisis in the 1970s that posed a serious threat to the industrial prison. The threat became an opportunity for innovation which introduced CAPIC, the Correctional Agency Prison Industry Cooperative, as a new resource (see chapter 5).

Prolonged Preparation for Change

When framed in 1908, the Prison Law was progressive, but now it is outdated: "It has become clumsy and cumbersome in the implementation of contemporary treatment programs for prisoners as well as in the clarification of the legal status of prisoners. Some provisions do not even accord with the contemporary international standards, such as the United Nations Standard Minimum Rules for the Treatment of Prisoners" (Akatsuka 1989, 3).

Postwar changes in the Japanese society and increased complications in the operations of legal institutions convinced the Minister of Justice in 1956 to establish the Preparatory Commission for Revision of the Prison Law. Its draft was completed in 1961, but the minister initiated another study group that finished its draft in 1971 (Suzuki 1973). Reporting in 1982 that the preparatory deliberations had continued but that the Diet had yet to take any action, the Correction Bureau summarized the main principles of the proposed amendments to the Prison Law:

> (a) Prisoners' legal rights should be stated as clearly as possible in the new law. The new law should have well-defined provisions with respect to freedom of religion,

access to publications, contact with the outside world, security measures employed against prisoners, grievance mechanisms, and other matters closely related to the human rights of prisoners.

(b) Provisions in the new law related to administration and management in penal institutions should be appropriately differentiated according to the legal status of those who are in custody, such as suspects, defendants, convicted prisoners, and other detainees.

(c) The new law should include written statements for guaranteeing proper living standards for prisoners with respect to food, clothes, medical services, sanitation, etc.

(d) Provisions regarding the correctional treatment of convicted prisoners should be geared to the promotion of their successful resocialization. Therefore, the new law should incorporate clear statements on resocialization as the goal of imprisonment and the need for individualization of treatment; revise provisions with respect to classification, prison labour, academic education, living guidance, and therapeutic treatment; and introduce innovative correctional measures, such as work-release, daytime leave, and overnight leave. (Correction Bureau 1982, 14–15)

In 1985, the Correction Bureau reported that the Penal Institution Bill had been submitted to the 96th session of the Diet in 1982 but was discarded in the 100th session because of dissolution of the House of Representatives. A new bill following the principles summarized above was being prepared. Again in 1987, a bill was not approved by the Diet "due to various circumstances concerning changes in political situations and session schedules of the Diet" (Correction Bureau 1990b, 23). Scandals about political donations—including the distribution of stock of the Recruit Company—diverted the attention of the Diet members. In 1987 the draft of a Police Custodial Facilities Law also had been submitted to the Diet. The proposed law was intended to ensure the proper treatment of detainees in lockups of the prefectural police (National Statement Japan 1990). The new draft of the Prison Law was submitted the third time and was awaiting action in 1993.

A Major Obstacle: Substitute Prisons

The revision of the Prison Law would be approved by the Diet, a former director general of the Correction Bureau told me, if the issue of the "substitute prison" (the *daiyo-kangoku* system) were resolved. Article 1-3 of the Prison Law states: "The police jail may be substituted for a prison, provided that a convicted person sentenced to imprisonment at forced labor or imprisonment without forced labor shall not be detained therein continuously for one month or more" (UNAFEI n.d., 201–11). This "substitution" is relevant to revision of the Prison Law in that detention of suspects is conducted by both the police and the Correction Bureau. The linkage of the two agencies has historic roots; from 1885 to 1903 both the police and prisons were administered by the Police and Public Peace Bureau in the Ministry of Home Affairs (Correction Bureau 1967). As a second reason, Miyazawa (1992) says, the Prison Law of 1908 recognized the shortage of prisons at that time.

The Constitution of Japan (effective in 1946) specifies that no persons shall be detained without being at once informed of the charges against them, without the immediate privilege of counsel, or without adequate cause (Article 34). The constitution (Article 38) prohibits as evidence confessions made under compulsion, torture, or threat, and also confessions made after prolonged arrest or detention.

The Code of Criminal Procedure requires that the police, when detention is believed to be necessary, present evidence to the public prosecutor within forty-eight hours (Article 203). If the public prosecutor agrees that detention is appropriate, the prosecutor must request that a judge issue a warrant of detention within twenty-four hours (Article 205). The court may detain the accused when there is reasonable ground to suspect the person has committed a crime and the case falls under one of the following items: the accused has no fixed dwelling; there are reasonable grounds for suspecting the accused may destroy evidence; or the accused has previously escaped or there is a likelihood the accused may escape (Article 60). If a warrant is issued, prosecution must be initiated within ten days; when unavoidable circumstances exist, a judge (when requested) may extend detention for another ten days (Article 208).

The police prefer the daiyo-kangoku system over the Correction Bureau's detention facilities, Miyazawa (1990) discovered in his research on police practices in Japan. Among the reasons are the convenience of interrogation at the station, the greater possibility of confessions that are especially sought, the opportunity to a establish a "human relationship" with the suspect for effective interrogation, and a better chance that grounds for charges for additional crimes will be discovered in the course of interrogation. When additional charges are discovered, the police can extend the length of detention and time of interrogation for each charge.

The Japan Federation of Bar Associations (Nichibenren) insists that the substitute prisons are instruments for violating human rights and creating forced confessions (Japan Federation of Bar Associations 1990). The federation reports that the police can keep suspects for up to twenty-three days after arrest in their station lockups under physical and psychological conditions that press suspects to confess crimes even when innocent.[10]

The Ministry of Finance objects to the cost of constructing new detention facilities for the Correction Bureau. The existing detention houses are few when compared with the number of police lockups, and they may be located at a distance from the courts and police stations. Acquisition of land at appropriate locations would be difficult and very expensive. The national government would be expanding its functional obligations if the detention houses replaced all the police lockups. Opposing the claim of insufficient capacity, Igarashi (1989) says that the average daily population of the police lockups in 1982 was 5,885 and the Correction Bureau had more than enough space for them. In 1988 there were 154 detention centers and 1,254 substitute prisons, and the capacity of each type of facility exceeded the demand two or three times.

9

PROBATION: PUTTING CONVICTED OFFENDERS BACK ON THE STREET

While stemming the flow into prisons and juvenile training schools, the procuracy and judiciary return many offenders to the regularities of community life. In playing a part in this diversion, probation goes beyond simple restoration to freedom by adding supervision by representatives of the court. The monitoring duties are, first, to safeguard the community against any tendency of probationers to victimize its citizens again and, second, to guide and assist the probationers' search for a self-satisfying and responsible place in the community. Japan places heavy reliance upon volunteer probation officers to strike a fragile balance between the often opposing duties. That reliance is one of the special features of probation as practiced in Japan. We will explore other special features.

NATIONWIDE ADMINISTRATION: AN ASSESSMENT

Japan has seized the advantages of a centralized service by combining probation and parole responsibilities within the Rehabilitation Bureau. On a nationwide basis, a single agency handles all probation and parole activities (with certain exceptions noted below). Within the bureau, probation is administered by probation offices and the selection of parolees is handled by regional parole boards. The combined model, however, is followed in making supervision of both probationers and parolees the responsibility of probation officers.

A centralized service holds advantages. All parts of Japan probably receive the same level of services, policies and practices are rather uniform, and the economies of scale are obtained. Probationers and parolees are distributed unevenly about the country; the national agency is better prepared to offer the same level of service in both urban and sparsely-populated areas, especially when the same personnel supervise probationers and parolees.

Centralized service also raises the possibility that the national bureaucracy will be unresponsive to local perceptions, conditions, and qualities of clientele. Any resentment of "outsiders" will be aggravated by evidence that the local community has no influence over probation and parole programs. Social service agencies at the local area are indispensable allies, but the local agencies do not necessarily welcome the personnel and clientele of national agencies.

Combining supervision of probationers and parolees is justified by the similar arguments advanced by their respective advocates. Probation is supposed to save convicted offenders from the stigmatization and pain of forced confinement; it holds the possibility of synchronizing the release from prison with the time when the inmate is most ready to rejoin the community in a compliant temper. Probation and parole are less expensive to operate than imprisonment; they take advantage of the human services available in the community. They are more likely to have lasting influence on the offender than confinement in the artificial world of the prison. Parole and especially probation preserve family ties and enable offenders to support their dependents.

In qualities of clients and relationships with other components of the criminal justice system, probation and parole programs differ, especially in supervision of cases. If the courts divert the more promising convicted offenders from the prisons, persons under probationary supervision are better prospects than those sent to prison, but penal confinement inculcates in the prisoner a degree of docility, causing many to accept supervision apparently with less resistance than inexperienced probationers. Isolation from family and community tends to aggravate the prisoner's problems of reintegration into the community, whereas the probationer is removed from family and community rather briefly.

THE ADMINISTRATIVE NICHE ASSIGNED TO PROBATION

A fundamental difficulty for probation agencies is their marginal position between the judicial and executive branches of government; the Rehabilitation Bureau is not an exception. If probation were completely the responsibility of the courts, the judges would be able to manage probation services to their own satisfaction, might be more inclined to make use of the services, and could exert their influence in acquiring needed resources for the probation services. The Japanese courts already are strongly committed to minimizing imprisonment of convicted offenders.

In Japan, probation administration already is in the executive branch of government, but being a component of the Ministry of Justice, presumably enjoys some of the advantages of being associated with the public prosecutors. The courts are independent of the executive branch. As part of the executive branch, probation offices have reasonable access to the social services of other departments and agencies.

Administrative responsibilities usually assigned to probation agencies in other societies are not necessarily characteristic of Japan; a major example is the exclusion of Japanese probation offices from the preparation of presentence investigation reports for the courts. The presentence reports provide basic information for informed decisions by the judges whether to allow convicted offenders to stay in the community or send them to a prison or juvenile training school. Ideally, the presentence report should include a history of family, personal, social, and economic factors in the offender's life, a statement of the offense, a description of any criminal record, an evaluation of the offender's personality and potential, and a plan for treatment.

The exclusion means that the probation offices have had no previous experience with a case when it is referred to them. For juveniles, the investigators on the family court staff carry out presentence investigations, not members of the probation office. The investigators report any diagnostic information acquired by the juvenile classification homes that are in the Correction Bureau, not the Rehabilitation Bureau.

The adult courts in Japan combine fact-finding and assessing of punishment. In deciding whether or not to suspend a sentence, including the requiring of probationary supervision, the judges depend on the information provided by the public prosecutor and defense counsel, rather than gaining the advantage of the presentence report. According to Ogawa (1976, 620), "The system of presentence investigation has not been introduced in criminal courts except for juvenile delinquents who come before the family courts."[1]

Has the "Control Net" Been Widened?

Unnecessary sanctions should not be imposed on those offenders less likely to commit a serious crime if left without any formal intervention. The director general of the Rehabilitation Bureau recommends: "It is possible that a newly introduced community sanction leads to the widening of the net of social control, thereby restricting the liberty of offenders to an undue extent, increasing caseloads of criminal justice practitioners, and eventually claiming increased correctional personnel" (Sugihara 1994, 14–15). That objection has been raised generally against diversion and expanded use of probation: "The tendency of diversion and other community programs to widen the control net produces results that are increasing rather than reducing the number of individuals coming into contact with the formal criminal justice system" (Blomberg 1987, 219).

Compared to the West, Japan introduced full-fledged probation relatively recently. An upsurge of caseloads usually occurs in the early history of an innovative practice; until the 1970s, probation in Japan followed that trend (see table 9.1). Thereafter, the number of admissions stabilized and then dropped. A more precise measurement is given by the age-specific rates shown in table 9.1. For juvenile probationers, the rates have fluctuated over the decades but have dropped since 1980. Since 1960 the adult probationers have recorded a somewhat more consistent decline of age-specific rates.

A second issue centers on whether or not admissions to probation—as a form of diversion—increased at a greater rate than admissions to institutional corrections. Table 9.1 also presents the percentage share of probation admissions in the total of admissions to probation, prisons, and juvenile training schools. Juvenile probation as a share of total admissions rose considerably until 1975 and then stabilized. The same trend held until 1980 for adult probation. The early gains for probation were at the cost of institutional corrections, rather than representing a widening of the criminal justice net.

Table 9.1 also illustrates the great numerical superiority

Table 9.1
Juvenile and Adult Admissions to Probation, 1950–92

Year	No. of Admissions Juvenile	Adult	Rate of Probation[a] Juvenile	Adult	Age-Specific Rates[b] Juvenile	Adult
1950	13,291	221	65.9	0.4	128.0	0.5
1955	17,094	4,361	66.5	7.5	161.4	8.6
1960	24,408	8,525	73.1	17.2	225.6	15.2
1965	28,173	8,350	78.2	19.7	218.3	13.4
1970	27,383	6,908	87.3	21.1	256.7	9.9
1975	21,384	7,048	89.3	21.2	224.6	9.2
1980	25,684	8,058	84.5	22.1	264.3	9.9
1985	27,050	7,180	81.8	18.5	246.8	8.3
1990	23,481	4,793	84.7	17.4	198.2	5.3
1992	22,693	4,732	83.9	18.5	200.2	5.1

Sources: Shikita and Tsuchiya (1990); Research and Statistics Section (1993a; 1993b; 1993c).

[a]Admissions to probation (juvenile or adult) as a percentage of total admissions to training schools and prisons plus probation for that year.

[b]The number of admissions per 100,000 of the general population in a given age group: 14 to 20 years of age for juveniles; 20 and above for adults.

of juvenile probation over adult probation. That relationship, which is also characteristic of the West, suggests the Japanese inclination to emphasize especially the "protective" function of criminal justice when juveniles are concerned. The function is extended to the predelinquents in Japan, thereby raising the possibility of a wider control net. Japan is withdrawing from that policy. Predelinquents adjudicated by the family court were 5,096 in 1951, 7,153 in 1965, and dropped irregularly to 2,558 in 1987 (Shikita and Tsuchiya 1990, 247). The number of predelinquents on probation dropped irregularly from 1,163 in 1965 to 313 in 1993 (Research and Statistics Section 1966, 73; 1994, 73).

Two Philosophies:
Juvenile and Adult Probation

In emphasizing the "protective" function in placing juveniles on probation, the family court expresses the philosophy expressed in Article 1 of the Juvenile Law: "The object of this law is, with a view to the wholesome rearing of juveniles, to carry out the protective measures relating to the character correction and environmental adjustment of delinquent juveniles and also to take special measures with respect to the criminal cases of juveniles and adults who are harmful to the welfare of juveniles."

"In Japan there are two kinds of probationary supervision as alternatives to institutional treatment," Kouhashi (1985, 1) declares. "One is for juveniles, while the other is directed mainly toward adults." Article 24 of the Juvenile Law authorizes the family court to place juveniles under probationary supervision of the probation office.

The family court's philosophy of probationary supervision is fleshed out in Article 35 of the Offenders Rehabilitation Law: "The persons placed under probationary supervision shall be guided and supervised by the following methods: (1) to watch the behavior of the person under probationary supervision by keeping proper contact with him; (2) to give the person under probationary supervision such instructions as are deemed necessary. . . . (3) to take other measures necessary to aid him to become a law-abiding member of the society." The ideal of the Juvenile Law is not to administer punishment according to the nature and seriousness of the offense but to provide guidance, care, protection, and education. "Today, most juvenile delinquents are treated by non-punitive, protective measures rather than punitive measures," Kouhashi (1985, 7) explains. "Probationary supervision is the prevailing measure among the protective measures provided by the law."

The philosophy of adult probation takes a different tack

that takes it more toward the punitive end of the treatment versus punishment continuum. Probation of adult offenders emerged in Japan, rather incidentally, as a possibility of the judge's authority to suspend a sentence under certain conditions specified below. The suspensions may return the convicted offender to the free community without restrictions or may add the requirement that the individual be subject to probationary supervision. The severity of punishment in practice, Nishikawa (1990, 9) points out, "goes up from fine to suspended execution of sentence without supervision, probation, and actual imprisonment."

Along that continuum of severity among the court's dispositions, probationary supervision hovers between outright release of the convicted offender and the penalties associated with penal incarceration. In that context the judges see probation as more punitive than outright release. When extenuating circumstances exist beyond those justifying the suspension of a prison sentence, the judges prefer to return the convicted offenders to the streets *without* probationary supervision.

In addition to the inconvenience of being subject to supervision by the probation office, the offender will be denied another suspension if a new crime is committed while on probation. If granted a suspension for the earlier crime without being placed on probation, the person committing a new crime still has the possibility of receiving a suspension.

The authority to suspend is limited to sentences of no more than three years; the limitation restricts the use of probation. The period of suspension is not less than a year nor more than five years from the day when the sentence is finally binding.

The penal code specifies that the person either must not have been previously sentenced to prison or, if previously sentenced to prison, has not been sentenced again within five years from the day when the execution of that punishment was completed or remitted. In the first instance, the sentencing judge may order "protective supervision," but that order is mandatory only in the second instance. If a person had been sentenced previously to prison, and then receives a prison sentence of no more than one year within the period of the earlier suspension, a new suspension may still be granted in the event of extenuating circumstances.

SIGNIFICANCE OF
PROBATION RATES

Suspensions with probation, in the period 1981 through 1992, have declined in number (see table 9.2, column A). The rates of revocations of all suspended sentences (both columns C and D) have fluctuated but have declined to a modest extent. Over those twelve years, the rates of revocations for suspensions with probation (column D) have exceeded the rates for suspensions without probation (column C) by more than two and one-half times.

What may we conclude from the higher failure rate of probation cases? Perhaps the judges' doubts about those cases are confirmed, but transgressions in supervised cases are much more likely to be detected and reported than for unsupervised persons. Most of the revocations were ordered because of a new crime committed during suspension (a violation under the Penal Code, Article 26-2-1). The data specify reasons for a few of the revocations without attributing them to either of the two brands of revocation. For example, 158 revocations in 1981 were due to commission of a crime previous to the suspension (Article 26-2); 110 for violations of probation conditions (Article 26-2-2); and 16 entailed having received more than one prior suspension (Article 26-3), being fined (Article 26-2-1), or being under concurrent suspension for another crime (Article 26-3).

The Japanese judges' negative opinion of probation stands in sharp contrast to the Western tradition that probation is an instrument of casework practice for helping to

Table 9.2

Suspension of Prison Sentences with Probation and Revocation of Suspensions, 1981–92

Year	A	B	C	D	E	F	G
1981	8,338	18.5	10.4	26.2	158	110	16
1982	8,215	18.6	11.4	28.4	159	92	17
1983	7,711	17.0	9.9	29.8	121	108	18
1984	7,647	16.8	10.5	29.6	172	99	10
1985	7,136	16.0	10.0	28.8	155	101	20
1986	6,381	14.8	10.1	30.1	147	88	9
1987	6,438	15.2	9.5	28.4	114	109	12
1988	6,074	15.6	10.0	28.3	101	129	12
1989	5,179	14.3	8.9	28.5	94	90	10
1990	4,774	13.7	8.3	26.5	94	87	7
1991	4,647	14.2	8.3	25.5	69	111	9
1992	4,696	14.3	8.4	24.2	90	110	13

Sources: Research and Training Institute (1984; 1987; 1990; 1993).

Note: Column headings are as follows:
   A. Number of Suspensions with Probation
   B. Percentage of Total Suspensions with Probation
   C. Revocation of Simple Suspension for New Offense
   D. Revocation of Suspension with Probation for New Offense
   E. Revocation for Conviction for Previous Offense
   F. Violation of Suspension Conditions
   G. Other Reasons for Revocations

meet the offender's needs and thereby terminate the criminal career. Probation also has a control function; balancing the help and control functions raises difficulties for any kind of intervention with "problem people," whether medically ill, economically underprivileged, or lawbreakers. Recent developments in the West have turned probation work increasingly toward the control function and closer to the negative perception characteristic of Japanese judges.

The suspended sentence of imprisonment is one of the major dispositions of adult cases in England: 40 percent of those suspended cases involve another imprisonable offense within two years, and 75 percent of suspensions are tied to a new custodial sentence. Bottoms and McWilliams (1979, 182–83) conclude that "the suspended sentence is a distinctly two-edged weapon in terms of its apparent contribution as a diversionary sentence." When probation officers recommend a suspended sentence, they do not "appreciate" that, as an ultimate effect, the recommendations "could well be to send an offender where he might otherwise not have finished up."

Two American studies also have reached the conclusion that probation has become more punitive. In California the number of probationers has grown to exceed the prison population, especially for serious offenders, and probation officers are scrambling for resources: "The purpose of probation has changed from the use of treatment and rehabilitation to keep the offenders out of prison, to one in which the purpose is to use probation as a means of reducing pressure on prison populations" (Lemert 1993, 449). Couch (1993) notes two contrasting trends in the United States: the tougher conditions for probation and the amelioration of the deprivations of imprisonment. The result is that offenders are less likely to prefer probation to imprisonment. In his survey, two-thirds of male felons in Texas prisons preferred a year in prison to ten years on probation and 32 percent preferred a year in prison to three years on probation.

Differential Use of Probation among Crimes

Many factors enter the judge's decision: first, whether or not to suspend a prison sentence and, second, whether the suspension should entail probationary supervision. Although not a substitute for a study of the combination of factors in each case, a comparison of admissions to probation with the crimes for which they were granted offers a general summary of the court's probable evaluation of candidates for a suspension.

Table 9.3 permits an examination of the dual relationship between the crime and the decision to grant a suspension with probation. First, the various crimes take up different shares of the caseload; the percentage distribution of the crimes in table 9.3 records that representation among persons entering the program in 1993. Second, admissions to probation are compared with admissions to correctional institutions. The rates in the table reflect the courts' estimation of the offenders in selecting probation versus prison or training school. Japanese judges are reluctant to require probation when a prison sentence is suspended, but they also view commitment to a correctional institution to be more stern than referral to the probation office.

Juveniles have greater access to probation than adults, as table 9.3 indicates, both in the number of cases and also in the rate of probation admissions among admissions to probation and to correctional institutions combined.

The juvenile and adult programs differ in the percentage distribution of 1993 admissions according to major crime categories. Traffic offenders dominate all other categories of juvenile probationers at 47.6 percent but constitute only 15.8 percent of adult admissions; the special probation program for juvenile traffic offenders is discussed below. Property offenders draw the highest share (40.1 percent) of adult probationers, primarily for larceny and fraud. Larceny is also important in the juvenile cases (26.2 percent) but is in second place behind traffic violations.

Drug offenders are more prevalent among adults (24.5 percent) than juveniles (8.5 percent); stimulants are the primary choice of adults, and organic substances (especially paint thinner) of juveniles. Violence against persons held a small share of probationers but, mostly because of minor cases of bodily injury, were more numerous than societal

Table 9.3

Juvenile and Adult Admissions to Probation, by Crime, 1993

Offense	Juvenile Probation			Adult Probation		
	No.	%	Rate[a]	No.	%	Rate[b]
Violence Against Persons	1,691	8.5	72.9	371	7.5	11.4
Bodily Injury	(1,457)	(7.4)	(77.0)	(301)	(6.1)	(23.9)
Robbery, Simple	(62)	(0.3)	(53.9)	(35)	(0.7)	(11.3)
Robbery, Other	(166)	(6.8)	(59.9)	(5)	(0.1)	(1.7)
Homicide	(5)	(0.0)	(16.7)	(24)	(0.5)	(5.2)
Other	(1)	(0.0)	(66.7)	(6)	(0.1)	(15.9)
Societal Violence	984	5.0	76.0	298	6.01	16.5
Extortion	(638)	(3.2)	(74.6)	(204)	(4.1)	(21.0)
Violent Act	(170)	(0.9)	(73.0)	(29)	(0.6)	(8.6)
Assault	(116)	(0.6)	(84.7)	(15)	(0.3)	(16.5)
Firearms	(24)	(0.1)	(77.4)	(41)	(0.8)	(11.2)
Other	(76)	(0.2)	(92.3)	(9)	(0.2)	(16.7)
Property	5,180	26.2	74.7	1,993	40.1	20.0
Larceny	(4,893)	(24.1)	(74.3)	(1,636)	(32.9)	(21.8)
Embezzlement	(103)	(0.5)	(87.3)	(32)	(0.7)	(14.5)
Intrusion	(81)	(0.4)	(81.0)	(49)	(1.0)	(20.8)
Fraud	(36)	(0.2)	(78.3)	(198)	(4.0)	(12.3)
Other	(67)	(0.2)	(78.8)	(78)	(1.5)	(18.5)
Sex	167	0.8	49.0	135	2.7	18.6
Rape	(67)	(0.3)	(32.1)	(68)	(1.4)	(14.5)
Forcible Assault	(97)	(0.5)	(76.4)	(57)	(1.1)	(23.8)
Pornography	(3)	(0.0)	(60.0)	(10)	(0.2)	(23.8)
Drugs	1,606	8.1	73.2	1,192	24.0	16.8
Organic Substances	(1,243)	(6.3)	(84.3)	(91)	(1.8)	(100.0)
Stimulants	(358)	(1.8)	(50.3)	(1,088)	(21.9)	(15.8)
Narcotics	(5)	(0.0)	(62.5)	(13)	(0.3)	(13.5)
Traffic	9,420	47.6	94.6	786	15.8	28.5
Perdelinquency	313	1.6	73.1	—	—	—
Other[c]	435	2.2	84.8	193	3.9	16.0
Total	19,796	100.0	82.4	4,968	100.0	18.9

Sources: Research and Statistics (1994a; 1994b; 1994c).

[a]Juvenile probation admissions as a percentage of admissions to juvenile training schools and probation.

[b]Adult probation admissions as a percentage of admissions to prisons and probation.

[c]Includes crimes of prostitution, gambling, public order, other penal, and and special laws.

violence. The latter form of violence violates communal interests by physical aggression or disturbances of the peace. Sex crimes, especially rape, were a small share of probation cases, especially for juveniles. Predelinquents received juvenile probation but constituted a small number of the cases.

Measured by the rates in table 9.3, traffic offenses held the greatest advantage in receipt of probation over referrals to correctional institutions. The traffic crisis of Japan brought about criminalization of the most serious traffic law violators, but doubts lingered about imprisoning them. Property offenses, largely larceny, recorded a high proportion of probation cases and, especially for adults, a greater rate of probation over institutionalization than most other crimes. Societal violence drew a small share of juvenile probationers, mostly because extortion cases were proportionally fewer than for adults. The crime of assault held a small share of juvenile probation cases and would have been even less significant if that general offense did not include unlawful assembly with weapons. That form of misconduct covers the public disturbances of the bosozoku among juvenile traffic offenders. Juvenile violence against persons—as well as for adult offenders—had a lower rate.

Drug crimes of adults were heavily represented in the number of probationers, but the rates indicate that the judges preferred granting probation to traffic and property offenders. Rape offenses held down the rate of probation of sex offenders, whether juvenile or adult.

The distribution of crimes for which probation has been granted over the years may help to answer the question of whether or not the "control net" of probation has been widened. In the years 1970–90, drug and traffic crimes assumed unprecedented importance because of the passage of laws designed to control them. When the two offenses are removed, the remaining number of adult probationers declined consistently and considerably over the years (see table 9.4). The drop for juvenile probationers also was considerable but less consistent (see table 9.5).

Table 9.4

Adult Probation Admissions, by Crime, 1970–90

Offense	1970	1975	1980	1985	1990
	Percentage of Admissions for All Crimes[a]				
Property	46.2	46.3	37.9	41.1	41.8
Violence Against Persons	12.4	10.0	6.2	6.4	8.6
Societal Violence	14.4	10.2	6.0	5.1	5.1
Traffic	12.3	18.5	23.3	20.6	21.3
Sex	8.4	4.5	3.1	2.1	2.4
Gambling	2.7	1.6	0.7	0.5	0.6
Drugs	0.7	7.8	22.2	23.7	19.2
Prostitution	2.9	1.1	0.6	0.5	0.6
Total	100.0	100.0	100.0	100.0	100.0
No.	6,738	6,830	7,841	7,004	4,665
Age-Specific Rate[b]	9.9	9.2	9.9	8.3	5.3
	Percentage of Admissions Excluding Drug and Traffic Crimes[a]				
Property	53.1	62.9	69.5	73.7	70.3
Violence Against Persons	14.3	13.6	11.4	11.4	14.4
Societal Violence	16.5	13.8	11.0	9.2	8.6
Sex	9.7	6.1	5.8	3.8	4.0
Gambling	3.0	2.2	1.2	1.0	1.7
Prostitution	3.4	1.4	1.1	0.9	1.0
Total	100.0	100.0	100.0	100.0	100.0
No.	5,863	5,034	4,273	3,902	2,774
Age-Specific Rate[b]	8.4	6.6	5.3	4.5	3.0

Sources: Research and Statistics Section, *Annual Report of Statistics on Rehabilitation* for given years.

[a]Data excludes public order, other penal law, and other special law offenses.

[b]Rate of admissions per 100,000 Japanese, age 20 and over, for these crimes.

For admissions to adult probation, traffic and drug offenses sharply increased. About 12 percent of traffic offenders were admitted to probation in 1970 and 21 percent in 1990. Drug offenders were less numerous, but their upsurge as probationers was much greater: from less than 1 percent in 1970 to 19 percent in 1990. Violations of the stimulant-drug control law were the primary adult drug crime.

Age-specific rates relate probation granted in a given year to the total population from which the probationers are drawn. For adult probationers that population consists of all Japanese twenty years of age or older. As shown in table 9.4, the rates generally declined except in 1980. With drug and traffic cases removed, the rates were consistently reduced.

With traffic offenses included, property offenses of adults were most numerous in receiving probation. That pattern is expected; the irregular decline is noteworthy. Removal of traffic and drug crimes strengthens the numerical dominance and percentage share of property offenses. The trend represents a movement away from granting probation for more serious offenses. The decline in the violent crimes' share of probation cases was preserved. Violence against persons surpassed societal violence by 1990 because of an upsurge in bodily injury cases. Robbery and homicide cases were too few in number to raise the share of violence against persons among the total offenses of probationers. Extortion, the major offense classified as societal violence, dropped sharply over the years. Sex crimes were primarily rape and lost share consistently. Probationers were few for prostitution and gambling.

Juvenile probation maintained over the years its sizeable numerical superiority over adult probation, but the fluctuation in the number of juveniles was rather irregular (see table 9.5). Removal of the traffic and drug offenders greatly cuts the remaining number on probation, but the irregularity over the years persists. The age-specific rates for juvenile probationers, as expected, were higher than for

Table 9.5
Juvenile Probation Admissions, by Crime, 1970–90

Offense	1970	1975	1980	1985	1990
	Percentage of Admissions for All Crimes[a]				
Property	27.5	24.7	25.9	30.6	26.5
Violence Against Persons	6.4	5.2	6.2	6.6	7.1
Societal Violence	6.6	5.5	7.1	5.0	4.2
Traffic	52.6	59.2	45.2	43.7	48.8
Sex	3.9	2.8	1.9	1.2	0.9
Gambling	0.0	0.0	0.0	0.0	0.0
Drugs	0.0	0.3	10.6	9.4	9.9
Prostitution	0.1	0.1	0.0	0.1	0.1
Predelinquency	2.9	2.2	3.1	3.4	2.5
Total	100.0	100.0	100.0	100.0	100.0
No.	27,088	20,671	24,873	26,659	23,138
Age-Specific Rate[b]	253.9	217.1	256.0	243.2	195.3
	Percentage of Admissions Excluding Drug and Traffic Crimes[a]				
Property	58.1	61.0	58.5	65.2	64.1
Violence Against Persons	13.4	12.9	13.9	14.0	17.1
Societal Violence	14.0	13.6	16.2	10.7	10.2
Sex	8.2	6.9	4.3	2.5	2.3
Gambling	0.0	0.1	0.0	0.1	0.1
Prostitution	0.3	0.2	0.1	0.2	0.1
Predelinquency	6.0	5.3	7.0	7.3	6.1
Total	100.0	100.0	100.0	100.0	100.0
No.	12,825	8,360	10,992	12,497	9,564
Age-Specific Rate[b]	120.9	87.8	113.1	114.0	80.7

Sources: Research and Statistics Section, *Annual Report of Statistics on Rehabilitation* for given years.

[a]Data excludes public order, other penal law, and other special law offenses.

[b]Rate of admissions per 100,000 Japanese, age 14 to 20, for these crimes.

adults. The elimination of drug and traffic offenses halved the age-specific rates yet failed to improve their consistency over the years, but the general trend was downward.

Traffic offenders were especially represented among juvenile probationers, but drug offenses were initially fewer than for adults and only became numerous for juveniles after the 1970s. These were the offenses receiving most attention in official efforts to deal with a perceived crisis of escalating juvenile delinquency. In the fluctuating juvenile admissions to probation, property offenders are most numerous when traffic and drug cases are removed. In that respect, the elimination of the traffic and drug cases would leave the current probation caseload with property offenses in their usual preeminent position among the offenses of probationers. Bodily injury incidents were especially instrumental in the upsurge of violence against persons. Chiefly because of fewer cases of extortion among probation cases, societal violence lost importance over the years. Predelinquency, exclusive to juveniles, was rather stable in maintaining a modest share of probation admissions over the years. Sex offenses also had a modest share that declined consistently. Gambling and prostitution drew too few juvenile probationers to establish a trend.

Program for Juvenile Traffic Offenders

Since World War II, car ownership in Japan has expanded greatly and produced a crisis of traffic fatalities and injuries. Young reckless drivers (the bosozoku) became a target of official concern because they drove vehicles without mufflers, illegally modified automobiles and motorcycles as symbols of gang affiliation, raced on wide roads in urban centers, and fought for territorial control. The bosozoku are more prone to being sent to juvenile training schools than to being granted probation by family courts. In 1991 they held 11.7 percent of probation admissions and

19.4 percent of training school admissions (Research and Training Institute 1992, 167; 1993, 118).

A short-term program was introduced in 1977 for selected juvenile traffic offenders who had been convicted in family court for violations of the road traffic law and for traffic incidents causing death or injury. Admissions to the program were 33,083 in 1981, 44,361 in 1985, and 50,298 in 1990 (Research and Training Institute 1984, 160; 1987, 159; 1992, 166).

On recommendation of the family court, the probation office requires these juveniles to attend two group sessions conducted by professional probation officers (PPOs) and report to the probation office each month for four months. The verbal report is supplemented by a simple written report in which the juvenile is required to answer questions such as: What did you do this month? Did you drive this month? Do you have a problem that you should discuss with the probation officer?

At the intake session, the program is explained and the conditions specified. After three or four months, the second session deals with the responsibilities of drivers and the importance of traffic safety, and an audiovisual discussion of ways to avoid traffic accidents is presented. Discussion groups are organized to separate certain kinds of traffic offenders: those who operated vehicles without driver's license versus those possessing the license, the bosozoku versus the nonbosozoku, or offenders convicted of professional negligence causing death or injury versus those not resulting in death or injury. After the second session, the probation officer can terminate supervision if the monthly reports have been satisfactory. A few juveniles are kept under supervision for a usual maximum of six months. Probationary supervision for more than six months must be authorized by the family court.

For the eleven years 1981 through 1991, the juvenile traffic probationers grew from 44,698 to 58,657, while the nontraffic admissions declined from 14,516 to 12,027. The second important trend has been the growing dominance of the short-term program for juvenile traffic offenders over the regular handling of juvenile traffic probationers. Among all admissions to probation of juvenile traffic offenders, the short-term program drew 74 percent in 1981 and 81.9 percent in 1991 (Research and Training Institute 1984, 160; 1987, 159; 1990, 182; 1992, 166).

ADJUSTING TO CHANGE: CLASSIFICATION

Ideally, case classification will identify the needs and characteristics of the probationers and parolees at time of their first appearance at the probation office. Then the individual is assigned for supervision. In Japan, those purposes hold for both probationers and parolees whose supervision are the responsibility of the probation offices. The initial assessment is of particular importance in Japan because the probation offices do not have prior experience with the individuals now added to their caseload. As noted earlier in this chapter, probation officers in Japan do not prepare presentence reports (a responsibility usually assigned the probation officers in other countries) and have not contacted those persons who later appear at the probation office.

The new probationer or parolee is instructed to report immediately to the probation office for the first interview by the PPO. Juvenile and adult probationers arrive from court without appointment. The day of release of parolees is known in advance and, unlike probationers, information developed at the prison or training school is already available (Maruyama 1985).

After assessing the needs and special problems of the individual, the PPO prepares a treatment plan and mails a copy of the case record to the volunteer probation officer (VPO). The VPO submits a monthly report to the probation office and a special written report when an unusual incident occurs. The PPO may react with a letter, telephone call, or visit to the VPO, may summon the client to the probation office, or go to the client's home (Hirata 1985). The PPO meets with the probationer or parolee in such events as failure to find a job, suspicion of drug abuse, or missing a visit to the VPO (Maruyama 1985).

Implemented in 1971, a more sophisticated system of classification has been introduced in the probation offices in Tokyo and Osaka. For probationers and parolees, except traffic offenders, the classification system differentiates between group-A persons who are expected to raise behavioral difficulties requiring more intensive treatment and group-B persons expected to raise few behavioral difficulties because they do not have acute problems. The criteria for differentiation are as follows:

Juvenile probationers and parolees are grouped by ages 15, 16–17, and 18 years or more. Offenses are distinguished by paint-thinner abuse, property offenses, predelinquency, heinous crimes (murder and robbery), violent, sex, and stimulant-drug crimes, and other offenses. Also considered are family problems, the guardian's ability to protect the juvenile, problems such as running away from home and vagrancy, drug abuse history, and a history of institutionalization.

Adult probationers are grouped by ages 22 or less, 23–29, 30–39, and 40 or above. Offenses are distinguished by theft, heinous crimes, violent crimes, and others. Also considered are the family status, such as living with a spouse or parent versus in a hostel, marital status, frequent changes of address, unstable household income, or affiliation with yakuza, problems with personality or intelligence, history of institutionalization, inadequate conduct during prior supervision, and unstable employment.

Adult parolees are grouped by ages 29 or less, 30–39, 40–49, 50–59, and 60 or above. Offenses are distinguished by (a) theft, (b) property crimes except theft, (c) robbery, violent crimes, and drug related crimes, and (d) other offenses. Length of parole is for less than two months, less than six months, less than a year, or over a year. Adult parolees also are categorized according to family status: living with spouse, in a hostel, single and living with parents, or other arrangements. Other general criteria are frequent changes of address, affiliation with yakuza, drug or alcohol abuse, more than five convictions, inadequate conduct in prior supervision, and unstable employment.

As a resource supplementing the judgments of PPOs, a rating scale was developed for differentiating group-A from group-B probationers or parolees. Particular points are awarded according to specified qualities of the individual or his or her situation. If the total points exceed eighteen, the individual is considered a type-A requiring intensive supervision. The score is considered advisory and to be ignored, in favor of personal assessment, in certain situations. PPOs are authorized to change the ratings from A to B or from B to A when experience with a client justifies. When the score exceeds eighteen, the individuals nevertheless may be rated as type-B if they exhibit strong commitment to be rehabilitated, their lifestyles and activities are stable in a positive way, support persons or guardians exert positive influences, or PPO intervention is deemed unnecessary.

When the score is less than eighteen, the offenders nevertheless may be rated as type-A if they have marked drug or alcohol addiction, are members of an organized criminal group, or have strong antisocial attitudes or mental illness that complicates their social adjustment. Juveniles who have been violent in school or in family relations, or otherwise have grave difficulties with other members of these groups, and persons aged 14 to 16 who have been violent in peer relations may also may be rated as type-A; so too may parolees if they have served long prison terms or if the probation officer is expected to cope with other special conditions.

Eight items constitute the evaluation scheme for juvenile probationers and parolees, with the items varying in points awarded. The younger the offender is at admission to the program, the less favorable the rating: 15 years or less, three points; 16–17 years, two points; 18–20 years, zero points; but, if the individual has been sniffing paint thinner, four points are added.

The type of offense draws points: two points for a property crime (theft) because recidivism is likely and for predelinquency because a strong need for "protective measures" is implied. Because these offenses are very unlikely to be repeated, zero points are given for "heinous" offenses, violent offenses, sex offenses, and stimulant-drug abuse; other offenses draw three points.

Family conflict draws three points; no conflict, one point. When parents are unable to control their child, three points are awarded; one point when parents exert control. A history of running away from home draws two points; absence of this conduct, one point. Two points are awarded for a history of drug abuse; one point for no drug abuse. Previous experience at juvenile training schools receives five points; no such record receives no points.

For adult parolees, age at admission is supposed to have predictive value; two points are awarded for ages 29 years or less and 40–49 years of age. Ages 30–39 or 50–59 years receive one point; persons aged 60 years or more receive zero points. Adult property offenders (theft) are given four points; other property offenders and murderers, two points. Robbery, violent offenses, and drug offenses receive zero points because experience indicates recidivism is unlikely. Drug offenders who have been drug free in prison for a considerable time are expected to return to the habit while on parole; alcohol or drug addicts get an additional two points, and none are given for nonaddicts. Recidivists receive two points and none are given for the nonrecidivist.

If supervision will be less than two months, zero points are given; one point for a period two to six months; five points for a period of six to twelve months; and three points for more than a year. Persons rejoining a spouse receive no points; one point for residence in a hostel; two points for a single person living with parents; and three points for any other residential arrangement. Other social factors draw special points: five points for an unstable living situation in the family and employment sectors, four points for affiliation with an organized criminal group, and three points for a problem in the person's occupation and poor performance on previous probation.

USUAL PROCEDURES
IN SUPERVISION

Supervision is an exercise in interaction between two individuals: the first person representing the fragile balance between control and empathic assistance and the second person presumably trying to find acceptance and new ways of satisfying personal needs. Tacit bargaining seeps beyond the coercion usually attributed to representatives of criminal law. Official rules shape the relationship, but the inclinations of particular persons and the social situations of supervision shape the ultimate outcome of probation. The Japanese culture inserts benevolence and paternalism into the supervisory situation.

The Offenders Rehabilitation Law specifies certain conditions for the probationer: to live at a fixed residence and engage in an honest calling, to be of good behavior, to keep away from persons with criminal or delinquent tendencies, and to ask the supervisor for permission in changing residence or going on a long journey. In revocations, the chief of the probation officer submits a written report to the court and requests an arrest warrant.

The new probationer is instructed to report immediately to the probation office for the first interview by the PPO. After assessing the needs and special problems of the individual, the PPO prepares a treatment plan and mails a copy of the case record to the VPO. The VPO submits a monthly report to the probation office and a special written report when an unusual incident occurs. The length of supervision ranges from one to five years as specified by the court for suspension of sentence. For juveniles the legally prescribed maximum period of supervision is until age twenty or two years, whichever is longer (Rehabilitation Bureau 1990, 23).

Supervision is carried out chiefly by VPOs who report to the PPOs. Sometimes the PPO advises the VPO that certain actions should be undertaken. That arrangement has been customary; in 1992 there were 600 PPOs, about 50,000 VPOs, and 70,000 clients. PPOs were eager to try direct supervision, but the clients were too few for widespread supervision by the PPOs. The probation officers told me of the administrative tasks of the usual PPOs that, in my opinion, lack the pleasures and frustrations of "people work." Some two hundred monthly reports of VPOs are evaluated and filed, and inquiries of the courts and police are answered. Some reports necessitate direct PPO interviews of the probationer or parolee. Unsatisfactory conduct may require a formal revocation; favorable behavior involves a recommendation for early termination. New VPOs are given initial training; established VPOs are interviewed when case developments require.

In 1960 the Ministry of Justice issued an administrative note about the escalating number of serious crimes by juveniles and the necessity to strengthen supervision of juveniles prone to such offenses. In an experiment from 1961 to 1963, PPOs supervised 50 probationers; VPOs supervised 150 probationers and reported developments to PPOs. After the experiment, "onset supervision" was introduced in 1965 in Tokyo, Osaka, and Nagoya (Shikita and Tsuchiya 1990). In onset supervision, the PPOs supervise the especially difficult cases directly for one to three months. In that period, the PPO is expected to diagnose the probationer or parolee and assess the personal problems. When turning over supervision, the PPO advises the VPO on how to manage the case.

Direct Supervision by PPOs

Since 1974, Tokyo and Osaka have employed direct supervision, a new approach whereby several PPOs supervise cases selected as raising unusual difficulties.[2] For example, some sex offenders present themselves as though they were models of obedience while actually resisting the supervision. Direct supervision is sometimes undertaken when neighborhood stigmatization of the client is of unusual concern. New PPOs are assigned for two years to direct supervision as a phase of on-the-job training.

Five PPOs in the Tokyo office supervise an average of 20 cases, compared with the 150 or so cases managed through VPOs. In family counseling, members of the offender's family are invited to the probation office to determine whether they have contributed to the offender's misconduct and to cultivate a favorable family environment. Social-skill training is intended to teach the client ways of winning the cooperation of others.

At day offices PPOs meet briefly with selected probationers and parolees, members of their families, VPOs, school teachers, employers, and the like. Biweekly sessions are held in a municipal office, public hall, or youth center convenient to the interviewees. These day offices serve usual probation functions, unlike the eighty day centers that existed in England and Wales by the early 1980s. The British centers are intermediary between orthodox probation and incarceration for chronic but less serious offenders who lack living skills, are socially isolated, and often dependent on drugs and alcohol. Program content varies among instruction in social and living conditions, recreational activities, and practical skills such as carpentry and home duties. Massachusetts and Connecticut introduced similar centers in the late 1980s (Vass 1990; Parent 1990).

Japanese judges may recommend direct supervision, but the director of the probation office makes the decisions. The offenders receiving direct supervision are in group A in the classification system described above. They tend to exhibit certain characteristics. First, they may suffer from a mental disorder that is sufficient to complicate relationships with others but does not require hospitalization: antisocial personality, borderline personality, passive-aggressive, schizoid, or narcissistic personality. Second, the individual may suffer difficulties in interpersonal relationships or borderline intellectual functions that do not qualify as mental disorders. Third, gross environmental handicaps, such as parent-child conflict or mental disorder of parents, demand attention. Fourth, they may have difficulties in adjusting to Japanese society because they are foreigners. The probationers or parolees placed in direct supervision are juveniles, predominately. Four such cases illustrate the kinds of offenders selected for the program.[3]

A male, age nineteen, threatened a taxi driver with a knife and robbed him. He has been diagnosed as a borderline personality. His mother deserted the family when he was one year old; his alcoholic father died when the offender was thirteen. The youth is irrational, lacks emotional control, and is egocentric. After junior high school, he became dependent on a brother, aged twenty-one years, economically as well as psychologically. A suicidal gesture and the robbery were attempts to attract the brother's concern.

Diagnosed as a schizoid personality, an eighteen-year-old male seriously knifed another male who had addressed him abusively and assaulted him. He and his family fled to Japan from war-torn Cambodia when he was eleven. The family has been severely handicapped economically in Japan and otherwise has had serious adjustment difficulties. He has exhibited immaturity, pessimism, and introversion. He has failed to adjust himself in school and employment. Gradually, he became violent in interrelations with others.

An eighteen-year-old male has an IQ of 61 and suffers

a negative self-image affecting his relationships with the opposite sex, apparently motivating his offense: indecency through compulsion with a young girl. He shoplifted several times. In a sheltered workshop, his unsatisfactory relationships with colleagues imposed stress upon him.

Member of a well-to-do family, a seventeen-year-old male has been addicted to drugs. His parents are physicians and pressed him to become a doctor also. The demands are not matched by his abilities. He dropped out from school and has accepted his parents' judgment that he is a failure. He turned to drugs to fill the vacuum of his life.

Once a month, a psychologist from the National Mental Health Center, Ministry of Social Welfare, consults with the personnel of the Tokyo Probation Office. Dossiers on selected problematic cases are sent to the psychologist in advance. The case conferences are open to all personnel. The direct supervision unit contributes most of the cases. A former research specialist at the Mental Health Center, now a professor in social welfare, offers similar consultation services and instructs staff in interviewing and case management.

BRINGING SUPERVISION
TO AN END

The routine completion of probationary supervision appears to be signaled by the term "expiration of supervision," but the interpretation of the term must recognize two allied concepts: "extinction of punishment" and "statutory limitations." The allied concepts lend a message of forgiveness unusual in criminal justice administration, but they also obstruct reliable assessment of case outcomes.

Together extinction and statutory limitation are used to eliminate from administrative records, after passing of the appropriate time, certain probationers and parolees who have not satisfied the conditions for probationary supervision. For extinction of punishment, the Penal Code, Article 34-2 states in part: "When ten years have elapsed since a person served out his sentence of imprisonment without forced labor or a heavier punishment or he was excused from execution of such punishment without receiving another sentence to a fine or graver punishment, the sentence shall lose its effect." Article 27 states: "When a period of suspension elapses without the revocation of the pronouncement of suspension of execution of sentence, the sentence loses its effect." For statutory limitation, Article 32 sets the number of years that must pass before the satisfaction of a penalty for a crime will be declared: thirty years for a death penalty, twenty years for a sentence of prison for life, fifteen years for a prison sentence of ten years or more, ten years for a prison sentence of three years or more, and five years for a prison sentence less than three years (UNAFEI n.d., 41–80).

Through the two concepts, the state gives back to the offenders their respectable reputation after the specified period of time has passed. Escapes from prison are very rare, but escapes will not be prosecuted if the escapees are not apprehended within the statutory number of years related to the prison sentence from which they escaped. More to the point, a probation or parole case may be removed from the active files of the probation office after the required amount of time has passed for the given offense. Without a justification for case success, certain case developments are treated as expiration of term: disappeared, arrest, and other. In "other," the supervision period has been completed without the contracts for evaluation of conduct because the clients were hospitalized for illness or mental disorder or because of other unusual circumstances.

Probation in Japan makes unusual provisions for early lifting of supervision as a reward for meritorious behavior. For juvenile probationers, "suspension for good behavior" is authorized by the Offenders Rehabilitation Law. As table 9.6 illustrates, the device is rarely used. The chief of the pro-

Table 9.6
Outcome of Juvenile and Adult Probation, 1993

| | Juvenile Probation | | | | Adult Probation | |
| | General Program | | Traffic Program | | | |
Outcome	No.	%	No.	%	No.	%
Expiration	2,437	19.7	768	7.1	2,194	43.8
Good Behavior	(724)	(5.8)	(198)	(1.8)	(1,283)	(25.6)
Average Behavior	(1,618)	(13.1)	(535)	(5.0)	(876)	(17.5)
Bad Behavior	(95)	(0.8)	(35)	(0.3)	(35)	(0.7)
Extinction	614	4.9	184	1.7	555	11.1
Disappeared(A)	(406)	(3.3)	(122)	(1.1)	(390)	(7.8)
Arrest(A)	(82)	(0.7)	(12)	(0.1)	(20)	(0.4)
Other(A)	(126)	(1.0)	(50)	(0.5)	(145)	(2.9)
Revocation	1,880	15.2	615	5.7	1,357	27.1
Suspension	7,469	60.2	9,204	85.5	899	18.0
Good Behavior	(3)	(0.0)	(3)	(0.0)	(—)	(—)
Early Termination	(7,466)	(60.2)	(9,201)	(85.5)	(—)	(—)
Provisional	(—)	(—)	(—)	(—)	(899)	(18.0)
Total	12,400	100.0	10,771	100.0	5,005	100.0
Success Rate		84.0		94.2		69.5

Source: Research and Statistics Section (1994c).

bation office can employ "early termination" to advance the day when the state pronounces the juvenile's full satisfaction of probation. Supervision can be resumed if the suspension proves to be premature.

Adult probationers also may be rewarded for good conduct but not as completely as juvenile probationers. The probation office must ask the regional parole board (RPB) for permission to grant "provisional suspension." One agency, the RPB, has authority to decide whether or not another agency, the probation office, can reward its own clients (probationers, not parolees). The administrative paradox is a partial balance for another paradox, the probation office's exclusive authority for supervising parolees as well as probationers.

Provisional suspension does not qualify as termination of probation, but commendable conduct is rewarded by excusing adults from visiting the probation office or reporting to VPOs. The procedure is authorized by Article 25-2-2 of the Penal Code and Article 8 of the Law for Probationary Supervision of Persons under Suspension of Execution of Sentence. The word "provisional" has three implications: the RPB can reverse the decision if subsequent behavior deteriorates; the probation period continues until otherwise terminated; and, since probation is a version of suspended sentence, only the court can terminate the supervision completely.

One way to measure case successes of adult probationers terminated in 1993 (see table 9.6) would be to count "expirations" for good behavior (1,283), average behavior (876), and bad behavior (35), plus "suspensions" (899). Failures would be "revocations" (1,357). The outcomes under "extinction," disappeared (390), arrest (20), and other (145) appear at first glance to be case failures, but should these categories be charged to 1990 termination? These outcomes clear the probation office records of pending cases rather than necessarily denote 1990 case failures. Presumably, the decision has yet to be made on "arrests"; if the cases become failures they should be charged against the year when they occurred.

The items for case outcomes are grouped in table 9.6 as expiration of term, extinction, and suspension. When estimating successful outcome of probation cases for a particular year, extinction was ignored for the reason given above. For adult probation cases ending in 1993, expiration (2,194 probationers) and suspension (899) are considered successes, while revocations (1,350) are defined as failures (see table

9.7). The success rate of 69.5 percent engenders a highly favorable initial impression, especially in light of the 18 percent of cases granted provisional suspension.

The success rate of 69.5 percent is similar to the published data on revocations over the five-year period before the policy of "extinction" removes "disappeared," "arrest," and "other" cases from the active files. Of the 7,180 adults placed on probation in 1985, 2,188 (or 30.5 percent) had their probation revoked by 1990 (Research and Statistics Section 1991c, 128). The success rate on that basis would be 69.5 percent, roughly similar to my estimate of 72.2 for the outcome of probation cases in 1990.

An authoritative assessment of probation outcome in Japan, however, awaits the application of a more elaborate methodology, a sampling of the probationers' characteristics, and identification of the factors directly involved in case supervision. My methodology is excessively simple; the published data on case outcomes available to me do not capture the probationers' characteristics in multivariable fashion and do not identify the factors that affect the actual conditions of supervision. The heavy reliance on VPOs probably inflates the success rate in Japan, but that possibility has not been tested reliably.

After sentencing a convicted offender to prison for a term of no more than three years, a judge is authorized to suspend the sentence and return the individual to the free community with or without probationary supervision. The suspension presumably is granted to offenders who are more amenable and thereby more eligible to be excused from the pains of penal confinement, but the courts are inclined to believe that because of the inconvenience for the probationers, supervision is more punitive than outright release into the free community without supervision. The judges' premise casts doubt upon the estimates of probationers' success.

The policy of extinction removes arbitrarily most of the pending cases that would be defined as failures by probation agencies of the United States. The "other" cases entail circumstances of supervision other than observation of the conditions set by the agency for the probationers' conduct; those relatively few cases probably are not "failures."

The estimated success rates are even higher for juvenile probationers. The philosophy of Japan's juvenile justice system encourages optimism about the probability of rehabilitating juveniles whose personalities are expected to be susceptible to constructive change. Juvenile probation is dedicated to the wholesome rearing of juveniles; linked to the suspension of sentences and the judges' identification of adult probation with the punishment of offenders, adult probation is colored by relative pessimism about modifying the habitual conduct of adult offenders.

Practical considerations supplement any philosophical justification for the high success rate for juvenile probation. First, the length of probationary supervision is either until the juvenile probationer reaches age twenty or a maximum of two years of supervision, whichever is greater. Supervision of adult probationers is for at least one year and cannot exceed five years after the sentence to prison would have taken effect. Their shorter average length of supervision would reduce the possibility of the juvenile probationers either violating the conditions set by the family court or the probation office becoming aware of a transgression.

Second, as table 9.6 shows, almost half of the juvenile probationers in 1993 were on the short-term traffic program. Their 94.2 percent success rate is very high and helps to raise the overall rate for juvenile probationers to 88.8 percent. As explained earlier, the program is only four months in duration and the young probationers are required only to attend two group sessions and to submit a written report each of the four months. The brevity of supervision and the minimal requirements greatly diminish the probability of case failures.

The success rates for juvenile probationers have fluctuated between 83 and 92 percent in the 28 years represented

Table 9.7
Outcome of Juvenile and Adult Probation, 1965–93

Year	No.	Expiration (%)	Extinction (%)	Revocation (%)	Suspension[a] (%)	Total (%)	Success Rate (%)
			Juvenile Probation				
1965	22,086	48.7	11.2	15.2	24.9	100.0	82.9
1970	29,191	45.3	11.2	7.7	35.8	100.0	91.3
1975	21,518	35.9	6.2	7.0	50.9	100.0	92.5
1980	21,659	20.3	4.8	12.8	62.1	100.0	86.6
1985	27,181	13.9	4.3	12.4	69.4	100.0	87.0
1990	23,963	14.7	4.0	11.2	70.1	100.0	88.3
1993	23,171	13.8	3.4	10.8	72.0	100.0	88.8
			Adult Probation				
1965	8,307	51.4	16.3	27.6	4.7	100.0	67.1
1970	7,650	56.2	16.1	20.7	7.0	100.0	75.3
1975	7,006	52.2	11.8	25.7	10.3	100.0	70.9
1980	8,146	42.4	10.9	30.3	16.4	100.0	66.0
1985	7,904	37.1	11.1	29.8	22.0	100.0	66.5
1990	5,869	44.7	11.5	24.6	19.2	100.0	72.5
1993	5,005	43.8	11.1	27.1	18.0	100.0	69.5

Sources: Research and Statistics Section (1981; 1994c).

[a]For juvenile probation, two types of suspension are reported: early termination and suspension for good behavior. The latter type is rare and declining in importance over the years. For adult probation, only provisional

in table 9.7. Of course, the percentage of revocations were instrumental in shaping the fluctuations, but of greater significance were the sharp decline in routine expiration of supervision and, accompanying that, the great increase in early terminations for exemplary conduct. The separate but interrelated trends show that the juveniles were found to merit special commendation rather than being kept under supervision to the end of the period set by the Offenders Rehabilitation Law. The administrative actions listed as extinction were fewer and fewer over the years. Absconders, identified as "disappeared," were the most frequent administrative actions. The persistent and definite decline in the extinction of juvenile cases suggests that the administration of probation for Japanese juveniles is losing its orthodox features. Arbitrary transfer of "disappeareds" and "arrests" from the active files have distorted outcomes to a decreasing degree over the years.

From 1965 to 1993 the adult probationers scored success rates ranging from 66 to 75 percent but always less than the rates for juvenile probationers. The adults exceeded the juveniles in dependence on routine terminations of cases, or "expiration." Provisional terminations—the reward for exemplary conduct—were less common than termination on legal expiration of term. Case extinctions declined over the years but remained high in comparison with the juvenile probationers. The number of adults under supervision was far short of the number of juvenile probationers, for the simple reason that fewer adults are granted probation and fewer juveniles are sent to correctional institutions. The official tolerance applied in limiting the imprisonment rate was extended in the probation programs to juveniles more than to adults.

10

Exiting from Confinement: Parole and Hostels

Reentry of inmates into the free community is a crucial turning point determining the outcome of earlier actions. The released persons are tested in their attitudes, capacities, resourcefulness, and emotional flexibility. Have they been willing and able to take advantage of whatever resources the correctional institution had to prepare them for community life? Have the institutions carried out their responsibilities? Has the court been correct in electing incarceration for this particular offender? Has the community given fellowship and access to its socioeconomic opportunities?

Parole has two "faces": protection of the community against threats to life and property versus respecting the interests of the parolee. The first face must be respected. Japanese and American parole authorities experience public protests when parolees commit sensational crimes. Hyotani (1985) refers to several incidents in Japan. Paroled from a life sentence, a fifty-three-year-old man knifed two junior high school girls. A former policeman had served seven years of an eight-year sentence for robbery; while on parole, he killed another policeman to get his pistol and then killed a shop clerk with the gun. A third man had been paroled from a life sentence; while residing at a hostel, he killed several persons at an inn.

The second face is difficult to accomplish. The probationer or parolee often has had difficulties in social relationships. Long-term inmates discover that the situation of their families, and the community generally, has changed during their absence. Complications for parole supervision in the United States also exist in Japan (Matsumoto n.d.). The status of ex-prisoner handicaps the job search; irregular employment, inferior income, undesirable work schedules, and conflicts with employers and coworkers are conducive to job changes. The fear of being found out plagues the parolee who conceals a criminal past.

DUTIES OF
REGIONAL PAROLE BOARDS

The eight regional parole boards (RPBs) are in Tokyo, Osaka, Nagoya, Hiroshima, Sendai, Sapporo, Takamatsu, and Fukuoka where the high courts and high public prosecutors are located. RPBs have more than two but less than thirteen members appointed for three-year terms. The Minister of Justice appoints the board chair from its membership. Each board has its secretariat according to the organizational scheme set by the Ministry of Justice Ordinance (Offenders Rehabilitation Law, Articles 12–17).

The Kanto RPB in Tokyo is responsible for eleven prefectures and more transactions than any other RPB. Its secretariat has five sections: general affairs, research and liaison, and three investigative sections. The first investigative section (consisting of a chief and seven staff members) gathers information on parole applications from juvenile training schools; the second section (a chief and staff of eight) deals with adult parole applications; and the third section (a chief and staff of four) administers parole revocations and other terminations of parole supervision.

RPBs make four contributions to community corrections. First, they grant paroles, grant provisional release from detention houses, and revoke paroles from prisons. Penal detention is served in a detention house for one to thirty days. Persons unable to pay a fine in full may be detained from one day to two years; the length of detention is reduced by partial payment according to the ratio of the amount paid to the total fine originally imposed. The RPBs may grant provisional release. From 1980 through 1993, RPBs received only one application, in 1990, and that one was withdrawn (Research and Statistics Section 1994c, 4–5).

The RPB may revoke parole when the persons do not live where they claim to reside, have been issued a warrant of arrest (*inchi-jo*), or otherwise violate parole conditions. The parole period for an absconding adult parolee (one who has escaped from supervision) may be extended by the same amount of time the parolee was absent from supervision.

Second, the RPBs decide when inmates serving indeterminate sentences will be released. The court sets a minimum term and a maximum term, leaving the precise time of release from prison to correctional authorities. Of the 13,423 cases before the boards in 1993, only 40 were for indeterminate sentences. The respective wardens withdrew 4 cases from RPB consideration because of violations of prison rules, and the RPBs approved the remaining 39 cases (Research and Statistics Section 1994c, 31).

Third, the RPBs grant paroles and absolute (irrevocable) releases from juvenile training schools. The boards do not carry out supervision but have the right to maintain contact with the probation offices to see how parole supervision is being carried out. RPBs have the responsibility of asking the family court to rule that a juvenile parole violator, less than twenty-three years of age, be returned to the training school until age twenty-three. RPBs may release, early and unconditionally, juveniles from training schools upon recommendation of the superintendent or may permit

early termination of the juvenile paroles when the probation office chief requests.

Fourth, the Minister of Justice may delegate to the RPB
chair the power to appoint the VPOs. The authorization exists in spite of the RPBs' exclusion from supervision of parolees and probationers.[1]

PARDONS:
TYPES AND PROCEDURES

Before there were paroles in Japan, in the Nara Era
(710–84), pardons were granted for major events such as
deaths in the imperial or shogunate households. During the
Meiji Restoration, only the emperor could grant amnesty,
pardon, commutation of punishment, and restoration of
civil rights. General pardons, those granted by imperial order on special occasions, were dominant then and survive
in the pardons authorized by ordinances of the national
Cabinet and attested by the emperor. Pardons to individuals are granted on a limited basis (Shikita and Tsuchiya
1990).

The general pardons (amnesties) categorize offenders
according to offense, length of sentence, or other broad variables and arbitrarily benefit the offenders who fall into the
category. General pardons have been issued only nine
times. The last general pardon was on the occasion of Emperor Hirohito's death in 1989 and was for persons who violated the election law by failing to report political contributions. The general pardons may involve commutation of
sentence (reduction of the severity) or restoration of rights.

Individual pardons have greater correctional importance since they are awarded according to qualities of individuals or their cases. Prisoners can not apply directly for
pardons. Applications may be originated by the public
prosecutor, warden of a prison, or the director of a proba-

tion office at their own discretion or by certifying the application of an individual.

Pardon is the only means available to a probation office to discharge an adult parolee or probationer from supervision before the full term. This action can be accomplished through pardon as a special amnesty, commutation of sentence, or remission of execution of sentence. Prison wardens may recommend pardon of a prisoner; there are few such applications. Public prosecutors may initiate applications for an offender sentenced to a fine or awarded a suspended sentence without probation or an ex-prisoner released on expiration of a sentence.

The applications go to the Amnesty Division of the Rehabilitation Bureau and to the National Offenders Rehabilitation Commission (NORC).[2] Administrative details are carried out by the Tokyo headquarters of the Rehabilitation Bureau. The commission recommends individual pardons to the Minister of Justice and reviews complaints about RPB revocations of parole (Rehabilitation Bureau 1990). The ten or twenty complaints about parole revocations each year seldom receive a favorable decision.

NORC disposed of 4,543 cases in 1953—the greatest number of cases in any year. Since then, the number has ranged from 929 in 1969 to 55 in 1991. The approval rate varied from 40 percent in 1958 to 92 percent in 1969. In 1993 the rate was 83 percent, or 58 out of 70 cases. Since 1975 the approved cases have been almost entirely restoration of civil rights or commutation of sentences (Shikita and Tsuchiya 1990, 375; Research and Statistics Section 1994c, 170–71).

Restoration of civil rights gives the former prisoner access to certain occupations and the right to vote. Completion of the full term of parole or probation supervision restores civil rights. The criminal record is canceled if ten years elapse without further conviction after the sentence has been fully served. Criminal records are entered in the Criminal Record Book at the municipal office in the offender's place of permanent residence. Since only competent public agencies have access to records, the possibility of social stigmatization is muted. Restoration of civil rights has its greatest significance in the lifting of statutory barriers to being a medical practitioner, school teacher, practicing lawyer, real estate dealer, and the like (Rehabilitation Bureau 1990).

GENERAL REQUIREMENTS
FOR PAROLE

Adult prisoners are eligible to be considered for parole when at least one-third of a determinate sentence or ten years of a life sentence has been completed. The likelihood of additional crimes on parole must be deemed unlikely and the community be expected to tolerate the parolee. Repentance and "progress" must be demonstrated. Progress toward rehabilitation is demonstrated by the absence of rule violations, at least recently, and the recommendation of the warden or superintendent. Supervision of adult parolees is limited to the unserved portion of the prison sentence; it could be as little as one month.

For training-school applications, the requirements are attainment of the highest grade in the progressive stages and a prognosis of becoming "rehabilitated" through parole supervision. The first requirement is not necessarily enforced in practice. The Juvenile Law, Article 58, specifies that a juvenile may be granted a parole after seven years of a life sentence, three years of a determinate sentence of ten years or more, and one third of the minimum term of an indeterminate sentence. Juvenile parole ends at age twenty.

The general conditions imposed on all parolees are similar to those in Western programs: living at a specified residence, engaging in a lawful occupation, avoiding illicit conduct and questionable companions, and obtaining advance approval for long journeys or changes in residence. Three to five special conditions usually are added; the most frequent are abstinence from alcohol and gambling, regular contacts with the VPO, and being responsible for the financial support of dependents.

INITIATING SELECTION
OF PAROLEES

The investigative sections of the RPBs may be described as "preparole service units" attempting to coordinate parole with the optimum inmate capacity for law-abiding behavior. Attainment of the objective is muted by the requirement that one-third of the sentence be served. Also, the warden or superintendent, not the inmate, files the application; parole becomes a device for managing prisoners.[3] An RPB can initiate an application, but the procedure is seldom used because the RPBs, I was told, respect the warden's opinion.

The correctional institution is directly involved in the selection of parolees. Summarized information about the inmate is sent to the RPB. The prison classification committee uses reports from prison officers for evaluating promotions in the progressive-stage scheme and for parole applications. The committee's recommendations go to the warden who decides whether or not an application will be filed with the RPB.

A VPO is assigned to visit the prospective residence as specified in the inmate's employment-residence plan. The VPO assesses the family situation and any problems in the setting. When appropriate, the VPO advises the family on how any problems can be overcome. The VPO's report, including comments of the probation office's chief, goes to the prison and the RPB. If the family setting is unacceptable, the inmate is asked to submit another parole plan. Efforts toward "environmental adjustment" are reported every six months for adults and every three months for training school inmates until the date of release.

The investigative officers (ninety-four, as of 1990) of the RPBs visit the correctional institutions that are their responsibility. After interviewing inmates, they prepare reports containing the inmate's name and birthday, name of the institution, type of offense and probable cause, names of codefendants and their sentences, inmate's life history, mental and physical condition, progressive-stage grade, behavior in the correctional institution, rule violations, time in the community since any previous sentence, required compensation to the victim, victim's attitude about the offense, whether the inmate had or did not have visitors or correspondence, inmate's intended residence upon release, whether a job awaits, and job skills or qualifications. The family situation is outlined: economic status, membership (wife, parents, or others), whether intact or broken, and how members feel about the inmate's return. The investigative officer presents impressions during the interview and makes recommendations.

The preparole service units are expected to serve several principles. Preparation for parole should begin as early in the prison career as possible. Upon admission, the inmate is interviewed by the parole investigative officers about plans for the release. All relevant information, regardless of the originating agency, should be consolidated. Ideally, the inmate's situation in the institution should be related to what the inmate will encounter in the community; this principle, of course, can not be fully attained.

To promote those principles, full-time parole investigative officers were introduced in 1979 in ten correctional institutions and the services were extended to long-term prisoners—those serving eight years or more and life sentences. All are interviewed, instead of the usual waiting for the warden's applications, when two-thirds of determinate sentences or twelve years of life terms are completed.

Deliberations of Parole Boards

The RPB membership is divided into several panels, say three members in each of four panels. The number of members depends on the RPB's caseload. Each member is assigned to certain prisons or training schools for face-to-face interviews. On average, sixty-eight days were required in 1993 for cases ultimately approved, eighty-five days for those debated but denied, and sixty-one days when withdrawn either because the inmate had violated a prison rule or the proposed residential plan was unsatisfactory (Research and Statistics Section 1994c, 10).

After interviewing the inmates, the board member prepares a handwritten report. If the parole is approved, a copy of the handwritten report goes to the probation office. The standard form of the report calls for the following information: names of the inmate and institution, outline of the inmate's personal problems and criminal tendencies, conduct during any previous probation or parole, experience with hostels, behavior in prison, grade in progressive stages, number of rule violations, self-examination (the inmate's thoughts about the offense, former life, and the future), whether or not the victim feels vindictive toward the inmate, rating of the family environment, the board member's impression of the inmate and recommended parole conditions, and suggestions of specific matters to be emphasized in supervision.

A panel meets once a week when the members report on their interviews. Full consensus is necessary in decisions. Otherwise, the responsible member reinterviews the inmate to clarify any remaining issues or to obtain another impression of the inmate. Decisions are based on philosophy, I was told, not on actual data derived from accumulated statistics on the characteristics of previous parolees. "We do not like automatic decision making," a board member explained to me. "We do not have statistics that go back on violence and other offenses. The recidivists think they know the outward demeanor the officers expect of inmates. We encounter the same attitude in our interviews."

The case of a prison inmate, age twenty-five, from Gumma Prefecture illustrates RPB procedures. At age eighteen he killed a delivery boy while under the influence of paint thinner and alcohol. Sentenced to five to ten years for manslaughter, he entered Kawagoe Juvenile Prison in September 1983. In February 1990, the warden recommended he be paroled on 29 May 1990. The inmate had four rule violations: the first, in January 1987, was his refusal to work; in January 1988, it was a quarrel with another inmate, for which he received solitary confinement for forty days, and then, while in solitary confinement, failure to sit in a fixed position, for which he got another fifteen days; then in May 1988, another quarrel, and another solitary confinement for ten days.

Prior to the preparole interview, an RPB member asked the prison physician about the inmate's mental condition; the report showed no mental or physical effects of drug abuse. A VPO had supervised the inmate in an earlier drug-abuse case. The RPB asked the VPO to interview him at Kawagoe. The VPO believed the inmate's attitude had improved. Negotiations were conducted by the lawyer of the widowed mother of the victim and the lawyer of the offender's parents. They agreed that nine million yen would be just compensation.

The board approved the parole for 28 August 1990. The decision making had taken six months and three days. The VPO drove the family to and from Gumma. Initially, the parolee exhibited intense anxiety about police surveillance but accepted assurance that he was exaggerating. Supervision ended at expiration of his prison sentence on 17 October 1992. Two months later, the Kanto RPB was informed he was working diligently as a truck driver, was drug free, and had recovered from his intense anxiety. Neighbors reported favorably on his conduct.

APPLICATION RATES:
KEY FACTOR IN ADULT PAROLES

Over the years, the number of paroles granted adults and their share of total releases from prison have declined. The decline can be attributed to a special feature of parole administration in Japan: the prison warden or training-school superintendent, not the inmate, files the application for parole.

The parole rate measures the relative importance of paroles among all the releases from correctional institutions. Table 10.1 shows that the parole rate among adults released from prison was 73.1 percent in 1950 and dropped thereafter.

The RPBs are gatekeepers in that their approval is necessary for a successful application. The parole approval rate measures the number of favorable RPB decisions among the cases before the board. The rate has fluctuated between 70 and 94 percent over the last four decades. The high approval rate demonstrates that the boards have not closed the administrative "gate" very often. The parole application rate measures the percentage of parole applications filed by prison officials for all prisoners present at the end of the year. The preferred denominator would be the number of prisoners eligible for parole that year, but the statistic is not available. Application rates declined from 74.6 to 36.2 percent between 1950 and 1993.

The number of paroles of adults also declined sharply from 1950 to 1993. The parole rate did not drop as dramatically, in part because the number of discharges at expiration of sentence also dropped. (Reduction of the imprisonment rate was basic to both trends.) The rise in the approval rate among parole applications does not explain the declining trend of the parole rate. The application rate declined even more rapidly than the parole rate. In summary, the prisons' application rate—not the RPBs' approval rate—influenced the drop of the adult parole rate.

Table 10.1

Application, Approval, and Parole Rates for Adults, 1950–93

Year	Inmates at End of Year	Released from Prison		Application Rate (%)	Approval Rate (%)	Parole Rate (%)
		Discharged	Paroled			
1950	80,589	15,445	42,141	74.6	70.0	73.2
1955	67,813	18,322	32,198	51.6	91.9	63.7
1960	61,100	14,179	30,751	55.7	90.3	68.4
1965	52,657	15,546	19,432	46.2	79.8	55.5
1970	39,724	11,015	17,855	52.9	85.0	61.8
1975	37,744	11,736	14,933	46.6	84.9	56.0
1980	41,835	14,140	15,202	43.4	83.8	51.8
1985	46,105	14,143	17,795	44.1	87.6	55.7
1990	39,892	11,557	14,896	39.9	93.6	56.3
1993	37,164	9,504	12,532	36.2	93.1	56.9

Sources: Research and Statistics Section (1990a; 1991a; 1991c; 1994a; 1994c); for years prior to 1990, data provided by Rehabilitation Bureau.

Paroles had a very minor place in releases from prison before World War II ended: 3.7 percent of all releases in 1930 and 12.7 percent in 1940. Since then, paroles have assumed more importance. Japanese prisons were seriously overcrowded right after the war; parole was seized upon as a means of speeding release of inmates. The parole rate was at its apex in 1950 but dropped thereafter.

The number of admissions to juvenile training schools is only a fraction of those to prisons, inevitably affecting the number of candidates for parole, but as the years passed, the proportion of juvenile inmates among all those receiving parole became greater (see table 10.2). Measured as percentages of all releases, the trends for both juvenile and adult parole were irregular. To measure the changes in the relationship of the two types of parole over the years, we take the ratio of adult to juvenile parole admissions for each year. The figures show that the number of juvenile pa-

Table 10.2
Trends in Admissions to Parole for Juveniles and Adults, 1950–92

Year	Parole Admissions Juveniles	Adults	Age-Specific Rates[a] Juveniles	Adults	Parole as Percentage of All Releases[b] Juveniles	Adults
1950	2,915	42,141	28.1	93.2	97.6	73.2
1955	7,304	32,198	69.0	63.3	84.1	63.7
1960	7,804	30,751	72.2	54.9	83.2	68.4
1965	6,310	19,432	48.9	31.2	81.8	55.5
1970	3,163	17,855	29.6	25.6	71.4	61.8
1975	1,593	14,933	16.7	19.5	77.1	56.0
1980	4,063	15,206	41.8	18.7	91.5	51.8
1985	5,585	17,795	50.9	20.7	93.1	55.7
1990	4,333	14,896	36.6	16.4	94.4	56.3
1992	4,298	12,417	37.9	13.3	95.1	56.1

Sources: Research and Statistics Section (1993a; 1993b; 1993c).

[a]Parole admissions per 100,000 Japanese that year, age 14 through 19 (for juveniles) and age 20 or over (for adults).

[b]Releases from training schools (for juveniles) and prisons (for adults).

roles has gained on adult paroles, although the adults always retained the numerical advantage. The number of adult parole admissions was about fourteen times greater than the number of juvenile parole admissions in 1950, three times greater in 1965, over nine times greater in 1975, and then declined again to about three times greater in 1992.

The age-specific rates in table 10.2 trace the irregular pattern of the increase of juvenile parole when compared with adult parole. Juvenile parole admissions have risen in number since 1950 while adult parole admissions declined. Age-specific rates, which relate changes in the number of parolees to the demographic gains in the total Japanese population, have experienced a downturn in both juvenile

Table 10.3
Outcome of Juvenile and Adult Parole, 1993

Outcomes	Juvenile Parole						Adult Parole	
	General Program				Traffic Program			
	Long Term		Short Term					
	No.	%	No.	%	No.	%	No.	%
Expiration	1,467	59.3	761	48.3	136	42.2	11,432	89.7
Good Behavior	(574)	(23.2)	(391)	(24.8)	(72)	(22.4)	(3,967)	(31.1)
Average Behavior	(819)	(33.1)	(347)	(22.0)	(61)	(18.9)	(7,346)	(57.6)
Bad Behavior	(74)	(3.0)	(23)	(1.5)	(3)	(0.9)	(119)	(0.9)
Indeterminate Sentence	—	—	—	—	—	—	3	0.0
Extinction of Punishment	—	—	—	—	—	—	114	0.9
Early Termination	247	10.0	474	30.1	152	47.2	—	—
Administrative Action	319	12.9	118	7.5	10	3.1	288	2.3
Disappeared	(152)	(6.2)	(64)	(4.1)	(7)	(2.2)	(30)	(0.3)
Arrest	(102)	(4.1)	(27)	(1.7)	(1)	(0.3)	(25)	(0.2)
Other	(65)	(2.6)	(27)	(1.7)	(2)	(0.6)	(233)	(1.8)
Revocation	434	17.5	221	14.0	24	7.5	908	7.1
Return to JTS	5	0.2	2	0.1	—	—	—	—
Total	2,472	100.0	1,576	100.0	322	100.0	12,745	100.0
Success Rate		79.6		84.7		92.3		92.7

Source: Research and Statistics Section (1994c).

and adult categories. Declines in incarceration rates narrow the sweep of the criminal justice net and produce a smaller representation of parolees among all Japanese.

The juvenile paroles also surpass adult paroles in another way: in the share of parole among all releases from prisons or training schools. Except for escapes (almost nil in Japan), deaths (rather few), and pardons, discharges from prison consist of either release upon expiration of the sentence or parole. Table 10.2 traces over the years parole's share of all releases from either training schools or prisons.

Adult paroles have dropped from about 73 percent of all releases in about 1950 to about 56 percent more recently. Parole has been dominant among juvenile releases: from almost 98 percent of all juvenile training school releases in 1950, down to 70 percent in the 1970s, and back above 90 percent recently.

Juvenile parole resembles juvenile probation in providing special programs for traffic offenders. The juvenile probation program usually requires only two meetings at the probation office in a four-month period. The training schools introduced in 1977 a short-term program for juvenile traffic programs along with a short-term program for other juvenile offenders. Parolees from training schools have been categorized as parolees from long-term treatment, parolees from short-term treatment, and traffic parolees from short-term treatment (Correction Bureau 1990b).

Difficulties in
Measuring Outcome

The concepts used for the evaluation of probation outcomes discussed in chapter 9 also hold generally for parole outcome. For juvenile parolees and probationers, most categories are identical: good behavior, average behavior, bad behavior, early termination, revocations, and "other." Suspension for good behavior exists only for juvenile probationers and return to training schools only for juvenile parolees. Only adult probationers benefit from provisional suspension of supervision; only adult parolees from extinction of punishment and a few from the RPBs' action on indeterminate sentences (see table 10.3).

Just as they were for probation, those concepts are also the foundation for official statistics concerning parole; and just as they did for probation, concepts such as "extinction of punishment," "disappeared" and "arrest" also obscure evaluation of case outcomes in parole. The concepts are symptoms of the legal framework of probation and parole in Japan. Another symptom is the length of supervision. For juveniles, the length is determined by the age of the parolee when supervision begins; the term of supervision is usually until age twenty is attained. Early termination also shortens supervision. Adults, but not juveniles, are on parole only for the remaining portion of the prison sentence not served in prison. Because of the rather few months remaining on many of the sentences, the length of parole supervision on average is considerably shorter than for juvenile parolees. The mean length of supervision was only 6.1 months for adults. The mean length of supervision was greater for juveniles: 13 months for parolees from the long-term program of training schools, 15.7 months from the short-term program for traffic offenders, and 18 months from the general short-term program (Research and Statistics Section 1994c, 104–7). "Short-term" refers here to the length of stay in the juvenile training school, not in juvenile parole.

The rather brief length of supervision for most parolees casts doubt upon the excellent outcomes reported in table 10.3. The data are presumably correct, but the brevity of supervision covers only the initial period of return to the community when the former inmate's resolution to meet official expectations is at its zenith and the difficulties of reintegration into community life have not had their full impact. The two tendencies underlie the patterns of revocations traced for the five years of supervision after parole has been granted. Of the 4,063 juveniles paroled in 1980, 1,131 (27.8 percent) had been revoked by the end of 1985. In 1980, 15,206 adults were paroled; by the end of 1985, revocations ended 802 of the paroles (5.3 percent) (Research and Statistics Section 1994c, 128–31). Table 10.4 presents those long-term revocation rates to show that their size is greater than the optimistic short-term revocation rates reported otherwise.

The reports of outcomes of paroles should be rated for reliability and validity against the reality of supervision by unpaid volunteers. Chapter 9 summarizes the strengths and weaknesses of the VPO system. Evaluation of a fully professionalized service raises serious methodological difficulties seldom overcome; the VPO system raises at least equivalent difficulties.

Comparing Outcomes of Juvenile and Adult Parole

As table 10.2 shows, almost all releases from juvenile training schools have been on parole but a smaller proportion of adults leaving prison (from 52 to 73 percent) were parolees. In comparison to juvenile parolees, adult parolees have scored higher success rates. For those parolees leaving the programs in 1993, adults had a success rate of 92.7 percent, while the juvenile parolees from the training school programs had the following percentages: 79.6 for the long-term program, 84.7 for the short-term program, and 92.3 for the traffic program. The overall success rate for juvenile parolees was 82.5 (see table 10.3).

The relatively short average length of supervision for the adults must be taken into account. As explained above, differences in the length do not necessarily measure the quality of the parolees' conduct, but the shorter the period of supervision the greater are the chances that the parolee can successfully conceal any violations of the parole conditions or suppress any antisocial tendencies temporarily.

The longer average length of parole supervision for juveniles increases the chances for detection of any transgressions, but there are other explanations for their lower success rates. The graduates of the traffic program did as well on parole as the adults in spite of a longer exposure to parole supervision. Those juvenile parolees had enjoyed two favorable criteria when evaluated by the family courts. As traffic law violators they were believed to be less criminalistic than the usual offenders; and they had been rated as qualified for short-term programs designed for offenders believed to need only a brief loss of freedom to become resocialized. That second criterion also applied to those juveniles on the general short-term program, but as table 10.3 records, their performance on parole earned them fewer early terminations and more revocations.

Several other possible explanations for the inferior success rates of the general programs come to mind. The heavy use of juvenile parole weakens the quality of selection as revealed when the youngsters are tested by the realities of parole supervision. They are less experienced than adults in harnessing their conduct to the programmatic requirements or in disguising any antisocial tendencies. The family courts sent them to juvenile training schools originally either because of doubts about their future conduct or because of a necessity to remove them from an adverse living environment. The agencies of juvenile justice in Japan speak frequently of the environmental victimization of juveniles appearing before the family court. The social welfare orientation identifies parole as another "protective measure." When young parolees are victimized by adverse conditions in their living environment, returning them to the training school may be interpreted as another protective measure.

The long-term program of training schools is supposed to receive youngsters particularly difficult to resocialize. Their performance was the least satisfactory. They exceeded the other juvenile parolees in expiration of term outcomes. They were excused from further supervision because the legal length of supervision had expired, not because of exceptional conduct. They also received the least percentage of early terminations and the highest rate of revocations.

From 1965 through 1993, the juvenile parolees have consistently had lower success rates than the adult parolees (see table 10.4). The rates for the adults have hovered in the low 90-percent range, while the juvenile rates ranged from 68 to 82 percent of the outcomes. The trend for the juveniles has been toward greater use of suspensions as rewards for ex-

Table 10.4
Outcome of Juvenile and Adult Parole, 1965–93

Year	No.	Expiration (%)	Administrative Action (%)	Revocation[a] (%)	Suspension[b] (%)	Success Total (%)	Rate (%)
				Juvenile Parole			
1965	5,378	54.8	16.5	26.9	1.8	100.0	67.8
1970	4,453	58.7	24.1	14.2	3.0	100.0	81.3
1975	1,968	61.7	18.7	15.4	4.2	100.0	81.0
1980	3,361	48.5	13.2	21.1	17.2	100.0	75.7
1985	5,035	48.3	12.3	22.1	17.3	100.0	74.8
1990	4,534	51.9	12.3	19.3	16.5	100.0	78.0
1993	4,370	54.1	10.2	15.7	20.0	100.0	82.5
				Adult Parole			
1965	19,811	91.7	2.9	4.5	0.9	100.0	95.3
1970	18,257	92.7	2.2	4.4	0.8	100.0	96.0
1975	14,971	91.2	2.7	5.4	0.7	100.0	94.4
1980	14,932	92.7	1.9	5.0	0.4	100.0	94.9
1985	17,357	90.3	2.0	7.3	0.4	100.0	92.6
1990	15,393	90.6	1.6	7.2	0.6	100.0	92.7
1993	12,745	89.7	2.3	7.1	0.9	100.0	92.7

Sources: Research and Statistics Section (1981; 1994c).

[a]For juvenile parole, revocations include return to juvenile training schools.

[b]For juvenile parole, "early terminations" are listed; for adult parole, "indeterminate sentence" and "extinction of punishment" are listed.

emplary conduct and a lowering of the proportion of cases ending in revocation from 27 percent of completed paroles in 1965 to 10 percent in 1993. Meanwhile, the elimination of cases for administrative convenience (extinction) also declined.

Unlike the outcomes for juveniles, the high rates for adult cases were the consequence of expiration. Most of the parole careers of the adults ended with routine completion of the full period of supervision rather than with early termination, as was given to juvenile parolees. Adults were denied that reward for exceptional conduct enjoyed by the juveniles, but to a more limited extent were granted other means of early discharge from parole supervision. The Rehabilitation Bureau (1990, 43) attaches the term "early discharge" for adult parolees to the termination of an indeterminate sentence and the remission of execution of sentence.

Table 10.3 offers the more detailed breakdown of the various kinds of outcome for parole cases ending in 1993. Expiration was more dominant for the adults than for the juveniles removed from supervision. Indeterminate sentences and extinction of punishment (the equivalent of the Correction Bureau's "early discharge") fell far short of the early terminations that lifted the success rates for juvenile parole, especially from the traffic program. The various kinds of "administrative actions" (as I have labeled the category) also were considerably more characteristic of juvenile parole. The revocations of juvenile paroles definitely exceeded those of the adults. The juvenile parolees who had been in the traffic program of the training schools were an exception, but as noted above, the juveniles assigned to that program were especially amenable among the juvenile delinquents.

The success rate of adult parolees also exceeded that of adult probationers (see table 9.6). Nishikawa (1990, 47–48) explains that adult parolees are selected more carefully to exclude poor risks and that the shorter length of parole supervision on average prevents a clear distinction of good and poor adjustment by the end of supervision. Otherwise, he comments, "There is no basic difference in the method and intensiveness of the supervision of probationers and parolees except for small differences in the restrictiveness of the conditions imposed."

The ratings of parolee conduct are given by the VPOs when the cases complete the officially defined length of supervision (expiration). The ratings are vulnerable to the criticism that they suffer from subjectivity, but the evaluations of adults are consistently more favorable than those of juveniles in percentages of "good" and "average" behavior. The adults also come off more favorably in the relative importance of the various administrative actions.

The comparisons of juvenile and adult parole outcomes hold for the twenty-nine years covered by table 10.4. The success rates of the juveniles vary more over the years than the adults' but are consistently much lower. The adults trail the juveniles in gaining early release from supervision because their high success rate stems from completion of the full period of supervision (expiration). Conversely, revocations have been few although they have increased modestly over the years. Finally, the adults are far less inclined to disappear, be arrested, or be released from supervision after long-term hospitalization, frequent travel, or other legitimate obstructions to efficacious supervision.

BUFFERING FACILITIES: THE HOSTELS

In meeting the reentry crisis, the family is the primary buffering agency for a large share of released prisoners; for those without family support or other resources, Japanese rehabilitation aid hostels cushion the shock. The hostels are part of a system of assistance also offering emergency aid. The hostel is expected to serve four classes of persons in addition to parolees and discharged prisoners: those sentenced to prison who have an unserved portion of the sentence that has been excused for illness or other exceptional circumstances, those granted suspension of a prison sentence that is not yet final, those receiving a suspension of sentence without probation, and those not prosecuted because prosecution was not found necessary.

The chief of the probation office refers eligible persons and technically sets the time limit for the stay. For adult parolees, the maximum stay is determined by the unserved portion of the prison sentence. A discharged inmate is eligible for a maximum of six months from release from confinement. When suspending a sentence, the judge sets the length of probation, from one to five years; technically, the probationer may stay at the hostel for a full period of probation. In practice, the government subsidy covers an average of two months. In 1993 a quarter of the residents stayed only ten days or less, and 32 percent more than sixty days (Research and Statistics Section 1994c, 166).

Administrators of the hostels decide whether or not the resident may stay beyond the maximum time specified by law. The halfway house and the resident reach an agreement, but the resident is always responsible for the payments beyond the coverage of the government subsidy.

Most residents are single, divorced, or separated. If a man is married, usually the wife has refused to accept him. In one case at the Sinkou Kai Hostel in Tokyo, the wife of a first offender, the father of two boys age twelve and fifteen years, was shocked by the imprisonment of her husband for theft of a bag on a train, which he had stolen because he had lost his money gambling. The wife planned a divorce because of the shame of his crime, but she visited him at the halfway house trying to save the marriage. The guidance worker there explained that it was the first offense and that he worked diligently in a well-paid occupation. The couple was reunited.

Miyagi Tokakai in Sendai accepted a juvenile from Hokkaido who had been refused by hostels there because of his connection with the yakuza. He wanted to be a painter and was accepted for employment in construction although the employer worried about the boy's yakuza-style tattooing. After three months he left the Sendai hostel, but the staff members continue their personal ties with him. After completing parole and becoming a skilled painter, he was helped by the staff to obtain a driver's license. In 1991 he planned to bring his mother and sister from Hokkaido.

Referrals to Rehabilitation Aid Hostels

Parolees who entered hostels tended to have greater difficulties in the reentry crisis than parolees who did not (see table 10.5). Referral to the hostels is justified when released inmates lack housing initially and need other services to cope with the crisis, but the hostels do not cancel their difficulties. Adult hostel residents exceeded other adult parolees in the rate of revocations but, on the positive side, also in extinction of punishment. Whether juveniles or adults, the parolees in hostels were less frequently evaluated as having "good" behavior and more often evaluated as having "bad" behavior. Juvenile hostel residents, more often than other juveniles, fell into the "administrative actions" categories of "disappeared" and "arrest."

The reasons for referrals are in keeping with the Japanese expectation that the family is the primary buffering institution. The hostel is seen to be a viable substitute only when the family does not serve the purpose. For that reason, the family is highlighted in the Rehabilitation Bureau's examination of why parolees and probationers entered hostels in 1993. Among all parolees and probationers who arrived, 51.2 percent had no relatives upon whom to depend, 20.6 were refused shelter by relatives, and 22.2 percent did not want to live with relatives. About 3.5 percent came for the benefit of the hostel's help in coping with the reentry crisis, and 2.5 percent had other reasons (Research and Statistics Section 1994c, 126–27).

Parolees depend for shelter in the hostels more than probationers and adults more than juveniles. Of the 12,745 adult parolees terminated in 1993, 27.1 percent entered hostels, compared with only 4.2 percent of the 4,370 juvenile parolees. Probationers usually can resume their previous place in the community, since their removal from the community tends to be briefer than that of parolees. Among probationers, adults turn to hostels to a greater extent than juveniles who are more likely than adults to have access to

Table 10.5
Outcome of Juvenile and Adult Parole Termination and Referral to Hostels, 1993

| Outcome | Juvenile Parole | | | | Adult Parole | | | |
| | Termination | | Referral | | Termination | | Referral | |
	No.	%	No.	%	No.	%	No.	%
Expiration	2,280	54.5	84	45.4	8,656	93.2	2,776	80.3
Good Behavior	(1,020)	(24.4)	(17)	(9.2)	(3,631)	(39.1)	(336)	(9.7)
Average Behavior	(1,169)	(27.9)	(58)	(31.3)	(4,957)	(53.4)	(2,389)	(69.1)
Bad Behavior	(91)	(2.2)	(9)	(4.9)	(68)	(0.7)	(51)	(1.5)
Indeterminate Sentence	—	—	—	—	3	0.0	—	—
Extinction of Punishment	—	—	—	—	41	0.4	73	2.1
Early Termination	860	20.6	13	7.0	—	—	—	—
Extinction	387	9.2	60	32.4	211	2.3	77	2.2
Disappear	(182)	(4.3)	(41)	(22.2)	(9)	(0.1)	(21)	(0.6)
Arrest	(116)	(2.8)	(14)	(7.6)	(15)	(0.2)	(10)	(0.3)
Other	(89)	(2.1)	(5)	(2.7)	(187)	(2.0)	(46)	(1.3)
Revocation	652	15.6	27	14.6	376	4.1	532	15.4
Return to JTS	6	0.1	1	0.0	—	—	—	—
Total	4,185	100.0	185	100.0	9,287	100.0	3,458	100.0
Success Rate		82.7		77.6		95.8		83.9

Source: Research and Statistics Section (1994c).

Note: For the comparison of hostel parolees with parolees not referred to hostels, the number of parolees in hostels are subtracted from total parole.

a family or a social service agency. Of the 5,005 adult probation terminations, 2.7 percent required a hostel. Only 0.3 percent of the 23,171 juvenile probationers entered rehabilitation aid hostels (Research and Statistics Section 1994c, 126–27).

Hostels are of greatest service to persons over forty years of age and particularly for those older than sixty. The residents leaving hostels in 1993 averaged 48.9 years of age. As the population grows older, the greater becomes the impact of the trend toward the nuclear family in Japan and the reduction of its readiness to care for the elderly. In comparison, adults approved for parole in 1993 averaged 39.4 years. The older the hostel residents are, usually the longer their stay will be: 38.5 days for persons less than thirty years old, 46 days for persons in their thirties, 49.9 days for those in their forties, 49.1 days for those in their fifties, and 56.1 days for those sixty and above (Research and Statistics Section 1994c, 167).

Adult parolees were especially dependent on hostels because family ties did not exist (53 percent of the reasons for referral) or the relatives refused to receive them (18.0 percent) or they refused to live with their relatives (23.3 percent). Adult probationers were less likely to turn to the hostels; when they did, the absence of family ties (54.5 percent) and refusal of the family to receive them (18.7 percent) were major reasons; but the probationers' rejection of relatives was only 13 percent of the reasons.

There have been relatively few referrals of juvenile parolees, mostly because of refusal of relatives to receive the residents (43 percent) or because of the lack of relatives (29 percent). Of the few juvenile probationers entering rehabilitation aid hostels, a considerable share (39 percent) entered for hostel services; only 21 percent had no relatives and 16 percent were refused by relatives.

In 1993 two-thirds of the residents left the hostels after averaging fifty-one days and were self-supporting (see table 10.6). Another 2 percent had been there for forty-seven days

Table 10.6

*Outcome of Stay at Hostel Compared with Reason
for Referral, 1993*

		Reason for Referral to Hostel					
Outcome	No.	(1) %	(2) %	(3) %	(4) %	Total	(5) Days
Self-Support	1,727	71.9	12.6	14.6	0.9	100.0	50.6
Public Welfare	62	82.3	11.3	6.4	—	100.0	47.3
Asked to Leave	132	72.0	15.1	12.1	0.8	100.0	46.3
Left Without Notice	300	74.7	13.0	11.0	1.3	100.0	34.7
Left by Accident	40	80.0	7.5	10.0	2.5	100.0	47.9
Change of Aid	312	65.1	17.3	16.7	0.9	100.0	57.0
Other	150	80.0	8.7	11.3	—	100.0	43.7
Total	2,723[a]	72.2	13.0	13.9	0.9	100.0	48.9

Source: Research and Statistics Section (1994c).

Note: Headings for columns are as follows:
  (1) Had no relatives
  (2) Refused by relatives
  (3) Rejected relatives
  (4) Claimed desire for hostel services
  (5) Mean number of days at hostel

[a]The number of unreported outcomes was 380.

on average but went on the public dole. Another 10 percent left after fifty-seven days on average and switched to another kind of assistance other than public welfare Eleven percent were at the hostel for a shorter time on average (thirty-five days) and left without consulting the staff; attendance in a hostel is entirely voluntary, and these persons may have had successful reintegration. The staff asked a few residents (4 percent) to leave because their financial benefits were exhausted, their situation did not require the hostel's services, or their conduct was questionable.

Absence of family ties was the primary reason given by

the offender for referral to the hostels—supporting the basic presumption of the Japanese government that the family is the usual buffering institution. The reason was predominant in all outcomes of the stay in the hostels, but particularly so for those residents who went on public welfare after leaving the hostel. Residents who had rejected living with relatives or who had been refused assistance by relatives were most inclined to support themselves or to turn to other kinds of assistance (other than the dole). We get the tentative impression that grave difficulties in family relationships stimulate some residents to seek resources on their own. Referrals to gain advantage of hostel services were few in general and were most frequent for residents pressed by the staff to leave the hostel. They, it seems, had not benefited by their stay.

The Research and Training Institute, Ministry of Justice, published the findings of a follow-up study of 1,480 persons who had been hostel residents on 15 February 1979 (Ito et al. 1992). The longer the stay in the hostels, the more favorable the benefits for the former residents. Among favorable reasons for departure were independence of the resident, marriage, or improvement in family conditions; among unfavorable reasons were discord with other residents or absconding. Favorable situations represented 28 percent of the reasons for residence less than three months and 46 percent for residence ten to twelve months. To meet the reentry crisis, residents ideally should possess one hundred thousand yen or more. Of residents departing in less than three months, only 12 percent were qualified, compared with 35 percent of those at hostels for ten to twelve months.

Of the 1,480 former residents, 78 (5.3 percent) committed a crime while at the hostel and 312 (21.1 percent) during the year following departure. For the 312 subsequent recidivists, the percentage of persons with new offenses ranged from 42 percent for four-to-six-month hostel stays to 25 percent for ten-to-twelve-month stays.

The researchers decided that the hostels have some deterrent effect on recidivism "in spite of difficulties concerning employment conditions and ill-feeling among community members" (Ito et al. 1992, 139). In light of the superior results for longer lengths of stay, Ito and associates recommended that "accommodation in the hostel should be prospectively provided at least for one year and that financial support to meet this requirement should also be established" (138).

PROVISION OF
REHABILITATION AID

In addition to the hostels, Japan provides "rehabilitation aid" under certain conditions. Hostels are a service in themselves, but they also are vehicles for providing other forms of assistance. Probation offices also provide resources (food, clothing, medical treatment, or travel expenses) without referral to hostels. In addition to providing monetary assistance, the probation offices refer persons to the hostels, public employment agencies, and welfare agencies. The Law for Aftercare of Discharged Offenders, Article 3-2, places the aid under the supervision of the RPB but its administration under the chief of the probation office "who shall do such work by himself or by commissioning it to the local public entity or the person operating rehabilitation aid services."

The Offenders Rehabilitation Law, Article 40, authorizes part of what is called "Aid II" and connects rehabilitation aid with probationary supervision in helping parolees to obtain means for education and training, medical treatment, lodging, vocational guidance, and transportation to destinations most suitable for their rehabilitation. Article 40 calls for emergency help for parolees and juvenile probationers suffering from "injury or sickness or by lack of proper temporary lodging, residence, or job." The chief of the probation office is instructed to assist needy parolees and juvenile probationers in obtaining help from other agencies. If the effort is futile, the chief is told to help pay necessary expenses "within the limits of the budget."

The Law for Probationary Supervision of Persons under Suspension of Execution of Sentence, Article 6, authorizes Aid I for persons granted suspension and refers to the enlistment of aid from relevant public institutions such as health and welfare services. When necessary aid cannot be obtained from those agencies, Article 6-2 instructs probation offices to supply expenses for travel to the release destination, clothing, food, and so on, and to make medical treatment or living quarters available.

The Law for Aftercare of Discharged Offenders, Article 1, authorizes Aid II for inmates completing their prison sentence or penal detention, persons receiving a suspension of a prison sentence without probationary supervision or whose disposition has not been decided by the court, and persons whom the public prosecutor has decided not to refer for trial. Article 2 defines the objectives:

> In this Law "rehabilitation aid" shall mean to help the persons mentioned in each item of the preceding Article to become law-abiding good members of the society and assist them quickly to be rehabilitated, by such means as rendering them temporary aids, that is, helping them return home and furnishing or lending money or articles to them, or continuous aids, that is, placing them in institutions for rehabilitation aid to help them obtain necessary culture, training, medical treatment, recreation, or employment and effecting the betterment and adjustment of their environments, if such persons can not receive aid from their relatives, friends, etc. or when they can not obtain medical treatment, lodging accommodation, employment, or other protection from public health, welfare, or other institutions or in case it is feared that they may not be rehabilitated merely with such aid or protection. (UNAFEI n.d., 265)

Table 10.7
Rehabilitation Aid: Type of Completed Aid, by Type of Recipient, 1993

Recipient	Aid at Hostels	Aid at Probation Offices	Specific Types of Aid among All Aid Given at Probation Offices				
			Total	Food	Clothes	Travel	Medical
			Aid I				
Total Recipients	4,679	3,106	1,520	628	533	349	10
Adult Parole (%)	83.7	77.1	55.8	86.6	34.2	33.2	60.0
Adult Probation (%)	6.8	11.0	21.9	4.6	34.3	33.8	30.0
Juvenile Parole (%)	6.1	6.0	10.2	6.4	12.6	13.5	10.0
Juvenile Probation (%)	3.4	5.9	12.1	2.4	18.9	19.5	—
Total (%)	100.0	100.0	100.0	100.0	100.0	100.0	100.0
			Aid II				
Total Recipients	2,761	4,266	3,009	436	1,304	1,263	6
Terminated (%)	73.6	59.2	50.8	51.8	49.2	51.7	100.0
Suspended Sentence (%)	13.6	14.4	17.4	18.8	16.9	17.6	—
Suspended Prosecution (%)	12.8	26.4	31.8	29.4	33.9	30.7	—
Total (%)	100.0	100.0	100.0	100.0	100.0	100.0	100.0

Source: Research and Statistics Section (1994c).

Note: "Completed Aid" refers to the number of aid recipients in a given year.

The hostels delivered more Aid I to parolees and probationers than did the probation offices, but probation offices gave more Aid II. Table 10.7 specifies four kinds of need for Aid I that were only a portion of all the assistance given by the probation offices. For Aid I, adult parolees received the most assistance. Probationers, especially adults, depended more on the probation offices than hostels; their emergency assistance was limited mostly to meals and travel. Although medical treatment was rarely provided, adult parolees were most likely to need medical treatment, presumably because only they had been isolated from the free community. Adult probationers had three of the ten incidents. Juvenile parolees were about equal in applying for aid in hostels or probation offices, mostly for food and travel. Adult parolees made heavy demands for all kinds of aid authorized by probation offices, particularly for clothing; that need is characteristic of released prisoners who have been absent from life outside the prison.

Table 10.7 also documents the heavy representation of hostels in the provision of Aid II to the "terminated" (persons completing parole, primarily, and probation). Aid II provided at probation offices was distributed more widely than the aid given at the hostels. Persons not prosecuted because it was found unnecessary made up about a quarter of those receiving aid at the probation offices, especially in meeting their need for food and travel expenses. Terminated persons took up the greatest share of Aid II distribution. The individuals benefiting from a suspended sentence were the least represented among recipients.

GROUP HOMES OF
INCIDENTAL SERVICE

Although not their primary purpose, other residential facilities receive juveniles on probation or parole, incidental to serving their usual clientele. The Rehabilitation Bureau limits rehabilitation aid to emergency cases not served by other community agencies. Eight group homes in Japan provide temporary quarters for juveniles experiencing family disorganization. The homes receive juveniles from social welfare offices, child guidance homes, governor's guidance homes of prefectures, and family court.

The Association for the Purpose of Walking with Youth

operates three group homes in Tokyo, including the House of Rest (Ikoinoie), which I visited. Another association operates three other group homes in Tokyo, including the "Small House" used by the family court for tentative probation. The Tokyo homes became first involved with delinquents when one of them accepted a stimulant-drug abuser from an orphanage; family courts began to include delinquents among the referrals. The House of Rest has received homicide cases, but rejects arsonists and sex offenders. Persons with psychiatric problems are not referred.

The House of Rest occupies a large residence purchased in 1967 because of its location close to where persons attended a night school or had jobs, or where adolescent girls would be safe. The crux of the home's functions is to provide a family-like environment while the residents are employed in the neighborhood in income-producing jobs. The maximum stay is one year, with the average being six months. Learning the concerns of the juveniles through conversations, the staff endeavors to restore their trust in adults. Otherwise, the juveniles are expected to be employed and move to regular housing after a temporary stay. The boys usually work as assistant drivers, handymen at gasoline stations, or manual laborers in construction. Girls clerk in stores or work in clothing factories or laundries. If the residents lose their jobs, the staff helps them find another.

The residents are expected to behave as responsible adults without a formal code of conduct. The residents have no tasks other than washing their dishes. If the family court's investigating officer finds the juvenile is not doing well, the family court is asked to make a final disposition. The officer visits once a month on average and, when appropriate, summons a juvenile to the court's office for an interview.

The family court and the Tokyo Metropolitan Government meet 45 percent of the costs of operating the House of Rest. Flea markets produce some seventy million yen a year.

Residents are charged thirty thousand yen per month; if they are unemployed and without funds, the unpaid rent is treated as their debt.

As another resource, the probation homes serve family courts for tentative probation and temporary removal from an unsatisfactory environment. The persons operating the homes may be farmers, Buddhist priests, or operators of a small factory inside a home (M. Sato 1985). The Tateno family in Chiba Prefecture began to receive boys on their farm in 1957 in spite of the protest of neighbors. In 1966 two of the boys rescued two younger children who had fallen into a river; the attitude of the neighbors was reversed. A man named Sumimoto in Nara Prefecture, repatriated from China after World War II, obtained a piece of a barren mountain, cut down trees, and tilled the soil. The neighbors objected to his acceptance of boys from the family courts of Osaka and Sakai; later, farmers in three mountain villages joined him in employing city boys to raise cedar trees and tea bushes.

CONCLUSION

In tracing the what, how, and why of many facets of correctional work, the preceding chapters have sketched the influence of the cultural heritage of the Japanese. Western ideas and practices were imported but given indigenous interpretations, probably because the industrial revolution reached Japan only some century and a third ago. Full-scale community-based corrections—as usually defined—arrived even later. The Rehabilitation Bureau gives the following account of that history:

> Since the first pioneer attempts, it took many decades for probation, parole, and aftercare to become fully implemented in Japan as an integral part of corrections. In contrast to the long prelude, however, probation and parole have made steady progress after they were given

a legal basis about forty-five years ago. As in those other countries where community-based treatment of offenders has a far longer history, Japanese corrections have also arrived at the stage where probation and parole play a crucial part in the administration of criminal justice and in recent years nearly three-fifths of the offenders who are receiving correctional treatment are left in the community under the supervision of probation officers. (Rehabilitation Bureau 1990, i)

The concept of community is especially involved in the Japanese version of probation, parole, and aftercare. Unsalaried private persons carry out most of the supervision of probationers and parolees; private organizations are responsible for aftercare, receiving only a portion of their operating costs through governmental subsidies. A variety of justifications for public participation is offered, but the policy is consistent with the government's limitation on the size of its bureaucracy and its tendency to turn many of its functions over to the private sector.

In that sense, the community becomes an alternative to the government as a unit of social organization. Citizens are recruited—individually as volunteer probation officers or collectively as members of several associations—to become a collectivity. To serve the purposes of the Rehabilitation Bureau, the volunteers are stimulated by the Japanese sense of duty. Within the interdependent community typical of urban life, they are drawn from particular segments of the population. Many recruits ultimately perceive themselves as representatives of a fraternal community expressing a sense of communion and rushing to help their fellows, but that perception of community does not square with the earlier history of community sentiments in Japan and the conditions of contemporary urbanism.

Another perception of community is applicable to all facets of correctional work in Japan. By sharing a common culture and social experience, the Japanese are bound to one another in a rather consensual society. Their strong group solidarity is derived from the loyalty of individuals, their personal dedication to fundamental values, and their willing obedience to common expectations. Although that dedication is not universally strong, and although misconduct does occur, the remarkable degree of social solidarity deters crime and presses offenders to be repentant.

The repentance of the delinquent and the criminal usually sparks forgiveness from a public that believes that persons have the capacity for self-correction without further intervention of the criminal justice system. Sharing the faith in the repentant offender, the procuracy and judiciary filter out the "worthy" offenders so only the "least deserving" end up in correctional institutions. The distinction appears to be between those worthy of membership in the community and those who have violated the conditions for inclusion in a consensual society. "Rehabilitation" becomes an exercise in earning one's way back into membership.

NOTES
REFERENCES
INDEX

NOTES

1
INTRODUCTION

1. The American and Japanese imprisonment rates in table 1.1 are derived from data on the year-end population of prisons. Some of the other tables in this book use data on annual admissions to prison, in keeping with the assumption that admissions are the best reflection of changes over time in the use of imprisonment. "Flow studies using annual admission," says Lynch (1988, 184), "are not affected by the accumulation of more serious offenders."

2. Much of the information reported in this book was obtained in interviews of prison officials in Tokyo and many other places in Japan. The interviews were recorded on tape and transcribed for later use. In order to allay any suspicions these individuals might have about speaking frankly with me, I assured them of complete anonymity and in return received more cooperation than I could have reasonably expected. Hence, remarks quoted in the book from these persons will remain, as promised, unidentified.

2
PARSIMONY IN RESORT
TO IMPRISONMENT

1. The terms oyabun and kobun can have either positive or pejorative connotations in popular Japanese thinking, caution

Bennett and Ishino (1963). The terms may refer to a style of non-familial relationship typified by an authoritarian parent and submissive child. Another popular meaning conveys the image of an explosive, ruthless, quasi-legal or illegal organization dominated by an authoritarian boss.

2. There are, of course, parallels in the United States. Alcoholics Anonymous, for example, insists that the addictive drinker must realize actively that he or she has a problem and decide voluntarily to give up consumption of alcohol. However, Japanese values support extension of *official* leniency to the repentant offender on grounds that one is capable of self-correction.

3. See Johnson and Heijder (1983) for discussion of the Netherlands's application of the principle of discretionary prosecution.

3

THE TWO BUREAUS

1. Within the prison system, the classification centers for young adults (discussed below) are an exception among adult institutions in their emphasis on classification and diagnoses for therapeutic purposes.

2. All adult women are forwarded directly from detention facilities to women's prisons.

3. Two schools specialize in vocational training, two in education at the senior high school level, and four in medical care (Correction Bureau 1990b).

4. Admissions to women's guidance homes declined sharply over years until it became zero. In 1991 the juvenile classification home in Hachioji provided space and staff in the event of admission of a street-walking prostitute but none were present.

4

THE MANAGERS

1. "A high degree of job security has been a privilege reserved primarily for government employees and for managers and staff workers in selected large industrial organizations until around World War II. The privilege of 'career employment' was then extended gradually to the key male production workers in

large factories" (Whitehill and Takezawa 1968, 13). Also see Thompson and McHugh (1990, 205).

2. The *nenko* system, in step with age and seniority, regularly moves employees into higher ranks in accord with pay grades.

3. Interviews conducted at the central office of the Correction Bureau and during field visits are the basis of this discussion of the recruiting and training of psychologists.

4. The budget of the Correction Bureau has been modified to permit future recruitment of an additional seven psychologists.

5. The headquarters in Tokyo of both bureaus are in the open-office plan except for the offices of the directors general.

6. I witnessed the ceremonial departure of persons who were transferred from the headquarters of the Correction Bureau in 1991. After being received by the director general in his office, the smiling individuals passed between two rows of applauding colleagues.

7. The history of testing previous to the NPA examinations is traced to 1 February 1912, when the Japanese Prison Association prepared tests for job candidates. The test would be sent in a closed envelope to the wardens and opened simultaneously all over Japan. The applicants were required to write essay answers about penal law, the psychology of prison officers, and practical matters (Correction Bureau 1990a).

8. "Correctional families" are an unofficial form of recruitment insofar as personnel of the Correction Bureau include representatives of second and third generations of employees.

9. Candidates for prison officer positions must meet these requirements: Japanese nationality, no prison sentences served, no dismissal from public service in the previous two years, at least a high school education, height of at least 160 cm, weight of at least 47 kg, chest girth of at least 78 cm, acceptable eyesight and job performance, and no impairment of arms and legs.

10. In the multiple-agency model, training of correctional personnel occurs in an institute responsible also for instruction of personnel of other agencies such as law enforcement, courts, and the immigration service.

11. Information on in-service training of the Rehabilitation Bureau was obtained from interviews; see also Rehabilitation Bureau (1990) and Kubo (1990).

12. The independent-academy model has a separate physical

plant and a full-time faculty instructing correctional personnel only and receives personnel from all the offices and facilities of the correctional system (E. Johnson 1992).

13. The direct involvement of private organizations in correctional affairs is a key characteristic of Japanese policy and practice, especially in community corrections. The Japanese Correctional Association has a major role in prison industries.

14. While inspecting Japanese prisons in 1927, Gillin (1931) found three courses for employees being conducted. Inaugurated in 1908, a course for higher prison officers lasted two months and had graduated two thousand persons by 1925. A second course was for chief warders and jail personnel, including women jailers. Prison physicians were required to attend a two-month course on medical care of inmates.

5
THE INDUSTRIAL PRISON

1. Research for this chapter was especially assisted by Kazuo Kawakani, former director general of the Correction Bureau, Keisei Miyamoto, head of CAPIC, and Takehisa Kihara, director of the Industrial Division, Headquarters of the Correction Bureau.

2. Two developments should be noted that, to a degree, reverse the long-term decline of the prison industries in the United States (Hawkins 1983; Weiss 1987). The Federal Prison Industries is a corporation established by Congress in 1934 that employs some quarter of the Federal Bureau of Prisons inmates in production and services for various federal government entities. More recently, the Free Venture model, an experiment of the Law Enforcement Assistance Administration in the Department of Justice, has funded private involvement in the prison industries of seven states.

3. Although open opposition to contracting has not surfaced in Japan, the state of the nation's economy can jeopardize access of the prisons to subcontracting opportunities. At this writing, the Japanese economy is suffering a downturn. In 1990–92 the small open correctional facilities, in which private firms employ selected prisoners, already suffered from declines in certain sectors of the total economy.

4. "In large areas of Tokyo and Osaka back streets rarely visited by outsiders, one hears the same clickety-clack of small machines behind hundreds of wooden doors as one did ten or twenty years ago, but the clickety-clack produces entirely different things today" (Van Wolferen 1989, 171).

5. A private contractor even insisted that background music be played in one of Osaka Prison's workshops as a means of raising worker efficiency.

6. When released from prison in 1990, male inmates averaged 25,962 yen and women inmates 28,449 yen in accumulated remuneration. The averages increased consistently with length of sentence from 1,686 yen for less than three months to 53,923 yen for sentences over three years for males. The equivalent range for women was 1,500 to 54,897 yen (Research and Statistics Section 1991a, 180).

7. The progressive stage system grants prisoners greater privileges according to their demonstrated improvement in conduct. The scheme's invention has been attributed to Alexander Maconochie in Australia in the 1840s and to Joshua Jebb and Walter Crofton who elaborated the scheme as the "Irish system" (Barnes and Teeters 1945). The system of conduct grades was a component in the experiments at Elmira (New York) Reformatory, established in 1877 as a prototype (McKelvey [1936] 1977).

8. MOF collects monies from several governmental institutions, primarily postal savings, insurance, national pensions, and welfare pensions (Woronoff 1986).

9. Chalmers Johnson points out that public corporations pay their own way, provide services, and thus contribute to keeping the Japanese tax rate lower than in other countries (C. Johnson 1978).

10. By improved administrative and accounting methods, the prisons were able, by the end of 1992, to stabilize those costs that previously had been increasing.

6
THE ORDERLY PRISON

1. The prison in Kosuge near Tokyo was modeled after the *maisons centrale* of France, and the prison at Miyagi duplicated the Central Prison of Leuven, Belgium. Miyagi Prison is a national

treasure today; portions of the moat and the ancient trees are remnants of the feudal castle of a daimyo.

2. In an opinion survey of 2,648 prisoners conducted by the Research and Training Institute, Ministry of Justice, 51.2 percent agreed that the prison is a "place to provide enforced labor for compensation of an offense" (Research and Training Institute 1987, 175).

3. As in the West, factories in Japan have tried in the past to enforce rules intended to encourage production efficiency. In 1927 a Japanese automobile plant displayed an announcement: "Don't lose your spirit for work. Don't look around while working. Don't think about anything else while working. Talking to someone who is working is prohibited in this factory" (Allinson 1975, 104).

4. Japanese prisoners continue to be far less inclined to file grievances than American prisoners. Japanese prisoners filed 58 civil-rights suits in 1986 and prisoners of the U.S. Federal Bureau of Prisons (FBP) 770 cases (Correction Bureau 1989, 101; Thomas 1988, 56). In 1982, FBP inmates filed 13,187 complaints (Baker 1985, 68), many more than the Japanese petitions to the Minister of Justice (see table 6.5).

7

THE JUVENILE
JUSTICE SYSTEM

1. The history recounted in this section draws primarily from Soejima (1974).

2. The practice resembles contemporary day-fines that differentiate monetary penalties according to the seriousness of the offense and the offender's level of income.

3. Tara Ogawa became superintendent of the Kanto Medical Training School, Kazuo Sato recalled, and introduced new ideas there he had learned from Lloyd W. McCorkle (later director of New Jersey's prisons), who was a member of the American army during the occupation.

4. Information on intake was obtained during field visits to the Tokyo and Urawa family courts.

5. Prison Law, Article 20, calls for the family court's referral of a case to the public prosecutor if the court finds, after proper

investigation, that the offense is punishable with the death penalty or imprisonment with or without forced labor. If the offense has been committed by a juvenile less than sixteen years of age, the article forbids referral to the public prosecutor.

6. In the 1960s the Correction Bureau experimented with short-term treatment in JTSs. Official introduction of that program came in 1977 as part of a new policy agenda stemming from two general developments. First, the family courts had reduced the number of commitments to the JTSs, contending that the length of stays in the schools was excessively long and had negative effect on some juveniles. Second, the Correction Bureau recognized that new kinds of delinquency—such as varieties of juvenile gangs—had appeared. To meet the new circumstances, greater flexibility of programming was sought in distinguishing between the more amenable youngsters from those needing more prolonged treatment.

7. The arrangement is similar to weekend arrest as practiced in Belgium and New South Wales (Johnson and Herreman 1975; E. Johnson 1981). In those programs the officials complain that concentration of inmates in the prison on weekends complicates staff work assignments, which usually are only on weekends, because inmates vacate quarters on weekday evenings. Japanese training schools alleviate such difficulties because, first, few inmates are on the special open-treatment program and, second, the duration of the open treatment is only two weeks. Most of the four-month total program is spent in the JTS; open treatment is a kind of prerelease.

8. Paraphrased from the Director General's Regulation 1285, "On the Criteria of Evaluating Grades at Training Schools," 24 June 1980.

9. Masaki (1964), director of the Prison Bureau during World War II, tells of the showing of an American film about Father Flanagan's Boys Town. Mr. Ichijima, deputy chief prosecutor, arranged the showing at a public meeting when funds were collected for purchase of five hectares of land.

10. In an experiment in the 1860s, American reformers introduced "ship schools" for teaching the rudiments of seamanship to male delinquents. Life at sea was expected to "purify" wrongdoers, but the experiment failed due to the youths' lack of discipline, excessive financial costs, and unemployment of adult seamen during an economic depression (U.S. Department of Justice 1976).

8
COMMUNITY-BASED CORRECTIONS

1. "Japan is a good illustration of a developed capitalist society where community involvement is extensive," Gill and Mawby (1990, 7–9) conclude from reviewing an international literature. They point out that Japan features "a bureaucratic, central state, which is partly a reflection of Confucianism" that "permeates local neighborhoods through a series of complex networks."

2. The oil shocks in the 1970s stimulated a particular effort to slice government expenditures; prison industries were targeted and CAPIC emerged (see chapter 5).

3. Spitzer (1983, 317–18) argues that the gonin-gumi strategy is an example of the weaknesses of central government: "The fact that local elites had to be kept in place and manipulated under Tokugawa law, rather than totally destroyed, is one indication of the political and ideological weaknesses characteristic of certain types of pre-capitalist states."

4. In this respect, Ben-Ari refers to Janowitz (1967) and his concept of "communities of limited liability."

5. The use of VPOs is remarkable in its extent. Volunteers are involved in corrections elsewhere. For example, "patronage societies" partly funded by the state expanded rapidly in France after 1885 (O'Brien 1982).

6. A precedent for the VPO system has been noted: the government's Ex-Convicts Protection System of the early 1900s helped ex-convicts under government sponsorship. Most volunteers were Buddhist monks (Wagatsuma and De Vos 1984).

7. "Environmental adjustment" requires investigation of the family and employment situation the parole candidate will encounter upon release; the conditions should be congenial to "rehabilitation."

8. Most halfway houses simply offer a supportive environment allowing time to have a restorative effect after leaving a domiciliary institution; any genuine therapy is to be offered elsewhere. Some halfway houses go beyond the simple transitional purpose to try to initiate changes in the residents within a sensitive environment.

9. In a letter to the author dated 9 September 1994, Hiroyasu Sugihara, director general of the Rehabilitation Bureau, writes:

> The recent economic recession in our country precluded firms and individuals from making donations to these hostels, leaving them to face difficulties in fund raising activities.... We, at the Rehabilitation Bureau, decided to make a revision of the administrative law which would allow the government to subsidize the hostels in need of financial assistance for the maintenance of their facilities.... Thanks to the support of the parliament ... the annual budget for 1994 to subsidize the hostels was allotted to our Bureau.... Although the government subsidies ... are limited to half the costs needed for facility maintenance and there still remains much to be done to further improve functions of the rehabilitation hostels, we are expecting that some progress will be made in this area."

10. Three bar associations of Tokyo formed a joint committee to study police practices in interrogating accused persons held in police cells during investigation of crimes. Daiyo-kangoku (substitute prisons) are cells in police stations that may be used for accused persons as substitutes for detention centers of the Correction Bureau (Prison Law, Article 1). The committee reported on treatment of thirty falsely accused detainees. The respondents told of a variety of police techniques, such as being forced to sit in uncomfortable chairs, being shouted at, and being denied access to an attorney.

9
PROBATION

1. The penal code specifies the conditions for suspension of sentences by criminal courts (see chapter 2).

2. As an example of "banked caseloads," direct supervision resembles the Western practice of concentrating quality-supervision on selected probation.

3. Kayo Konagai, head of the Direct Supervision Unit in the Tokyo Probation Office, provided the case histories.

10
EXITING FROM CONFINEMENT

1. In another administrative paradox, the RPB has authority to terminate probationary supervision, when requested by the chief of the probation office, that the court had required when suspending a prison sentence (Article 8 of the Law for Probationary Supervision of Persons under Suspension of Execution of Sentence).

2. The Offenders Rehabilitation Law, Articles 3–6, defines the functions and organization of the National Rehabilitation Commission: The chair and four members are appointed by the Minister of Justice with the consent of the Diet; the term of office is three years; two members are part-time; the chair and members shall not be officers of a political party or any other political organization and shall not engage in political activities during tenure of office; and they can not have other duties receiving remuneration or run a business enterprise while in office.

3. The use of parole for managing prisoners is not unusual. Beginning at Elmira Reformatory in 1869 as an element in prison reform, parole by the 1930s "had reverted to its earliest form as a means of controlling and managing convicts within the prison sentence and outside while on license" (Bean 1981, 158).

REFERENCES

Abe, Hakaru. 1963. "Education of the Legal Profession in Japan." In *Law in Japan: The Legal Order in a Changing Society*, edited by Arthur Taylor Van Mehren. Cambridge: Harvard University Press.

Abe, Haruo. 1963. "The Accused and Society: Therapeutic and Preventive Aspects of Criminal Justice in Japan." In *Law in Japan: The Legal Order in a Changing Society*, edited by Arthur Taylor Van Mehren. Cambridge: Harvard University Press.

Abegglen, James C. 1973. *Management and Worker: The Japanese Solution*. Tokyo: Kodansha International.

Akatsuka, Ko. 1989. "Problems of Japanese Contemporary Corrections." Unpublished paper. Tokyo: United Nations Asia and Far East Institute for Prevention of Crime and Treatment of Offenders (UNAFEI).

Allinson, Gary D. 1975. *Japanese Urbanism: Industry and Politics in Kariya, 1872–1972*. Berkeley: University of California Press.

———. 1979. *Suburban Tokyo: A Comparative Study in Politics and Social Change*. Berkeley: University of California Press.

Ancel, Marc. 1971. *Suspended Sentence*. London: Heinemann Educational Books.

Andenaes, Johannes. 1975. "General Prevention Revisited: Research and Policy Implications." *Journal of Criminal Law and Criminology* 66: 338–65.

Angata, Shizuo. 1990. "Some Aspects of Volunteer Probation Officer (Hogoshi) System in Japan." Unpublished paper. Tokyo:

United Nations Asia and Far East Institute for Prevention of Crime and Treatment of Offenders.

Aoyagi, Kiyotaka. 1983. "Variable Traditions in Urban Japan: *Matsuri* and *Ohonaikai*." In *Town-Talk: The Dynamics of Urban Anthropology*, edited by Ghaus Ansari and Peter J. M. Nas. Leiden, The Netherlands: E. J. Brill.

Azumi, Koya. 1974. "Voluntary Organizations in Japan." In *Voluntary Action Research*, edited by David Horton Smith. Lexington, Mass.: Lexington Books.

Baker, J. E. 1985. *Prisoner Participation in Prison Power*. Metuchen, N.J.: Scarecrow Press.

Barnes, Harry E., and Negley K. Teeters. 1945. *New Horizons in Criminology*. New York: Prentice Hall.

Bean, Philip. 1981. *Punishment: A Philosophical and Criminological Inquiry*. Oxford, England: Martin Robertson.

Beasley, William G. 1972. *The Meiji Restoration*. Stanford: Stanford University Press.

———. 1990. *The Rise of Modern Japan*. Tokyo: Charles E. Tuttle.

Beckman, George M. 1957. *The Making of the Meiji Constitution*. Lawrence: University of Kansas Press.

Befu, Harumi. 1992. "Introduction: Framework of Analysis." In *Otherness of Japan: Historical and Cultural References on Japanese Studies in Ten Countries*, edited by Harumi Befu and Josef Kreiner. Munich: Iudicum.

Bellah, Robert N. 1971. "Continuity and Change in Japanese Society." In *Stability and Social Change*, edited by Bernard Barber and Alex Inkeles. Boston: Little, Brown.

Ben-Ari, Eyal. 1991. *Changing Japanese Suburbia: A Study of Two Present-Day Localities*. London: Routledge and Kegan Paul.

Bennett, John W., and Iwao Ishino. 1963. *Paternalism in the Japanese Economy: Anthropological Studies of Oyabun-Kobun Patterns*. Minneapolis: University of Minnesota Press.

Bestor, Theodore C. 1985. "Tradition and Japanese Social Organization: Institutional Development in a Tokyo Neighborhood." *Ethnology* 24: 121–35.

Bixby, F. Lovell. 1971. "Two Modern Correctional Facilities in Japan." *Federal Probation* 35: 13–15.

Blomberg, Thomas G. 1987. "Criminal Justice Reform and Social Control: Are We Becoming a Minimum Security Society?" In

Transcarceration: Essays in the Sociology of Social Control, edited by John Lowman, Robert J. Menzies, and T. S. Polys. Alderholt, England: Gower.

Blumstein, Alfred. 1988. "Prison Populations: A System Out of Control?" In *Crime and Justice: A Review of Research*, vol. 10, edited by Michael Tonry and Norval Morris. Chicago: University of Chicago Press.

Bottoms, A. E., and William McWilliams. 1979. "A Non-Treatment Paradigm for Probation Practices." *British Journal of Social Work* 9: 159–202.

Braibanti, Ralph J. D. 1948. "Neighborhood Associations in Japan and Their Democratic Potentialities." *Far Eastern Quarterly* 7(2): 136–64.

Buendia, Hernando-Gomez, ed. 1989. *Urban Crime: Global Trends and Policies*. Tokyo: United Nations University.

Burks, Ardath W. 1964. *The Government of Japan*. 2nd ed. New York: Thomas Y. Crowell.

Campbell, John Creighton. 1985. "Governmental Responses to Budget Scarcity: Japan." *Policy Studies Journal* 13: 506–16.

Caves, Richard E., and Masu Uekusa. 1976. *Industrial Organization in Japan*. Washington, D.C.: Brookings Institution.

Ch'en, Paul Heng-Chao. 1981. *The Formation of the Early Meiji Legal Order*. Oxford: Oxford University Press.

Cheng, Man Tsun. 1991. "The Japanese Permanent Employment System: Empirical Findings." *Work and Occupations* 18: 148–71.

Christopher, Robert C. 1983. *The Japanese Mind: The Goliath Explained*. Tokyo: Charles E. Tuttle.

Cole, Robert E. 1979. *Work, Mobility, and Participation: A Comparative Study of American and Japanese Industry*. Berkeley: University of California Press.

Colignon, Richard A., and Chikako Usui. 1994. "Japanese Response to the Current Economic Resession." Paper delivered at annual meeting of the Southern Sociological Society, Raleigh, N.C.

Collick, Martin. 1988. "Social Policy: Pressures and Responses." In *Dynamic and Immobilist Politics in Japan*, by J. A. A. Stockwin et al. Honolulu: University of Hawaii Press.

Correction Bureau. 1967. *Correctional Administration in Japan*. Tokyo: Ministry of Justice.

———. 1982. *Correctional Institutions in Japan*. Tokyo: Ministry of Justice.

———. 1985. *Correctional Institutions in Japan*. Tokyo: Ministry of Justice.

———. 1989. "Statistics on Inmate Grievances." *Hoanjouhou* (Security Information) 61: 101–6.

———. 1990a. "A Centennial History of Training for Correctional Personnel in Japan" (in Japanese). *Bulletin of Training Institute for Correctional Personnel* 5: 154–66.

———. 1990b. *Correctional Institutions in Japan*. Tokyo: Ministry of Justice.

Couch, Ben M. 1993. "Is Incarceration Really Worse? Analyses of Offenders' Preferences for Prison Over Probation." *Justice Quarterly* 10: 67–88.

Craig, Albert M. 1961. *Chosu in the Meiji Restoration*. Cambridge: Harvard University Press.

Crawcour, Sydney. 1978. "The Japanese Employment System." *Journal of Japanese Studies* 4: 225–45.

Dale, Peter N. 1986. *The Myth of Japanese Uniqueness*. London: Crom Helm.

De Vos, George A., 1973. *Socialization for Achievement: Essays on the Cultural Psychology of the Japanese*. Berkeley: University of California Press.

De Vos, George A., and Keiichi Mizushima. 1973. "Criminality and Deviancy in Premodern Japan." In *Socialization for Achievement: Essays on the Cultural Psychology of the Japanese*. Berkeley: University of California Press.

Dore, Ronald P. 1958. *City Life in Japan: A Study of a Tokyo Ward*. Berkeley: University of California Press.

———. 1987. *Taking Japan Seriously: A Confucian Perspective on Leading Economic Issues*. London: Athlone Press.

Duffee, David E. 1990. "Community Corrections: Its Presumed Characteristics and an Argument for a New Approach." In *Community Corrections: A Community Field Approach*, edited by David E. Duffee and Edmund F. McGarrell. Cincinnati: Anderson.

Duke, Benjamin. 1986. *The Japanese School: Lessons for Industrial America*. New York: Praeger.

Duus, Peter. 1969. *Feudalism in Japan*. New York: Alfred A. Knopf.

Fishman, Gideon, and Simon Dinitz. 1989. "Japan: A Country with Safe Streets." In *Advances in Criminological Theory*, vol. 1, edited by William S. Laufer and Freda Adler. New Brunswick, N.J.: Transaction Publishers.

Flanagan, Timothy J., and Kathleen Maguire. 1992. *Sourcebook of Criminal Justice Statistics—1991*. Washington D.C.: Bureau of Justice Statistics, U.S. Department of Justice.

Flanagan, Timothy J., Ann L. Pastore, and Kathleen Maguire. 1993. *Sourcebook of Criminal Statistics—1992*. Washington, D.C.: Bureau of Justice Statistics, U.S. Department of Justice.

Flynn, Frank T. 1951. "Employment and Labor." In *Contemporary Corrections*, edited by Paul W. Tappan. New York: McGraw-Hill.

Fosgate, Blanchard. 1866. *Punishment*. Auburn, N.Y.: N. J. Moser.

Foucault, Michel. 1977. *Discipline and Punish: The Birth of the Prison*. Translated by Alan Sheridan. New York: Pantheon Books.

———. 1980. "Prison Talk." In *Power/Knowledge: Selected Interviews and Other Writings by Michel Foucault, 1972–1977*, edited by Colin Gordon. Brighton, England: Harvester Press.

Fox, James G. 1982. *Organizational and Racial Conflict in Maximum Prisons*. Lexington, Mass: Lexington Books.

Friedman, David. 1988. *The Misunderstood Miracle: Industrial Development and Political Change in Japan*. Ithica, N.Y.: Cornell University Press.

Funke, Gail S., Billy L. Wayson, and Neal Miller. 1982. *Assets and Liabilities of Correctional Industries*. Lexington, Mass: Lexington Books.

Fuse, Toyamasa. 1975. "Japan's Economic Development: Success, Stress and Prospects for the Future." In *Modernization and Stress in Japan*, edited by Toyamasa Fuse. Leiden, The Netherlands: E. J. Brill.

Gaes, Gerald G., and William J. McGuire. 1985. "Prison Violence: The Contribution of Crowding Versus Other Determinants of Prison Assault Rates." *Journal of Research in Crime and Delinquency* 22: 41–65.

Galtung, Johan. 1961. "Prison: The Organization of Dilemma." In *The Prison: Studies in Institutional Organization and Change*, edited by Donald R. Cressey. New York: Holt, Rinehart and Winston.

George, Aurell A. 1988. "Japanese Interest Group Behaviour: An Institutional Approach." In *Dynamic and Immobilist Politics in Japan*, by J. A. A. Stockwin et al. Honolulu: University of Hawaii Press.

George, B. J., Jr. 1988. "Discretionary Authority of Public Prosecutors in Japan." In *Law and Society in Contemporary Japan: American Perspectives*, edited by John O. Haley. Dubuque, Iowa: Kendall-Hunt.

Gill, Martin, and Rob Mawby. 1990. *Volunteers in the Criminal Justice System*. Buckingham, England: Open University Press.

Gillin, John L. 1931. *Taming the Criminal*. New York: Macmillan.

Goffman, Erving. 1961. *Asylums*. Garden City, N.Y.: Doubleday Anchor.

Griffiths, Arthur. N.d. *Oriental Prisons: Prisons and Crime in India, the Andaman Islands, Burmah, China, Japan, Egypt, Turkey*. London: Grolier Society.

Haley, John O. 1989. "Confession, Repentance, and Absolution." In *Mediation and Criminal Justice*, edited by Martin Wright and Burt Galaway. Newbury Park, Calif.: Sage.

Hamilton, V. Lee, and Joseph Sanders. 1992. *Everyday Justice: Responsibility and Individual in Japan and the United States*. New Haven, Conn.: Yale University Press.

Hane, Mikiso. 1982. *Peasants, Rebels and Outcasts*. New York: Pantheon Books.

Hashimoto, Noboru. 1983. "Japan's Use of Volunteers in Community-Based Treatment." College Park, Md: Proceedings of 12th Annual Congress of Corrections, American Correctional Association.

Hattori, Takaaki. 1963. "The Legal Profession in Japan: Its Historical Development and Present State." In *Law in Japan: The Legal Order in a Changing Society*, edited by Arthur Taylor Van Mehren. Cambridge: Harvard University Press.

Hawkins, Gordon. 1983. "Prison Labor and Prison Industries." In *Crime and Justice: An Annual Review of Research*, vol. 5, edited by Michael Tonry and Norval Morris. Chicago: University of Chicago Press.

Hayashi, Shuji. 1988. *Culture and Management in Japan*. Translated by Frank Baldwin. Tokyo: University of Tokyo Press.

Hiramatsu, Yoshiro. 1972. *History of Penalty Theory and Practice of Penalties* (in Japanese). Tokyo: Sobunsha.

———. 1973. "History of Penal Institutions in Japan." *Law in Japan* 6: 1–48.

Hirata, Keiko. 1985. "Collaboration Between the Probation Officer and the Volunteer Probation Officer in Japan." Unpublished paper. Tokyo: United Nations Asia and Far East Institute for Prevention of Crime and Treatment of Offenders.

Hirono, Ryokichi. 1969. "Personnel Management in Foreign Corporations." In *The Japanese Employee*, edited by Robert J. Balloon. Tokyo: Charles E. Tuttle.

Hyotani, Toshiyuki. 1985. "Rehabilitation Services and Criminal Policy." Unpublished paper. Tokyo: United Nations Asia and Far East Institute for Prevention of Crime and Treatment of Offenders.

Igarashi, Futaba. 1989. "Abolish Substitute Prisons: Regular Detention Centers Are Not Full" (in Japanese). *Horitsu Jiho* 61: 103–5.

International Association of Traffic and Safety Sciences. 1987. *Statistics '86: Road Accidents in Japan*. Tokyo: International Association of Traffic and Safety Sciences.

Ishida, Takeshi. 1971. *Japanese Society*. New York: Random House.

―――. 1983. *Japanese Political Culture*. New Brunswick, N.J.: Transaction Books.

Ishii, Ryosuke. 1980. *A History of Political Institutions in Japan*. Tokyo: University of Tokyo Press.

Ito, H., A. Saisyo, O. Sera, and K. Hosoki. 1992. "Study of the Characteristics of the Residents and the Treatment Programmes in the Rehabilitation Aid Hostels." Abstract of 2nd and 3rd reports in *Summary of Research Monographs in the Bulletin of the Criminological Research Department Published in 1981–1990*, Research Material Series, no. 40. Tokyo: Research and Training Institute, Ministry of Justice.

Janowitz, Morris. 1967. *The Community Press in an Urban Setting*. Chicago: University of Chicago Press.

Japan Federation of Bar Associations. 1990. *What's Daiyo-Kangoku?* Tokyo: Japan Federation of Bar Associations.

Japanese Correctional Association (JCA). N.d. *Japanese Correctional Association*. Tokyo. Brochure.

―――. Correctional Association Prison Industry Cooperative. N.d. *A Guide to CAPIC*. Tokyo.

Jeffery, Clarence Ray. 1969. "The Development of Crime in Early English Society." In *Crime and the Legal Process*, edited by William J. Chambliss. New York: McGraw-Hill.

Johnson, Chalmers A. 1978. *Japan's Public Policy Companies*. Washington, D.C.: American Enterprise Institute for Public Policy Research.

Johnson, Elmer H. 1961. "Sociology of Confinement: Assimilation and the Prison Rat." *Journal of Criminal Law, Criminology, and Police Science* 51: 528–33.

———. 1963. "The Present Level of Social Work in Prisons." *Crime and Delinquency* 9: 290–96.

———. 1965. "Administrative Statistics in Corrections as a Tool for Theoretical Research." *Prison Journal* 45: 34–43.

———. 1966a. "In-Service Training: A Key to Correctional Progress." *Criminologica* 4: 16–36.

———. 1966b. "Pilot Study: Age, Race and Recidivism as Factors in Prisoner Infractions." *Canadian Journal of Corrections* 8: 268–83.

———. 1967. "Work-Release: A Study of Correctional Reform." *Crime and Delinquency* 13: 521–30.

———. 1968. "Correctional Research as a Bridge Between Practice and Theory." *Canadian Journal of Corrections* 9: 545–52.

———. 1969. "Work Release: Conflicting Goals Within a Promising Innovation." *Canadian Journal of Corrections* 12: 67–77.

———. 1973. "Felon Self-Mutilation: Correlates of Stress in Prison." In *Jail House Blues: Studies in Suicidal Behavior in Jail and Prison*, edited by Bruce L. Danto. Orchard Lake, Mich: Epic Publications.

———. 1981. "Work Release and Periodic Detention in New South Wales: The Custodial Model and Role Experimentation." *Journal of Criminal Justice* 9: 375–81.

———. 1992. "Preliminary Survey of Personnel Training in American State Prison Systems." *Journal of Correctional Training* (summer): 7–11.

Johnson, Elmer H., and Alfred Heijder. 1983. "The Dutch Deemphasize Imprisonment: Sociocultural and Structural Explanations." *International Journal of Comparative and Applied Criminal Justice* 7: 3–19.

Johnson, Elmer H., and Josef Herreman. 1975. "Work Release in Belgium: Tolerance and the Urban Job Market." *International Journal of Criminology and Penology* 3: 367–80.

Kasai, Akio. 1973. *Some Causes of the Decrease of Crime in Japan.* Resource Material Series, no. 6. Tokyo: United Nations Asia and Far East Institute for Prevention of Crime and Treatment of Offenders.

REFERENCES

Kawashima, Takeyoshi. 1967. "The Status of the Individual in the Notion of Law, Right, and Social Order in Japan." In *The Japanese Mind: Essentials of Japanese Philosophy and Culture*, edited by Charles A. Moore. Honolulu: University of Hawaii Press.

Keefe, William J., William H. Flanigan, Morris S. Ogul, Henry J. Abraham, Charles O. Jones, and John W. Spanier. 1990. *American Democracy: Institutions, Politics, and Policies*. 3rd ed. New York: Harper and Row.

Keiichi, Sakuta. 1978. "The Controversy over Community and Autonomy." In *Authority and the Individual in Japan: Citizen Protest in Historical Perspectives*, edited by J. Victor Koschmann. Tokyo: University of Tokyo Press.

Keirstead, Thomas. 1990. "The Theater of Protest: Petitions, Oaths, and Rebellion in the *Shoen*." *Journal of Japanese Studies* 16: 357–88.

Koschmann, J. Victor, ed. 1978. *Authority and the Individual in Japan: Citizen Protest in Historical Perspectives*. Tokyo: University of Tokyo Press.

Kouhashi, Hiroshi. 1985. "Courts' Selection of Offenders to Be Placed Under Probationary Supervision." Unpublished paper. Tokyo: United Nations Asia and Far East Institute for Prevention of Crime and Treatment of Offenders.

Kubo, Takashi. 1990. "Training System of the Rehabilitation Bureau of the Ministry of Justice in Japan." Unpublished memorandum. Tokyo: Tokyo Probation Office.

Kuriyama, Yoshihiro. 1973. "Terrorism at Tel Aviv Airport and a 'New Left' Group in Japan." *Asian Survey* 13: 336–46.

Kyokai, Keimu. 1943. *Manuscript for History of Japanese Prison Administration in Modern Age*, vols. 1 and 2 (in Japanese). Tokyo: Keimu Kyokai.

Lauen, Roger J. 1990. *Community-Managed Corrections*. 2nd ed. Washington, D.C.: American Correctional Association.

Leiserson, Michael. 1973. "Political Opposition and Political Development in Japan." In *Regimes and Oppositions*, edited by Robert Dahl. New Haven: Yale University Press.

Lemert, Edwin M. 1993. "Visions of Social Control: Probation Considered." *Crime and Delinquency* 39: 447–61.

Levy, Marion J. 1970. "Contrasting Factors in the Modernization of China and Japan." In *Comparative Perspectives: Theories and Methods*, edited by Amitai Etzioni and Frederic L. Dubow. Boston: Little, Brown.

Lewis, Orlando F. [1922] 1967. *The Development of American Prisons and Prison Customs, 1776–1845.* Montclair, N.J.: Patterson Smith.

Lincoln, James R., and Arne L. Kalleberg. 1990. *Culture, Control, and Commitment: A Study of Work Organization and Work Attitudes in the United States and Japan.* Cambridge: Cambridge University Press.

Lopez-Rey, Manuel. 1958. "Some Considerations of the Character and Organization of Prison Labor." *Journal of Criminal Law, Criminology and Police Science* 49: 10–28.

Luhmann, Niklas. 1979. *Trust and Power.* New York: John Wiley.

Lynch, James P. 1988. "A Comparison of Prison Use in England, Canada, West Germany, and the United States: A Limited Test of the Punitive Hypothesis." *Journal of Criminal Law and Criminology* 79: 180–217.

McKelvey, Blake. [1936] 1977. *American Prisons: A History of Good Intentions.* N.J.: Patterson Smith.

Maguire, Kathleen., Ann L. Pastore, and Timothy J. Flanagan. 1993. *Sourcebook of Criminal Justice Statistics—1992.* Washington, D.C.: Bureau of Justice Statistics, U.S. Department of Justice.

Maruyama, Haruo. 1985. "Probation Officers' Routine Work and Some Urgent Problems." Unpublished paper. Tokyo: United Nations Asia and Far East Institute for Prevention of Crime and Treatment of Offenders.

Masaki, Akira. 1964. *Reminiscences of a Japanese Penologist.* Tokyo: Japanese Correctional Association.

Masland, John W. 1946. "Neighborhood Associations in Japan." *Far Eastern Survey* 15: 355–58.

Matsumoto, Masaru. N.d. "Some Aspects of Probation, Parole, and Aftercare Service." Unpublished paper. Tokyo: United Nations Asia and Far East Institute for Prevention of Crime and Treatment of Offenders.

Melossi, Dario, and Massimo Pavarini. 1981. *The Prison and the Factory: Origins of the Penitentiary System.* Translated by Glynis Cousin. London: Macmillan.

Miyazawa, Setsuo. 1990. "Learning Lessons from the Japanese Experience: A Challenge for Japanese Criminologists." In *Crime Prevention and Control in the United States and Japan,* edited by Valarie Kusuda-Smick. Dobbs Ferry, N.Y.: Transnational Juris Publications.

————. 1992. *Policing in Japan: A Study on Making Crime.* Translated by Frank G. Bennett, Jr. and John O. Haley. Albany, N.Y.: State University of New York Press.

Mouer, Ross, and Yoshino Sugimoto. 1986. *Images of Japanese Society: A Study in the Structure of Reality.* London: KPI.

Muramatsu, Michio, and Ellis S. Krauss. 1984. "Bureaucrats and Politicians in Policy Making: The Case of Japan." *American Political Science Review* 78: 126–46.

Nagashima, Atsushi. 1990. "Criminal Justice in Japan." In *Crime Prevention and Control in the United States and Japan*, edited by Valarie Kusuda-Smick. Dobbs Ferry, N.Y.: Transnational Juris Publications.

Nakamura, Hachiro. 1968. "A Re-examination of *Chonaikai* (Urban Ward Association)." In *Readings in Urban Sociology*, edited by R. E. Pahl. Oxford, England: Pergamon Press.

Nakamura, Hajime. 1964. *Ways of Thinking of Eastern People: Asia, China, Tibet, Japan*, edited by Philip P. Wiener. Honolulu: East-West Center Press.

Nakamura, Takafusa. 1981. *The Postwar Japanese Economy.* Tokyo: University of Tokyo Press.

Nakane, Chie. 1984. *Japanese Society.* Tokyo: Charles E. Tuttle.

National Police Agency. 1991. *The White Paper on Police, 1990 (Excerpt).* Tokyo: Japan Times.

————. 1992. *The White Paper on Police, 1991 (Excerpt).* Tokyo: Japan Times.

National Statement Japan. 1990. *International Cooperation in Crime Prevention and Criminal Justice for the Twenty-First Century.* Havana, Cuba: Eighth United Nations Congress on Prevention and Treatment of Offenders.

Nishikawa, Masakazu. 1990. "Adult Probation in Japan: A Case Study of Alternatives to Imprisonment." Unpublished paper. Tokyo: United Nations Asia and Far East Institute for Prevention of Crime and Treatment of Offenders.

Noda, Tosiyuki. 1976. *Introduction to Japanese Law.* Translated by Anthony H. Angelo. Tokyo: University of Tokyo Press.

O'Brien, Patricia. 1982. *The Promise of Punishment: Prisons in Nineteenth-Century France.* Princeton, N.J.: Princeton University Press.

Ogawa, Shigejiro, and Kosuke Tomeoka. [1910] 1970. "Prisons and

Prisoners." In *Fifty Years of New Japan*, 2nd ed., vol. 1, compiled by Count Shigenobu Okuma, English version edited by Marcus B. Huish. New York: Kraus Reprint.

Ogawa, Taro. 1976. "Japan." In *Criminology: A Cross-Cultural Perspective*, vol. 2, edited by Dae Chang. Durham, N.C.: Carolina Academic Press.

Okochi, Kazuo, Bernard Karsh, and Solomon B. Levine, eds. 1973. *Workers and Employers in Japan: The Japanese Employment Relations System*. Tokyo: University of Tokyo Press.

Ooms, Hermon. 1985. *Tokugawa Ideology: Early Constructs, 1570–1680*. Princeton, N.J.: Princeton University Press.

Ozaki, Robert S. 1978. *The Japanese: A Cultural Portrait*. Tokyo: Charles E. Tuttle.

Parent, Dale C. 1990. *Day Reporting Centers for Criminal Offenders— A Descriptive Analysis of Existing Programs*. Washington, D.C.: National Institute of Justice, U.S. Department of Justice.

Passim, Herbert. 1968. "Japanese Society." In *International Encyclopedia of the Social Sciences*, vol. 8, edited by David L. Sills. New York: MacMillan.

Pempel, T. J. 1982. *Party and Politics in Japan: Creative Conservatism*. Philadelphia: Temple University Press.

Pharr, Susan J. 1990. *Losing Face: Status Politics in Japan*. Berkeley: University of California Press.

Plath, David W. 1964. *The After Hours: Modern Japan and the Search for Enjoyment*. Berkeley: University of California Press.

Porporino, Frank J. 1986. "Managing Violent Individuals in Correctional Settings," *Journal of Interpersonal Violence* 1: 213–37.

Powers, Gershom. 1826. *A Brief Account of Discipline of the New York State Prison at Auburn*. Auburn, N.Y.: Doubleday.

President's Commission on Law Enforcement and Administration of Justice. 1967. *Task Force Report: Corrections*. Washington, D.C.: U.S. Government Printing Office.

Rehabilitation Bureau. N.d. *The Rehabilitation System in Japan*. Videocassette.

———. 1990. *Community-Based Treatment of Offenders in Japan*. Tokyo.

Research and Statistics Section. 1966. *Annual Report of Statistics on Correction for 1965*. Tokyo: Secretariat, Ministry of Justice.

———. 1971. *Annual Report of Statistics on Correction for 1970*. Tokyo: Secretariat, Ministry of Justice.

———. 1976. *Annual Report of Statistics on Correction for 1975*. Tokyo: Secretariat, Ministry of Justice.

———. 1981. *Annual Report of Statistics on Rehabilitation for 1980*. Tokyo: Secretariat, Ministry of Justice.

———. 1986. *Annual Report of Statistics on Rehabilitation for 1985*. Tokyo: Secretariat, Ministry of Justice.

———. 1988. *Annual Report of Statistics on Correction for 1987*. Vol. 2. Tokyo: Secretariat, Ministry of Justice.

———. 1990a. *Annual Report of Statistics on Correction for 1989*. Vol. 1. Tokyo: Secretariat, Ministry of Justice.

———. 1990b. *Annual Report of Statistics on Correction for 1989*. Vol. 2. Tokyo: Secretariat, Ministry of Justice.

———. 1991a. *Annual Report of Statistics on Correction for 1990*. Vol. 1. Tokyo: Secretariat, Ministry of Justice.

———. 1991b. *Annual Report of Statistics on Correction for 1990*. Vol. 2. Tokyo: Secretariat, Ministry of Justice.

———. 1991c. *Annual Report of Statistics on Rehabilitation for 1990*. Tokyo: Secretariat, Ministry of Justice.

———. 1993a. *Annual Report of Statistics on Correction for 1992*. Vol. 1. Tokyo: Secretariat, Ministry of Justice.

———. 1993b. *Annual Report of Statistics on Correction for 1992*. Vol. 2. Tokyo: Secretariat, Ministry of Justice.

———. 1993c. *Annual Report of Statistics on Rehabilitation for 1992*. Tokyo: Secretariat, Ministry of Justice.

———. 1994a. *Annual Report of Statistics on Correction for 1993*. Vol. 1. Tokyo: Secretariat, Ministry of Justice.

———. 1994b. *Annual Report of Statistics on Correction for 1993*. Vol. 2. Tokyo: Secretariat, Ministry of Justice.

———. 1994c. *Annual Report of Statistics on Rehabilitation for 1993*. Tokyo: Secretariat, Ministry of Justice.

Research and Training Institute. 1984. *Summary of the White Paper on Crime*. Tokyo: Ministry of Justice.

———. 1987. *Summary of the White Paper on Crime*. Tokyo: Ministry of Justice.

———. 1990. *Summary of the White Paper on Crime*. Tokyo: Ministry of Justice.

———. 1992. *Summary of the White Paper on Crime*. Tokyo: Ministry of Justice.

———. 1993. *Summary of the White Paper on Crime*. Tokyo: Ministry of Justice.

Rohlen, Thomas P. 1974. *For Harmony and Strength*. Berkeley: University of California Press.

Rothman, David J. 1971. *Discovery of the Asylum*. Boston: Little, Brown.

Sakuma, Ken. 1988. "Change in Japanese Style Labor-Management Relations." *Japanese Economic Studies* 16: 3–48.

Sansom, George. 1963a. *A History of Japan to 1334*. Tokyo: Charles E. Tuttle.

———. 1963b. *A History of Japan, 1334–1615*. Tokyo: Charles E. Tuttle.

———. 1963c. *A History of Japan, 1615–1867*. Tokyo: Charles E. Tuttle.

Saso, Mary, and Stuart Kirby. 1982. *Japanese Industrial Competition to 1990*. Cambridge, Mass.: Abt Books.

Sato, Mitsuka. 1985. "Community-Based Treatment for the Delinquents by Volunteers." Unpublished paper. Tokyo: United Nations Asia and Far East Institute for Prevention of Crime and Treatment of Offenders.

Sato, Tsuneo. 1990. "Tokugawa Villages and Agriculture." In *Tokugawa Japan*, edited by Chie Nakane and Shizaburo Oishi, translated by Conrad Totman. Tokyo: University of Tokyo Press.

Satoh, Kunpei. 1989. "Rehabilitation Services in Japan: Present Situation and Problems." Unpublished paper. Tokyo: United Nations Asia and Far East Institute for Prevention of Crime and Treatment of Offenders.

Satsumae, Takeshi. 1977. "The Practice of Suspension of Prosecution." Unpublished paper. Tokyo: United Nations Asia and Far East Institute for Prevention of Crime and Treatment of Offenders.

Scalapino, Robert A. 1953. *Democracy and the Party Movement in Prewar Japan*. Berkeley: University of California Press.

Schade, Thomas. 1986. "Prison Officer Training in the United States: The Legacy of Jessie O. Stutsman." *Federal Probation* 50: 40–46.

Sellin, Thorsten. 1935. "Historical Glimpses of Training for Prison Service." *Journal of Criminal Law, Criminology, and Police Science* 15: 594–600.

Shihgetoh, Hozumi. 1943. "The *Tonari-Gumi* of Japan." *Contemporary Japan* 12: 984–90.

Shikita, Minoru. 1972. "The Rehabilitative Programmes in the

Adult Prisons of Japan." *International Review of Criminal Policy* 30: 11–19.

———. 1985. "Violence and Urbanization: The Experience in Large Japanese Cities." In *Crime and Criminal Policy,* edited by Pedro N. David. Rome: United Nations Social Defense Research Institute.

Shikita, Minoru, and Shinichi Tsuchiya. 1990. *Crime and Criminal Policy in Japan from 1926 to 1988.* Tokyo: Japan Criminal Policy Society.

Shinkai, Hiroyuki. 1992. " 'Litigious Inmates' in Japanese Correctional Associations." Unpublished paper. Tokyo: United Nations Asia and Far East Institute for Prevention of Crime and Treatment of Offenders.

Shiono, Vasuyoshi. 1969. "Use of Volunteers in the Non-Institutional Treatment of Offenders in Japan." *International Review of Criminal Policy* 27: 25–31.

Singer, Kurt. 1973. *The Mirror, Sword, and Jewel: The Geometry of Japanese Life.* Tokyo: Kodansha International.

Smith, Robert J. 1961. "The Japanese Rural Community: Norms, Sanctions, and Ostracism." *American Anthropologist* 63: 522–33.

Smith, Thomas C. 1955. *Political Change and Industrial Development in Japan: Government Enterprise, 1868–1880.* Stanford: Stanford University Press.

———. 1959. *The Agrarian Origins of Modern Japan.* Stanford: Stanford University Press.

Soejima, Kazuho. 1974. "History of Regulations for Juvenile Delinquents in Japan." Unpublished paper. Tokyo: United Nations Asia and Far East Institute for Prevention of Crime and Treatment of Offenders.

Spitzer, Steven. 1983. "The Rationalization of Crime Control in Capitalist Society. In *Social Control and the State: Historical and Comparative Studies,* edited by Stanley Cohen and Andrew Scull. Oxford, England: Martin Robertson.

Stastany, Charles, and Gabrielle Trynauer. 1982. *Who Rules the Joint? A Study of the Changing Political Culture of Maximum Security Prisons in America.* Lexington, Mass: Lexington Books.

Steiner, Kurt. 1965. *Local Government in Japan.* Stanford: Stanford University Press.

Steinhoff, Patricia, Ellis Krauss, and Thomas Rohlen. 1984. *Conflict in Japan.* Honolulu: University of Hawaii Press.

Stutsman, Jesse O. 1926. *Curing the Criminal*. New York: Macmillan.

———. 1931. "The Prison Staff." *Annals of American Academy of Political and Social Science* 157: 62–71.

Sugihara, Hiroyasu. 1994. "Some Aspects of Criminal Sanction and Community-Based Correction." Unpublished paper. Tokyo: United Nations Asia and Far East Institute for Prevention of Crime and Treatment of Offenders.

Supreme Court. N.d. *Justice in Japan*. Tokyo: Supreme Court.

———. 1989. *Guide to the Family Court of Japan*. Tokyo. Brochure.

Suzuki, Yoshio. 1973. "Politics of Criminal Law Reform—Japan." *American Journal of Comparative Law* 212: 287–303.

———. 1979. "Corrections in Japan." In *International Corrections*, edited by Robert J. Wicks and H. H. A. Cooper. Lexington, Mass.: Lexington Books.

———. 1982. Correctional Administration in Japan. Tokyo: Third Asian and Pacific Conference of Correctional Administrators. Mimeographed.

———. 1983. *Correctional Administration in Japan*. Tokyo: Correction Bureau.

Sykes, Gresham M. 1958. *The Society of Captives: A Study of a Maximum Security Prison*. Princeton: Princeton University Press.

Tadao, Kiyonari. 1979. "Small Businesses." In *Politics and Economics in Contemporary Japan*, edited by Murakani Hyoe and Johannes Hirschmeier. Tokyo: Japan Culture Institute.

Takigawa, Seijiro. 1972. *A History of Prison Administration in Japan* (in Japanese). Tokyo: Seikeibou.

Tamiguchi, Tasuhei. 1984. "The Post-War Court System as an Instrument for Social Change." In *Institutions for Change in Japanese Society*, edited by George De Vos. Berkeley: University of California Press.

Tatai, Kichinosuke. 1983. "Japan." In *Suicide in Asia and the Near East*, edited by Lee A. Headley. Berkeley: University of California Press.

Thomas, Jim. 1988. *Prisoner Litigation: The Paradox of the Jailhouse Lawyer*. Totowa, N.J.: Rowman and Littlefield.

Thompson, Paul, and David McHugh. 1990. *Work Organizations: A Critical Introduction*. London: Macmillan.

Toch, Hans. 1976. "A Psychological View of Prison Violence." In *Prison Violence*, edited by Albert K. Cohen, George F. Cole, and Robert C. Bailey. Lexington, Mass: Lexington Books.

Tomita, Shozo. 1971. *How to Utilize Volunteers in the Field of Proba-tion.* Resource Material Series, no. 1. Tokyo: United Nations Asia and Far East Institute for Prevention of Crime and Treatment of Offenders.

Tonomura, Hitmi. 1992. *Community and Commerce in Late Medieval Japan: The Corporate Village of Tokuchin-Ho.* Stanford: Stanford University Press.

Totman, Conrad. 1980. *The Collapse of the Tokugawa Bakufu, 1862–1868.* Honolulu: University of Hawaii Press.

Tsubouchi, Toshihiko. 1973. *Diversion in the Criminal Justice System of Japan.* Resource Material Series, no. 6. Tokyo: United Nations Asia and Far East Institute for Prevention of Crime and Treat-ment of Offenders.

Udo, Goro. 1990. "Rehabilitation Aid Hostels in Japan." Unpub-lished paper. Tokyo: United Nations Asia and Far East Institute for Prevention of Crime and Treatment of Offenders.

United Nations Asia and Far East Institute for Prevention of Crime and Treatment of Offenders (UNAFEI). N.d. *Criminal Jus-tice Legislation of Japan.* Tokyo: United Nations Asia and Far East Institute for Prevention of Crime and Treatment of Offenders.

U.S. Department of Justice. Law Enforcement Assistance Admini-stration. 1976. *Two Hundred Years of American Criminal Justice.* Washington, D.C.

Van Wolferen, Karel. 1989. *The Enigma of Japanese Power.* London: Macmillian.

Vass, Anthony A. 1990. *Alternatives to Prison: Punishment, Custody, and the Community.* Newbury Park, Calif.: Sage.

Wagatsuma, Hiroshi, and George A. De Vos. 1984. *Heritage and En-durance: Family Patterns and Delinquency Formation in Urban Japan.* Berkeley: University of California Press.

Wagatsuma, Hiroshi, and Arthur Rosett. 1986. "The Implications of Apology: Law and Culture in Japan and the United States." *Law and Society Review* 20: 461–98.

Watanuki, Joji. 1986. "Is There a 'Japanese-Type Welfare Society'?" *International Sociology* 1: 259–69.

Weiss, Robert P. 1987. "The Reappearance of the Ideal Factory: The Entrepreneur and Social Control in the Contemporary Prison." In *Transcarceration: Essays in the Sociology of Social Control,* edited by John Lowman, Robert J. Menzies, and T. S. Polys. Alderholt, England: Gower.

REFERENCES

Whitehill, Arthur M., Jr., and Shin-Ichi Takezawa. 1968. *The Other Worker: A Comparative Study of Industrial Relations in the United States and Japan*. Honolulu: East-West Center Press.

Wines, Enoch Cobb. 1880. *The State of Prisons and of Child-Saving Institutions in the Civilized World*. Cambridge, England: John Wilson and Son.

Woronoff, Jon. 1986. *Politics the Japanese Way*. Tokyo: Lotus Press.

Yanaga, Chitoshi. 1956. *Japanese People and Politics*. New York: John Wiley and Sons.

Yanagimoto, Masaharu. 1970. "Some Features of the Japanese Prison System." *British Journal of Criminology* 10: 209-24.

Yokoyama, Minoru. 1982. "How Have Our Prisons Been Used in Japan?" Paper delivered at World Congress, International Sociological Association, Mexico City.

Yoshino, Michael Y. 1968. *Japan's Managerial System: Tradition and Innovation*. Cambridge: MIT Press.

Zellick, Graham. 1982. "The Offense of False and Malicious Allegations by Prisoner." *British Journal of Criminology* 22: 21-35.

INDEX

Elmer H. Johnson was born in Racine, Wisconsin, and received his Ph.D. in sociology from the University of Wisconsin at Madison in 1950. He taught at North Carolina State University at Raleigh from 1949 to 1966. To gain practical experience, he worked in the summer of 1956 as a parole supervisor for the North Carolina Board of Paroles and later took academic leave to serve as assistant director of the North Carolina Prison Department, 1958–60. He taught at Southern Illinois University at Carbondale, where he attained the rank of Distinguished Professor in the Center for the Study of Crime, Delinquency, and Corrections, and the Department of Sociology, from 1966 until his retirement in 1987. He has authored numerous articles and several books, including *Social Problems of Urban Man* (1973) and *Crime, Correction, and Society*, 4th ed. (1978), and edited the two-volume *International Handbook of Contemporary Developments in Criminology* (1983) and the *Handbook on Crime and Delinquency Prevention* (1987). He has also published extensively on comparative criminal justice of Europe, Australia, Korea, China, and Japan.